中國面面談

上冊

Discussing Everything Chinese

Volume 1

鄧立立
Li-li Teng Foti

李戎真
Rongzhen Li

王郁林
Yu-lin Wang

MyChineseClass LLC

Preface

Deep learning involves not simply the mastery of content, but also involves establishing the learner's initial engagement, fostering the learner's motivation and enthusiasm, and supporting the learner's subsequent transfer of understanding into action. Our goal is a textbook that can provide learners high challenge with low stress. We also hope that this textbook helps active learning to occur through exploration and discoveries both in the classroom and after classes. Following the guidelines of foreign language teaching, we bring Communication, Cultures, Connections, Comparison and Community to the center of our design and use a variety of topics and class activities to engage learners. In the course of helping them take language into practice by developing advanced language skills through integrated activities in listening, speaking, reading and writing, we provide clear notes and rich sample usages while also constantly review and reinforce vocabulary and patterns in different contexts and activities. Authentic tasks are also brought to learners through video materials and supplementary readings.

We would like to give thanks to our students for their feedback and support during the five years of testing and revising this book. Yale Chiense150 year 2005 students Veronica Ip, Daniel Thies, Paull Randt, Jee Hye Kim, Yumiko Sheard, and Derrick Sutter, and year 2004 students Matthew Magliocco, Rachel Gretencord, Jessica Cheng, Nathaniel Puksta, and others improved the English part of this book; Sam Doyon from Williams College shared his term paper and helped us write the lesson *Chinese society in the movie "To live."* We also sincerely thank the Chinese branch of Voice of America and Ms. Yi-ru Wang for providing us the video material for the lesson *Taipei and Shanghai from the eyes of scholar Long Yingtai.*

We also want to thank our Yale colleagues for their support, especially Mr. Kai Zhang for his contributions to the listening project, and Prof. John Montanaro for his help with the translation exercises. Many thanks to Li-li's professors and classmates from the Graduate Institute of Chinese as a Second Language at National Taiwan Normal University, her colleagues and teachers Neil Kubler, Cecilia Chang from Williams college, Yu Feng, Baozhang He, Wenze Hu, Aimin Li, Yuhua Liu, and Craig Butler from Harvard University for their guidance. We appreciate Wen-lin Su and Hsiu-fen Chien for their contributions in the earlier stages. We are also grateful that Prof. Kai Li and Prof. Jen-mei Ma kindly corrected our errors and mistakes. We thank our teaching assistants Shirui Shang, Yong Mei, Mark Levin, Shr-tzung Shie, and Xiaochuan Wang for helping with this project. Any errors in this book are the responsibility of authors.

The publication of this book wouldn't be possible without the understanding of our families. We deeply appreciate their love and support.

Li-li Teng Foti, Rongzhen Li and Yu-lin Wang, July, 2007

前言

海外漢語教學的課時與課堂之外的語言環境都十分有限。教基本詞彙和語法之外，怎麼能夠在不增加學生詞彙負擔的情況下，系統地介紹常用口語表達，並循序漸進地提高學生的聽說和讀寫能力，是編寫本套教材的初衷之一。另外，我們也希望學生通過教材中詳細的詞語例句和語法解釋，有效做好課前準備和課後複習，使課堂時間得以充分應用於語言實踐和課堂互動。更重要的是，我們希望提高學生的學習興趣，讓他們在學習溝通與表達之外，更能將語言學習與文化、生活結合，並與同儕不斷切磋、探索，相互激發學習的動力。教學中，我們強烈感受到，趣味性、討論性、以及主題的多樣性對激發學生的積極參與是必不可少的。此外，語言的學習需要不斷重複。在與二年級教材達成銜接之外，我們也力求每一課新學的重要詞彙和語法在聽力、課文、例句、練習、課堂討論中以及隨後的單元中反複出現。同時，我們希望創造自然或接近自然的語言情景，讓學生在原有基礎上自然吸收和應用新的詞彙和語法。

這套集聽說讀寫為一體的教材，從醞釀到今天的出版，修訂，前後歷經五年。感謝多年來耶魯大學中文 150 的學生和我們一路走過，激勵我們不斷增修、刪改、完善。05 年的 150 學生葉瑋妍、羅丹尼、雷杰、金智惠幫我們做了最後英文部分的修訂及校對。其中，葉瑋妍同學還豐富了書中的例句，羅丹尼在編排上也提了一些專業的建議。在這五年的編寫試用中，不少學生也對排版及英文注釋都提供了很大幫助，包括 04 年學生麥特、古瑞秋、陳定煦、雷子揚，05 年學生川上由美子、蘇德立等。另外也要特別感謝維廉大學 (Williams College) 東亞系學生 Sam Doyon 為我們提供他的英文影評，協助我們撰寫《從電影<活著>看近代中國》一課的課文。

在此還要特別感謝耶魯大學東亞系同仁的支持、臺灣師大華研所的師長及同學、維廉大學顧百里、張曼蓀老師、哈佛大學馮禹、何寶璋、胡文澤、李愛民、劉月華、白瑞戈等老師的引領。特別是馮禹老師在三年級中文教學上傳授的精辟見解，以及孟老師(John Montanaro) 在下冊翻譯練習所給予的協助。另外，蘇文霖、簡秀芬老師曾參與初期的編寫和討論，Oberlin 大學李愷老師，Augustana 大學馬真梅老師指正了我們的筆誤和某些例句的瑕疵，IUP 張凱老師幫助了聽力講解的制作，歷年來的助教尚世睿、梅詠、Mark Levin、謝世宗、王笑川等人，也都對此書有所貢獻。記者王怡茹促成美國之音中文部提供《文人龍應臺談臺北與上海》一課的視聽材料，我們在此都致上最深的謝意。

最後，當然是要感謝我們三位老師的家人和另一半。沒有他們的鼓勵和支持，這本書不可能順利完成。然而，對於此教材的不足之處，還望各位老師、同行不吝指正，多提寶貴意見。

編者　2007 年 7 月

前言

目錄

上冊 (Volume 1)

下冊 (Volume 2)

第一課　中國人眼中的英雄

Let's warm-up with a review exercise!

Match the words in characters with Pinyin and English:

漢字	拼音	英文	哪兒學過
認為			二年級
其實			二年級
故事			二年級
許多			二年級
討論			二年級
關心			二年級
文化			二年級
漸漸			二年級
安靜			一年級
歷史			一年級
年輕			一年級
頭發			一年級

拼音

1. ānjìng	2. guānxīn	3. gùshi	4. jiànjiàn
5. lìshǐ	6. niánqīng	7. qíshí	8. rènwéi
9. tǎolùn	10. tóufa	11. wénhuà	12. xǔduō

英文

a. actually	b. to care for	c. culture	d. gradually
e. hair	f. history	g. many; much	h. quiet
i. story	j. to discuss	k. to think; to regard as	l. young

聽力&口語

聽錄音回答問題

對話一

1.	2.	3.	4.	5.

生詞：職業，球員，賺錢，球隊，球賽，場
複習：年輕，籃球，足球，加油

對話二

1.	2.	3.	4.	5.

生詞：不幸，車禍，去世，孤兒，一生
複習：關心，認為

對話三

1.	2.	3.	4.	5.

生詞：沉默，頑皮，踢，存錢，恢復，行李
貧窮，流行，捐錢，無私，自私，懷念
複習：安靜，來自，後來

根據對話一回答問題：

1. 對話中說到的麥可喬丹(Màikě Qiáodān) 是做什麼的？
2. 女兒的學校有什麼樣的球隊？人多嗎？常有活動嗎？
3. 爸爸為什麼說他“打不動了”？女兒後來怎麼讓爸爸決定跟她一起去打球的？

根據對話二回答問題：

1. 對話裏，小麗發生了什麼事？
2. 說話人覺得這件事對小麗有什麼樣的影響？他們準備怎麼幫小麗？

根據對話三回答問題：

1. 女孩小李和男孩小王小時候都是活潑、愛說話的孩子嗎？
2. 小王小時候有一次做了什麼壞事？為什麼他要那麼做？他給媽媽帶來什麼樣的麻煩？
3. 男孩的媽媽為什麼不給他買比較好的衣服？她只想自己，不想別人嗎？她去世以後，男孩常想她嗎？
4. 女孩的母親是有錢人家的孩子嗎？她為什麼不讓女孩的爸爸給孤兒捐錢？

口語用法

1. 你看看我，都已經快五十歲了，哪還能打籃球啊？ (“哪” or “哪兒” “哪裏”can be used in a rhetorical question to negate instead of meaning “place”. In this sentence, the speaker means he is too old to play basketball).

他就會說那麼一兩句中文，哪能給你翻譯(fānyì)中文小說啊？
He can only speak a few Chinese phrases. How can he translate a Chinese novel for you?

我哪裏跟你說過一定會買你的東西了？
When did I tell you that I'd definitely buy your stuff?

2. 女兒：…
父親：好吧，我這個星期六就跟你們一起打！
(“好吧” can be translated as “all right,” or “okay” here. It is used to show that a previous request or suggestion is not perfect but is nevertheless acceptable to the speaker).

A: 外面太冷了，我們別去打籃球了，待在家裏看電視吧！
B: 好吧！
A: It is too cold outside. Let's not go to play basketball and stay at home watching TV instead.
B: Ok.

學生：老師，真對不起，我忘了把功課帶來了，明天給你行嗎？
老師：好吧！下次別再忘了。
Student: Teacher, I'm really sorry. I forgot to bring my homework. Would it be alright if I gave it to you tomorrow?
Teacher: That's fine. Next time don't forget it. (Don't let it happen again).

小張：二十五塊太貴了，算二十塊吧！
小販(xiǎofàn): 好吧！便宜賣給你啦！
Little Zhang: $25 is too expensive, but I'll take it for $20.
Vender: Fine. I'll sell it to you at the cheaper price.

3. 人家麥可喬丹打到三十多歲就不打了，你看看我，都已經快五十歲了，哪還能打籃球啊!

"人家" is used very often in spoken language. It refers to two different meanings depending on the context:

1) "人家" means "the other people." It can stand alone or is used in front of a noun or pronoun to which "人家" refers.

人家小李三點就來了，你怎麼現在才來？
Xiao Li was here as early as three o'clock. How can you come now?

人家能做到，我們也能做到。
If other people can do it, so can we.

2) "人家" can also refer to the speaker himself. In this context it carries a sense of complaint.

人家話還沒說完，他就把電話掛了。
I haven't finished speaking and he already hung up the phone!

你怎麼才來，人家已經等你半個小時了！
How come you are so late? I have been waiting for you for half an hour!

4. 女兒：你還年輕得很呢，別總說自己老了。("Adj+ 得很" is used in a statement of personal opinion. It can be translated as "very" . It is more colloquial and stronger in tone than "很 Adj.")

那家店的東西貴得很，你到別的地方去買吧！
That store's goods are extremely expensive. Shop at another place!

你怎麼那麼喜歡那部電影? 我覺得它難看得很。
How can you like that movie so much? I think it's so bad.

5. 我早就告訴她爸爸喝了酒以後開車會出車禍，可是他就是不聽。
("就" in the second clause of the above sentence expresses strong determination).

我讓他休息一會兒再工作，可他就是不休息。
I asked him to take a break before continuing his work, but he would not take a rest.

我就不相信我學不好中文。
(Although being against all the odds, still) I don't believe I can't learn Chinese well.

6. A: 小麗的父母都在車禍中去世了，真是太不幸了，還好，小麗沒事。
B: 沒事是沒事，可她以後怎麼辦呢？才三歲，就沒有父母成了孤兒
("還好" means "fortunately" or "under this bad circumstance, it is fortunate that …")

他身上一毛錢也沒有，還好，這家店收信用卡。
He didn't even have a penny with him; fortunately, the store accepted credit cards.

我出門時忘了把毛衣帶上了，還好，天氣不是太冷。
When we walked out the door, we forgot to bring sweaters. Fortunately, the weather wasn't too cold.

7. 沒事是沒事，可她以後怎麼辦呢？("X是X" means "it is true…" It is used in the first sentence clause to show an affirmation while emphasizing additional information in the second clause. The two clauses are usually connected by " 但是/可是/不過") .

A: 今天晚上的晚會你去，對吧？
B: 去是去，可是得晚點去。
A: You will come to tonight's party, won't you?
B: Yeah, but I have to be a little late.

這東西好是好，可是貴了點。
It is true that this thing is good; however, it's a little expensive.

8. 那當然，但我認為最重要的還是幫小麗再找一個家。
("那當然" is used at the beginning of a sentence when continuing a conversation, meaning "of course" or "that is for sure").

A: 你兒子真聰明 (cōngmíng)!
B: 那當然! 他有個聰明的媽媽。
A: Your son is so smart!
B: Of course! He has a smart mother.

A: 哎呀，電影已經開始了！
B: 那當然。電影應該八點開始。現在已經八點十分了。
A: Wow, the movie already started.
B: Of course. The movie is supposed to start at 8:00 and now it is already 8:10.

9. 小李，怎麼這麼沉默，半天都不說話，是不是不高興啊？

(“半天” literally means “half day” . However, it is often used in the spoken language to indicate that it seems like a long time to the speaker, even if the period is actually very short).

小張說今天下午跟我一起打籃球，可是我等了他半天他也沒來。
Xiao Zhang said he would play basketball with me this afternoon. However, I waited for quite a long time and he didn't even show up.

10. 我跟你可不一樣，我小時候整天又跑又跳的。

“可” can be used as an adverb to emphasize tones of speaking in a few ways:

1) to imply the speakers' intention to clarify the matter or to highlight the focus of the matter.

在學校要好好學習，可不要跟那些壞孩子一起玩。
Work hard at school. By no means should you hang out with those bad kids.

我可沒有你那麼頑皮。
I am NOT as mischievous as you.

2) to imply the unusualness, rareness, or unexpectedness of the case

那個孩子可聽話了，你說什麼他就做什麼。
That kid is really obedient. She does whatever you tell her.

這個農村可窮了，有時候他們連吃的東西都不夠。
This village is really poor. Sometimes they don't even have enough food to eat.

3) to emphasizes the speaker's sincerity and degree of care when giving a warning, a request, or a reminder, usually with use of an auxiliary verb such as “要”、會”、“得”、or “别”).

大夫啊！你可得幫我們把他的病給治好啊！
Oh, Doctor, in any case you have to help us cure his illness.

你今天晚上可要按時來啊！
Make sure you will come on time tonight, ok?

這個商店的東西很貴，你可別到哪兒去買東西。
Things in this store are very expensive. By no means should you shop there.

11. 真的啊，小王，你怎麼能這樣？
("怎麼能這樣呢？" means "how can [the subject] do this?" A verb phrase may occur after "這樣"in this expression).

政府官員怎麼能這樣呢？說讓人下崗(xiàgǎng) 就讓人下崗！
How can those government officials be like this? They lay off people however they please.

你媽媽有困難才來找你呢，你怎麼能這樣對她呢？
Your mother came to you because she was in trouble. How can you treat her like this?

12. 這個孩子也真是的，怎麼能說這樣的話？
("真是的" is a very colloquial phrase used to express one's complaint or one's dissatisfaction. The subject of the complaining is before "真是的". There can be an additional clause to add more detail to the complaint).

A: 今天晚上爸爸又出去喝酒了。
B: 爸爸也真是的。(總是把家裏的事留給媽媽一個人做，太自私了。)
A: This evening Dad went out to drink again.
B: That is very bad of Dad. (He always leaves the housework to Mom alone. That is very selfish of him).

13. 哎，我媽媽已經去世了，說真的，我好懷念她啊。
("說真的" means "to tell you the truth; no kidding").

說真的，我真不想把我的錢捐給孤兒。
To tell you the truth, I am really loath to donate my money to those orphans.

說真的，我這次得到這個工作可真不容易啊！
No kidding, it was not easy for me to get this job.

口語練習：請用聽力對話中學到的生詞和口語用法討論下面的問題：

rhetorical 哪/　　好吧,…/　　人家/　　　___Adj.得很呢
可是他就是不聽/　　還好，…/　　XX 是 XX，但…/　　那當然/
半天都不說話/　　我跟你可不一樣/　　你怎麼能這樣 /　　真是的/　　說真的

1. A—你喜歡麥可喬丹(Michael Jordan)，你想讓孩子長大後打籃球。
   B—你喜歡老虎伍茲(Tiger Woods)，你想讓孩子長大後打高爾夫球。

2. A,B— 你們得一起想個辦法讓你們的朋友小張喝了酒後別開車。

3. A—你賺的錢不多，但是你很想給孤兒們捐點錢。
   B—你覺得把錢存下來比較好，不應該捐出去。

課文

第一部分

二零零三年，在青島某所中學裏，一位來自美國的年輕老師在英文課上問她的學生"誰是你的英雄？"。一開始，大家都很安靜，後來，終於有位學生舉了手說："雷鋒！雷鋒是英雄。"

頭一個學生開了口，其他的學生也就不再沉默了。"老師教我們要學習雷鋒精神。"一位長頭發的女同學站起來說。這時，坐在她後邊的男同學，頑皮地踢了一下她的椅子，笑著說："雷鋒才不是英雄呢！"另一位同學說"你怎麼跟我爺爺一樣，把雷鋒當英雄啊？"大家跟著笑了起來。

"別吵！別吵！"年輕的美國老師讓大家先安靜下來，然後問："誰知道雷鋒是誰？認為他是英雄的，請舉手。"

只有四五個同學舉手。看來這位老一輩中國人心中的英雄對這些孩子們來說已經很陌生了。

雷鋒於一九四零年十二月出生在一個貧窮的農村家庭裏，七歲的時候成了孤兒，二十二歲就不幸在車禍中去世了。說起他的一生，其實也沒什麼特別偉大的事，他的故事，不是幫老太太提行李，就是把自己存的錢捐給了黨。但他的無私和他對黨的愛，似乎永遠值得學習，永遠受到尊敬。許多老一輩的中國人，還都很懷念雷鋒精神。

生詞用法

1	英雄	英雄	yīngxióng	hero	
	青岛	青島	Qīngdǎo	Qingdao (a city in China)	
2	某	某	mǒu	certain; some	某一天/某個學生/某些工作
3	所	所	suǒ	measure word for school, house, and hospital, etc.	一所大學/兩所房子/一所醫院
	来自	來自	láizì	to come from	見語法
4	终于	終於	zhōngyú	finally; eventually	等了半天，你終於來了。/ 我終於把功課寫完了。
5	举	舉	jǔ	to raise; to lift; to hold up	舉手問問題/把手舉起來/把杯子舉得很高
	雷锋	雷鋒	Léi Fēng	name of an exemplary communist (1940-1962)	
6	头(一个)	頭(一個)	tóuyígè	the first	頭一次/頭三天/頭一所教中文的美國學校
7	开口	開口	kāikǒu	to open one's mouth; to start to talk	別人不開口，他是不會第一個開口的。/他想說但開不了口。
8	其他	其他	qítā	other; else	其他事情/其他地方/ 怎麼只來了你一個，其他的學生呢？
9	沉默	沉默	chénmò	to be silent; silent ; silence	沉默的人/三分鐘的沉默/ 她沉默了兩分鐘。/ 聽了他的話，大家都很沉默。
10	精神	精神	jīngshén	spirit; mind; vitality	愛國精神/雷鋒精神/無私的精神/昨天沒睡好，今天一點精神也沒有。
11	顽皮	頑皮	wánpí	naughty; mischievous	頑皮的孩子/不要頑皮！/他頑皮地打了我一下。
12	踢	踢	tī	to kick	踢了一下前邊的椅子。/踢足球/把球踢過來/把球踢進了球門。
13	吵	吵	chǎo	to make noise; to quarrel; noisy	這孩子吵得很厲害。/ 裏邊太吵，我們到外邊說吧！/他和太太每天都為小事吵。
14	老一辈	老一輩	lǎoyíbèi	the older generation	年輕一輩/ 新一輩
15	陌生	陌生	mòshēng	strange; unfamiliar	陌生人:stranger / 對 XX 感到陌生/這個城市對我來說還很陌生

16	于	于	yú	in; on (written expression)	雷鋒於一九四零年出生。/雷鋒死於一九六二年。
17	贫穷	貧窮	pínqióng	poor (adj.); needy	貧窮的地方/他們生活很貧窮。
18	农村	農村	nóngcūn	countryside; village	農村生活/農村人/住在農村/他是農村長大的
19	孤儿	孤兒	gū'ér	orphan	一所孤兒院
20	不幸	不幸	búxìng	unfortunate; unfortunately; misfortune; adversity;	不幸的孩子/發生了不幸後，他一直很沉默。 /他不幸在車禍中去世了。
21	车祸	車禍	chēhuò	traffic accident	兩起車禍/出了一場(/一起)大車禍/在車禍中去世
22	去世	去世	qùshì	to pass away	父母去世後他成了孤兒。
23	一生	一生	yìshēng	a lifetime; all of one's life	誰是你一生中最重要的人。 /他的一生很不幸。
24	伟大	偉大	wěidà	great (for achievement or personality); mighty	偉大的國家/雷鋒是個偉大的英雄。/這麼無私的想法，真是偉大！
25	提	提	tí	to carry (in one's hand below the shoulders)	提行李/提箱子/提不動
26	行李	行李	xínglǐ	luggage; baggage	一件行李/行李車/行李票/存行李
27	存	存	cún	to save or accumulate (for future use); to store; to deposit	存錢/把錢存起來/把錢存到銀行/存行李
28	捐	捐	juān	to donate	捐錢/把錢捐出去/把書捐給圖書館。
29	党	黨	dǎng	political party	共產黨/ 他是一名黨員。
30	无私	無私	wúsī	selfless; disinterested	無私的精神/無私的黨員/他把錢無私地捐給了孤兒。
31	似乎	似乎	sìhū	it seems; as if; it looks like	他似乎沒聽見我說的話。 /這事似乎跟他沒什麼關係。 /他似乎不高興。
32	永远	永遠	yǒngyuǎn	forever; always	永遠的朋友/他永遠離開家了。/我永遠愛你。
33	值得	值得	zhídé	to be worth; to deserve	這本書不值得你買。/這次旅行很值。/這部電影值得再看一次。

34	尊敬	尊敬	zūnjìng	to respect; to honor	他尊敬老人，但對老師不夠尊敬。
35	怀念	懷念	huáiniàn	to cherish the memory of; to think of	懷念過去的日子/懷念他已去世的母親/懷念中學生活

課文

第二部分

討論完雷鋒，突然有位同學說："老師，他們說的雷鋒你大概沒聽過，可你一定知道小巨人姚明吧！我覺得姚明才是中國人的英雄。"

姚明是一位籃球運動員。在二零零二年六月二十六日，他加入了美國火箭隊，成為美國籃球聯盟歷史上第一位在首輪被選上的外國球員。從此以後，姚明為火箭隊打的每一場球賽，都受到了海內外華人的熱情關注，姚明也漸漸被無數年輕人看成中國的驕傲，而雷鋒精神離這些年輕人卻越來越遠了，有的人甚至不知道雷鋒是誰。他們追求的是個人享受，關心的是流行文化，是怎麼賺錢。在他們看來，自私比無私更實際。

一九七二年，當雷鋒還是所有中國人眼中的英雄的時候，中國第一次派出乒乓球隊到美國進行友好訪問，所謂的"乒乓外交"使中美兩國開始多項交流，並加速恢復了兩國之間的外交關係。那時的中國人一定沒想到，三十年後，大家眼裏的英雄會是一位替美國職業籃球隊打球的中國球員。

生詞用法

36	突然	突然	tūrán (also as túrán in Taiwan)	sudden; unexpected; suddenly	他的去世很突然。/怎麼突然下起雨來了呢？/我突然想不起他的名字來。
37	大概	大概	dàgài	general; approximate; probably; most likely	她沒來上課，大概生病了。/這是我們大概的計劃。
38	巨人	巨人	jùrén	a giant	巨大 (huge; gigantic): Lesson 15
	姚明	姚明	Yáo Míng	name of a famous Chinese basketball player	
39	运动员	運動員	yùndòng yuán	sportsman; athlete 運動：to exercise; to work out	一名籃球運動員
40	加入	加入	jiārù	to join	加入了這個球隊/加入黨/加入聯盟
41	火箭	火箭	huǒjiàn	a rocket	
42	队	隊	duì	a team; a row of people	籃球隊/一隊學生/ 買票的隊排(pái)得很長。/請排隊買票
43	联盟	聯盟	liánméng	alliance; coalition; league	籃球聯盟/歐洲(Ōuzhōu)聯盟=歐盟
44	首轮	首輪	shǒulún	the preliminary round (of election) (首 = first; highest; supreme)	第一輪/三輪
45	选	選	xuǎn	to select; to choose	選一名運動員/選出最好的球隊/選一家飯館/ 她被選為美國小姐/我想去，可是我沒被選上。
46	球员	球員	qiúyuán	ballplayer	
47	从此以后 從此以後		cóngcǐ yǐhòu	since then (此 = “this” in written expression)	他的父母在車禍中去世了，從此以後，他的生活很不幸。
48	场	場	chǎng	measure word for sports and recreation	一場球賽/一場電影/一場表演(biǎoyǎn)/一場車禍
49	球赛	球賽	qiúsài	ball game (比賽 = game; to take part in the game)	籃球賽/足球賽/打一場球賽/看兩場球賽
50	海内外	海內外	hǎinèiwài	inland and overseas	海外華人/改革開放對海內外的中國人都有影響。

51	华人	華人	huárén	Chinese people (including those who aren't Chinese citizens)	
52	热情	熱情	rèqíng	enthusiastic; warm; enthusiasm; warmth	他是個熱情的人。/他對學生很熱情。/他的熱情給我留下了很深的印象。
53	关注	關注	guānzhù	to follow with interest; to pay close attention to	他對今年的球賽非常關注。/華人電影受到大家的關注。
54	骄傲	驕傲	jiāo'ào	to be proud of; arrogant; pride	他是父母的驕傲。/他的父母為他驕傲。/他太驕傲了，以為他自己最聰明。
55	无数	無數	wúshù	countless; innumerable	無數個學生/無數輛車
	却	卻	què	but; yet (used as an adverb. Also written as 却)	見語法
56	甚至	甚至	shènzhì	even; so much so that	他每天都跑步，甚至下雨天也跑。/你會把錢借給一個不熟、甚至陌生的人嗎？
57	追求	追求	zhuīqiú	to pursue; to seek; to woo	追求知識(zhīshi)/追求享受/追(or 追求)漂亮女孩
58	个人	個人	gèrén	an individual; personal	個人問題/個人興趣/這是我個人的看法。/ 這件事你個人負責，公司不管。
59	享受	享受	xiǎngshòu	to enjoy; enjoyment	享受生活/享受很好的學習條件/享受得到/享受不到/ 他只追求個人享受，不關心國家發展。
60	流行	流行	liúxíng	prevalent; popular; fashionable	流行音樂/流行文化/流行性感冒/今年不流行紅色了，流行黑色。
61	赚钱	賺錢	zhuànqián	to make money; to make a profit	現在賺錢不容易。/他這次生意賺了很多錢。/現在錢不容易賺。/做這個生意不賺錢。
62	自私	自私	zìsī	selfish	自私的想法/自私的孩子/ 你這樣做太自私了。
63	实际	實際	shíjì	practical; realistic; actual (實際上 = actually)	他只說不做，很不實際。/他是個很實際的人。/ 他父母很實際，不讓他學畫畫，讓他學電腦。/他大學剛畢業，還沒有什麼實際經驗。

64	派	派	pài	to send, to dispatch, to assign	派球隊出去比賽/派出了三個球員/ 老板派他去買東西給大家吃
65	乒乓球	乒乓球	pīngpāng qiú	Ping-Pong; table tennis	
	进行	進行	jìnxíng	to process, to carry out; to be in progress	見語法
66	友好	友好	yǒuhǎo	friendly; amicable	友好關係/ 他對我很友好。
67	访问	訪問	fǎngwèn	to visit and have an interview with; visit (n.)	訪問中國/進行訪問/一個友好的訪問
68	所谓	所謂	suǒwèi	what is called; so-called	所謂"乒乓外交"是...。/中國人所謂的"美女"和美國人所謂的美女不一樣。/他所謂的無私實際上還是很自私。
69	外交	外交	wàijiāo	diplomatic; diplomacy; foreign affairs	外交關係/外交活動/他做外交方面的工作。/臺灣雖不是一個國家，但和中南美的一些小國有外交關係。
70	使	使	shǐ	to make; to cause; to enable (written expression. Similar to "讓")	他的熱情使我不舒服。/ 他的去世使每一個人都很難過。
71	项	項	xiàng	item; sub-category (measure word)	一項活動/一項工作/一項表演 (biǎoyǎn)
72	交流	交流	jiāoliú	to exchange; to communicate; communication; exchange; interchange;	大家交流一下想法。/經濟交流/文化交流/政治上的交流/生意上的交流/朋友之間的交流
73	加速	加速	jiāsù	to accelerate; to speed up (加速 = 加快 速度 – sùdù- speed)	加速進行/加速了經濟發展
74	恢复	恢復	huīfù	to recover; to resume	恢復健康/恢復友好關係/恢復外交關係/恢復到原來的樣子
75	替	替	tì	to replace; for ; on behalf of	你休息，我替你做飯。/媽媽替我高興。/別替我擔心。

76	职业	職業	zhíyè	occupation; profession; vocation	你的職業是什麼？/打球是他的職業。/職業婦女(a career woman)/ 他是一個職業球員。

句型和語法

- 來自 **(to come from)**

王朋的父母來自中國，但他是在美國出生的。
Wang Peng’s parents are from China, but he was born in the U.S.

這位年輕的老師來自一個非常有錢的家庭(jiātíng), 他從來沒有過過貧窮的日子。
This young teacher is from a very rich family. He has never experienced poverty.

你知道美國最早的白人是從哪兒來的嗎？
(回答問題) =〉

- 才不…呢！/ 才…呢！ **(This colloquial expression is used to indicate the speaker’s strong disagreement with a previous statement. What comes after “才” is the “right information” the speaker wants to emphasize).**

小張：你的女朋友呢？怎麼沒來？
小李：你說昨天你看到的那個女的啊？她才不是我的女朋友呢！我的女朋友比她漂亮多了。
Where is your girlfriend? Why didn’t she come?
You mean the girl you saw yesterday? She is not my girlfriend. (How can she be my girlfriend?) My girlfriend is much more beautiful than her.

小王：你別那麼自私，賺了錢應該給我一點吧！
小陳：我自私？我看你才自私呢！自己不去賺錢讓我賺了給你！
Don’t be so selfish. You made some money. Give me some!
Am I selfish? You’re the selfish one. You don’t make money yourself and want me to make money for you.

大家都說哈佛(Hāfó) 是最好的大學，你覺得呢？
(回答問題) =〉

- **把…當(成)/ 看成 (To see something or someone as, to take something or someone as).**

  老一輩的人大多把雷鋒當成英雄。
  Most people from the older generation see Lei Feng as a hero.

  他們家沒有桌子，一到吃飯時間，孩子就坐在地上，把椅子當桌子用。
  They don't have a table in their family. When it is mealtime, the children sit on the floor and use stools as a table.

  (完成句子) => 她從小就沒有媽媽，但有個大她九歲的姐姐, ____________

- **說起 ("說起" is often used to start a topic in the same way that English uses "Speaking of XX").**

  說起國內外的籃球球員，我覺得麥可喬丹(Màikě Qiáodān)最值得大家尊敬。
  Speaking of domestic and international basketball players, I feel Michael Jordan is the most respectable one.

  說起那次不幸的車禍，沒有一個人不難過。
  Speaking of the tragic car accident, not a single person doesn't feel sad about it.

  說起幫別人找房子，我想李老師比我有經驗得多
  Speaking of helping people with housing, I think teacher Li is much more experienced than I.

  A: 聽說中國的改革開放已經開始了快二十年了。
  (完成對話) => B:
  ____。

- **受到 vs. 受 (受到 is usually followed by a disyllabic nominalized verb, such as "關注", "歡迎", "影響", or "注意" and takes the meaning "to receive"; "受"is used in front of these verbs as a passive structure and gives them the meaning "to be noticed," "to be welcomed,"…etc).**

  他的每一場球賽，都受到海內外中國人的關注。
  Every single game of his receives close attention from domestic and overseas Chinese.
  這首流行音樂受到很大的歡迎。
  This pop song received a great welcome (was very popular).

大家很注意這項外交訪問。
(也可以說) =>

- **..., 而...("而" can be used as a conjunction either to indicate opposition or to introduce two complementary sides of one thing).**

年輕人開始把姚明看成英雄，而漸漸忘了雷鋒。
Young people started to see Yao Ming as a hero and gradually forgot who Lei Feng was.

你怎麼能不加入中國隊而加入美國隊呢？
How can you not join the Chinese team while joining the American team?

(完成句子) =>哥哥想把錢捐出去而弟弟想________________________

- **卻 (卻 is used in a second clause as a cohesive device to indicate a contrastive situation. It is used as an adverb and thus can never be put in front of a subject.)**

老一輩把雷鋒當成英雄，年輕一輩卻連雷鋒是誰都不知道。
The old generation takes Lei Feng as a hero, but the younger generation has not even heard of him.

別人是想當律師卻當不了律師，她卻是能當律師卻不想當律師。
Some people want to be lawyers but don't have the ability, whereas she has the ability but doesn't want to be one.

A: 她父親跟她母親完全不一樣。
(完成句子) => B: 是啊，她的母親無私又偉大，________________________

- **在...看來(在...看來 is usually used to indicate one's opinion and is similar to the English expressions "from the perspective of ... " or "in the eyes of ...").**

在我爺爺看來，小孩頑皮大人不能不管。
From my grandfather's perspective, adults have to step in when kids are naughty.

在年輕人看來，追求什麼樣的精神不重要，追求個人享受才是最重要的事。
From the perspective of young people, what philosophy (spirit) one follows is not important; instead, pursuing personal enjoyment is the most important thing.

海內外的許多華人把姚明當成中國人的驕傲。
(也可以說) =>

- **進行 ("進行" is a verb used with polysyllabic activities that continue for a period of time to give the meaning "to conduct" or "to carry through." It is usually used for more formal activities and not for common, everyday actions. The activity that accompanies "進行" can function as either a subject or as an object. Normally, "著" or "過" doesn't occur in "進行" sentences. The polysyllabic words we use in "進行" sentences are often gerunds. If there are "objects" of these gerunds, we can either use "對"to introduce them before "進行" or use "的" to transform them as modifiers of the gerund).**

她的工作面談進行得很順利。
Her job interview went smoothly (was carried through smoothly).

他們才剛打完這一場球賽，就開始為下一場球賽進行準備了。
They just finished this game and immediately began to conduct the preparation for the next game.

美國的乒乓球隊在中國進行的只是友好訪問，不是外交訪問。
The U.S. Ping-Pong troop only conducted a friendly visiting in China. It wasn't a diplomatic visiting.

他們在這個問題上討論了很多次。
(也可以說) =>

- **..., 並(並且)(並 or 並且 are conjunctions meaning "and," "and also," or "moreover." The second clause that follows 並 or 並且 indicates a further progression. Unlike "和," which is used to connect only nouns or noun phrases, 並 and 並且 are used to connect verb phrases).**

他舉了手，並(且)站了起來。
He raised his hand and stood up.

他們討論並(且)通過了公司的發展計劃。
They discussed and adopted the development plan of their company.
這裏房子便宜並且交通方便。
In this neighborhood the houses are cheap and the commuting is convenient.

買到便宜並且實用的攝像機(shèxiàngjī)不容易。

It is not easy to buy a camera that's both cheap and practical.

他把錢捐給孤兒，並(且)在週末的時候去孤兒院幫助他們。
Besides donating his money to the orphans, he also goes to the orphanage and helps them on weekend.

所謂的"乒乓外交"讓中美兩國開始多項交流，並(且)加速恢復兩國的友好關係。
So-called "Ping-Pong diplomacy" started many different interactions between China and the U.S. and accelerated the rekindling of their friendship.

姚明加入了美國職業籃球聯盟以後，開始替火箭隊打球。
(也可以說) =〉

課堂活動

(一) 用課文裏學到的生詞和句型回答問題：

- 從課文中，你知道中國孩子上課跟美國孩子上課有什麼不一樣的地方？你覺得中國孩子上課時比美國孩子安靜嗎？為什麼？你小時候上課時是什麼樣子？
- 雷鋒是誰？為什麼有人把他當英雄？老一輩的人和年輕一輩的人對雷鋒有什麼不同的看法？
- 姚明是誰？中國人喜歡他嗎？為什麼？
- 什麼是乒乓外交？乒乓外交對中美關係有什麼影響(yǐngxiǎng)？

(二)從不同的角度**(jiǎodù)**來討論**:**

- 課文裏說，自私比無私實際一點，你同意這樣的說法嗎？
  - 交朋友方面
  - 讀書考試方面
  - 找工作方面

- 姚明為美國球隊打球是件好事嗎？
  - 老一輩的中國人
  - 年輕的中國人
  - 美國人

(三) 你的看法
- 在你看來，下邊這些人誰最應該算是英雄？為什麼?

- 甘地 Gāndì Gandhi
- 羅斯福 Luósīfú president Roosevelt
- 希拉裏 Xīlālǐ Hilary Clinton
- 歐巴馬 Ōbāmǎ Barack Obama
- 塔瑞莎修女 Tǎruìshā xiūnǚ Mother Teresa
- 達賴喇嘛 Dálài Lǎma Dalai Lama
- 愛因斯坦 Àiyīnsītǎn Einstein
- 蘇格拉底 Sūgélādǐ Socrate
- 比爾蓋茨 Bǐěr Gàicí Bill Gates

練習題

一.　詞彙練習：(選擇最合適的詞完成句子或段落)

(一) *(項 所 隊 場)*

1. 幫助孤兒找到一個新家是一____很重要的工作。
2. 這一____穿紅色運動服的球員看起來很有精神。
3. 這____中學常常跟別的學校互相交流，互相訪問。
4. 昨天那____球賽，他打得很漂亮。

(二) *(踢 吵 派 選 舉 存 捐 提 使)*

1. 請安靜一會兒，要是你再____，我就要____你的腿(tuǐ-leg)。
2. 我決定______老一輩運動員張帥去訪問美國籃球聯盟，誰不同意，請___手。
3. 火箭隊要在這幾個學生中____一個作職業籃球運動員。
4. 我要把錢____起來，以後買所大房子。我不想把錢____給那些陌生人。
5. 去年旅行的時候，老王總讓小王幫他____行李，____小王很不高興，從那以後， 小王再也不跟老王一起出去旅行了。

(三)

1. *(似乎　不幸　車禍　恢復　甚至)*

靜靜以前很喜歡開車，而且喜歡開得特別快。________的是，去年她出了一次________。一年以來她的身體已經完全________了，可是對她對開車的興趣卻________永遠________不了了。

2. *(尊敬　貧窮　無私　沉默　驕傲　頑皮)*

先生: 我覺得我們兒子太______了,你看他什麼時候安靜過?在學校常常打同學，對老師也不________。

太太: 他頑皮是頑皮， 可是很熱情，也很________， 他常常幫助那些生活________的孩子。說真的，我們應該為我們的兒子感到________。

3. ***(外交　偉大　一生　關於　關注)***

張大明做了一輩子______工作，訪問過很多國家。他去世不久，他的______就被寫成了書，也有了______他的電影。但也有許多人認為張大明沒做過什麼特別______的事，只是個普通外交家。

二.　語法練習：(用提供的句型或詞彙完成句子或者改寫句子)

1. A: 農村人生活還很貧窮。
   B: ________________________。我認識很多農村人，他們每年賺的錢比我多多了。***(才不...呢！)***
2. 我認為毛澤東(Máo Zédōng) 是一位值得懷念的英雄，可是他不這麼認為。 ***(卻)***
3. 我太太覺得孩子學音樂很不實際，應該學電腦或者經濟。***(在...看來)***

三.　翻譯練習：(用提供的詞或句型翻譯下面的句子)

1. 某/ 來自/ 才…呢！/ 卻/ 把…當成/

   A student from the South raised his hand and said: "My grandfather is a hero." but the girl who sat behind him kicked his chair and said: "We don't take him as a hero at all."

2. 說起/ 不是…就是…/ 其實/ 所謂的

   Speaking of the life of the so-called professional player, he didn't actually do anything especially remarkable. Stories about him are either about exchanging basketball ideas with children or donating the money he saved to the party.

四.　閱讀練習：

我叫多多，是一個孤兒，住在一所孤兒院裏。我不知道我的父母是誰，沒有人告訴我他們還活著，或是已經去世了。每次一問起我的父母，這裏的叔叔(shūshu)阿姨就沉默了。孤兒院裏有很多和我一樣不幸的孩子。叔叔阿姨們非常熱情，對我們也很無私，但他們的無私精神並沒有使這裏的孩子變得無私。在很多孩子看來，叔叔阿姨為他們做的似乎都是應該的。而且，大概是因為我太瘦小(shòuxiǎo)了，很多孩子對我很不友好，有些頑皮的大孩子還常常打我，或者踢我。因此我很少跟他們交流。我要好好學習，長大後我要賺很多錢，然後把錢都捐給孤兒院，給叔叔阿姨買最漂亮、最流行的衣服，讓他們為我驕傲。

根據上文選擇正確答案：

1．關於"多多"的父母：(　)
　a. 叔叔阿姨說他們去世了
　b. 叔叔阿姨說他們很沉默
　c. 叔叔阿姨什麼都不說
2．"多多"覺得孤兒院的孩子不太：(　)
　a. 自私
　b. 友好
　c. 驕傲
3．"多多"不喜歡：(　)
　a. 孤兒院
　b. 孤兒院的孩子
　c. 孤兒院的叔叔阿姨
4．"多多"認為：(　)
　a. 叔叔阿姨們沒有很多錢享受
　b. 追求生活享受比幫助孤兒更重要
　c. 叔叔阿姨為孤兒做的是應該的
5．根據對話下面哪個不對？(　)
　a. 孤兒院的很多孩子和多多一樣不幸
　b. 孤兒院的孩子都和多多交流很多
　c. 孤兒院的一些孩子比多多高大

五.　作文：(從下邊幾個題目中, 選擇一個, 寫一篇不少於 500 字的作文。你至少要用四個所提供的句型或詞彙)

來自	在...看來，	從此以後	說起...
受到	所謂	並	卻

1. 談談你心中的英雄。
2. 你是一位中國人，你個人認為姚明不應該給美國球隊打球。請你給姚明寫一封信。
3. 你同意"自私比無私實際"這樣的想法嗎？為什麼？
4. 你可能剛剛從中國回來，請談談你對中國的印象，並談談這次經歷(jīnglì-experience)對你的影響。

第二課　女人能頂半邊天

Let's warm-up with a review exercise!

Match the words in characters with Pinyin and English:

漢字	拼音	英文	哪兒學過
傳統			二年級
律師			二年級
觀念			二年級
馬上			二年級
社會			二年級
完全			二年級
改變			二年級
願意			二年級
不幸			第一課
卻			第一課
流行			第一課
加入			第一課
所謂			第一課
似乎			第一課
農村			第一課
享受			第一課

拼音

1. chuántǒng	2. gaǐbiàn	3. guānniàn	4. liúxíng
5. lǜshī	6. mǎshàng	7. nóngcūn	8. què
9. shèhuì	10. sìhū	11. suǒwèi	12. wánquán
13. xiǎngshòu	14. búxìng	15. yuànyì	16. jiārù

英文

a. lawyer	b. to be willing to	c. farming village	d. but, yet
e. society	f. as if	g. so-called	h. completely
i. to enjoy	j. to join	k. immediately	l. unfortunate
m. traditional	n. to change	o. concept	p. fashionable

聽力&口語

聽錄音回答問題

對話一

1.	2.	3.	4.	5.

生詞：色情，行業，陪，性感，講究
複習：陌生，賺錢，農村，開口，沉默，交流，(願意，城市，竟然)

對話二

1.	2.	3.	4.	5.

生詞：獨生子女，政策，控制，增長，比例
複習：(漸漸，政府，社會，傳統，觀念，改變，嚴格，人口)

對話三

1.	2.	3.	4.	5.

生詞：女強人，娶，嫁，反對，墮胎，懷孕
　　　性別，重男輕女，平等，世紀，接受，傷腦筋
複習：賺錢，(律師，照顧，馬上，千萬，孫子，能幹)

根據對話一回答問題：

1. "色情行業"是什麼？在你看來，為什麼城市裏這個問題比較大呢？
2. 你覺得幹色情小姐的一定都長得很好看嗎？除了長得好看不好看以外，什麼樣的色情小姐更受歡迎？

根據對話二回答問題：

1. 中國的人口問題為什麼沒有印度(Yìndù)的嚴重呢？2035年以後，這個情況有可能改變嗎？
2. 在中國，男人找女朋友容易還是女人找男朋友容易？為什麼？
3. 中國人口還有哪些問題？中國政府為此做了什麼？

根據對話三回答問題：

1. "嫁"和"娶"有什麼不一樣？對話裏，兒子結婚的時候，老太太高興嗎？為什麼？
2. 對話中的老太太現在為什麼事傷腦筋？她的兒子和兒子的太太為什麼要這樣做？

口語用法

1．哎呀！連色情行業你都沒聽說過？
("哎呀" can be translated as "oh" or "oh my dear." It is a Chinese interjection used to show surprise. Sometimes the surprise is followed by worries or frustration).

哎呀！我教給他的是個錯的用法！
Oh no!(I just realized that) I gave him a wrong instruction

哎呀，好大的雨啊！
Wow! What a downpour!

哎呀，你怎麼還不睡覺呀！
Dear me, how can you stay up till this late!

2. 這些女人為什麼喜歡往色情行業裏跳，在別的行業裏找個工作不行嗎？("不行嗎" can be tagged to the end of a statement or a suggestion to form a rhetorical question. This sentence can be translated as "why don't they find another kind of job?")

不派他參加外交訪問不行嗎？
Do we have to send him on the diplomatic visit?

我喜歡幫職業籃球聯盟工作，不行嗎？
I like working for the National Basketball Association. Is there something wrong with that?

3．你說，在餐廳裏做服務員的，一個月才能賺多少錢啊？(When we use "你說" in front of a question, we may have an answer already and need the listener to support our opinion, or we may feel that it is important to hear the answer from the listener. The sample sentence is the former case, the speaker doesn't think waiting tables in the restaurant can make good money, and he wants the listener to support his opinion).

他只有母親這一個親人，現在她去世了，你說，他能不懷念他的母親嗎？
His mom was the only person he had in the family, and now she passed away. You tell me, how can he not cherish the memory of his mother?

他總給自己買衣服，從來不管他的太太，你說，他這個人自私不自私？
He always buys himself clothes and never cares about his wife. You tell me, is he selfish or not?

4．話是沒錯，但你給我再多錢，我也不願意陪陌生男人跳舞，喝酒，睡覺。
(“話是沒錯” is used to continue a conversation by showing acknowledgement of a previous statement before bringing out a different point of view. It is usually followed by “但是，不過，可是....” . It can be translated as “You are right, however...”).

A: 雷鋒是個那麼無私的人，他值得我們永遠尊敬。
B: 話是沒錯，但我不想成為雷鋒，我想當個實際一點的人。
A: Lei Feng is such a selfless person. He is worthy of everlasting respect.
B: You’re right. However, I don’t want to become Lei Feng. I want to be a practical person.

5．好在我是美國人，要不然我爸爸媽媽就只有我哥哥，沒有我了。
(“好在..., 要不然...” means “fortunately/luckily..., otherwise...” . “好在” and “要不然” may be used either together or separately).

好在我的孩子不那麼頑皮，要不然我的麻煩就更多了。
Luckily my kids aren’t that mischievous; otherwise, I would have a lot more trouble.

他昨天出車禍了，好在人沒事。
He had a car accident yesterday. Fortunately he is alright.

你能來幫我太好了，要不然我今天一定做不完。
It is great that you can come to help. Otherwise, I definitely wouldn’t be able to finish it today.

6．...., 更別說我妹妹了。
(“更別說”means “not even to mention.” It is used to explain one’s point by giving a further comparison).

A: 你還年輕，應該再要一個孩子。
B: 一個孩子已經夠我忙了，更別說兩個了。
A: You are still young. You should consider having one more child.
B: One child already makes me busy enough, not to mention two.

你再給我三天我也看不完這本書，更別說今天了。
Even if you give me three more days I won’t be able to finish this book, let alone to finish it today.

7．中國政府也是沒辦法，你知道，中國的人口太多了。("沒辦法" means "to have no choice" or "there is nothing I can do about it." "也" or "也是" here eases the tension of an accusation or confrontation).

我知道我派你去訪問那個農村你不高興，可我也沒辦法呀。
I know that you are unhappy about me sending you to visit that village, but you know that I have no choice.

8．這樣下去，中國的男女比例問題會越來越嚴重。
("這樣下去" can be used as a cohesive device meaning "to continue like that…" or "to go on like that." Sometimes you can use a verb in front of "下去," meaning "if the action continues like that."

姐姐：那孩子又踢你了嗎？
弟弟：嗯。
姐姐：這樣下去怎麼行呢？你得跟老師說啊！
Elder sister: Did the kid kick you again?
Younger brother: Yes.
Elder sister: We can't let things stay like that. You have to tell the teacher.

(In the car) 你別再喝了，這樣喝下去，一定會出車禍的。
Stop drinking. If you keep drinking like that, we will definitely get into an accident.

9．看來印度也得學中國，開始獨生子女政策嘍。
("嘍" here is a modal particle used at the end of a sentence to indicate that one is expecting a confirmation of his conclusion or suggestion from the listener. It is pronounced as "lo," like the sound combination of "了" and "喔" ["喔" pronounced as "aw" in "saw"]).

他給你打了三次電話你都不接，看來你是不打算接他的電話嘍！
He called you three times and you didn't answer. It seems that you aren't going to answer his call.

A: 那我下禮拜就離開嘍！
B: 好吧！
A: Well then, I'll leave next week.
B: Alright.

A: 那你是不願意嫁給我嘍！
B: 我沒說我不願意。

A: So, you are not willing to marry me, are you?
B: I didn't say I am not.

10. A: 老王，聽說你們家兒子娶了個律師做太太，每個月賺的錢比你兒子多多了吧?
B. 錢賺得多有什麼用？

("有什麼用", is a type of rhetorical question meaning "what is the use of it?" You can also say "…有什麼好," meaning "what is good about it?" Finally, you could also use "有什麼好+ verb + de.")

A: 你應該把錢存起來。
B: 把錢存起來有什麼好？我就要賺一塊花一塊。
A: You should save your money.
B: What good is saving money? I just want to spend every dollar I make.

A: 我想和你商量(shāngliang)一下這個問題。
B: 有什麼好商量的？你不是已經決定了嗎？。
A: Let's discuss this matter.
B: There is nothing to discuss. Didn't you already make a decision?

11. 老李，娶太太千萬不能娶女強人。
("千萬"is often used in an imperative sentence in conjunction with "要", "得", or "別". The word "可" is often used before "千萬" to emphasize sincerity or negation).

明天的討論會你千萬要來！
Be sure to come for tomorrow's discussion.

他在開玩笑，你可千萬別生氣！
He was joking. Do not get angry, please.

(If not in an imperative sentence, "千萬" is used to indicate the speaker's earnest desire or wish about something).

我希望這個週末千萬別下雨，要不然我們就不能出去玩了。
I so wish it wouldn't rain this weekend; otherwise, we can't go out for fun.

我得走了，今天千萬不能再遲到了。
I have to go now. I really can't be late again today.

12. 這麼說來，他們墮胎不是因為想要男孩？
("這麼說來" is used as a cohesive device. It can be translated as "according to what you said…" or "so, in that case,…" . What is stated after "這麼說來" is a conclusion or estimation based on the information given earlier in the discourse).

這麼說來，小李不是一個好丈夫。
In that case, Xiao Li wouldn't qualify as a good husband.

小李：中美乒乓球隊的互相訪問打開了兩國之間的對話。
小張：這麼說來，運動員對外交來說也很重要嘍！
Xiao Li: The Chinese and American Ping-Pong teams' mutual visit started the dialogue between the two countries.
Xiao Zhang: So, I guess I would say athletes are also important to diplomacy.

13. 那怎麼行？為了工作就不要孩子，這樣的觀念怎麼能讓人接受。
("那怎麼行" means "that is unacceptable" or "that is not ok" . It is a strong negative response).

A: 媽媽，晚上我跟朋友一起看電視籃球賽。我十二點回來， 你們別等我吃晚飯了。
B: 那怎麼行，你必須10點以前回來。
A: Mom, this evening I will watch basketball games on TV at my friends' house. I will be back at 12:00am so you needn't wait for me for dinner.
B: You can't do that. You must be back by 10:00pm.

14. 我看，你得跟你兒子他們好好說說。
("我看" is a colloquial expression meaning "I think". It brings up one's opinion, estimation, or suggestion. When you use "我看" you are a little surer than "我想").

我看，他不像是個頑皮的孩子。
I don't think he is a mischievous child.

這個老頭的生活沒那麼貧窮，我看，我們還是別把錢捐給他了
I don't think this old man's life is that poor. We had better not donate the money to him.

口語練習：請用聽力對話中所學的生詞和口語用法討論下邊的問題：

哎呀！/　…不行嗎？/　你說，…/　話是沒錯，…/　…,更別說…
好在…，要不然…/　…也是沒辦法/　這樣下去，…/　…嘍
有什麼 XX？/　千萬/　這麼說來，…/　那怎麼行？/　我看，…

1. A-你覺得城市裏不應該有色情行業
   B-你認為城市裏有色情行業沒什麼不好

2. A-你同意中國政府的人口政策
   B-你反對中國政府的人口政策

3. A-你要讓媽媽知道娶個女強人的好處
   B-你是 A 的母親，不希望他娶女強人

課文

第一部分

在十九世紀，當西方婦女開始組織活動，爭取政治權利的時候，中國婦女還纏著小腳，不幸地忍受著各種各樣的傳統束縛。在那個時代，有錢人娶兩三個太太是常見的事；而且，女人一旦嫁到男人家，就被視為男人家的財產。先生打太太不算犯罪，但太太如果對先生或先生的父母不夠客氣，卻會受到處罰。

二十一世紀的今天，討論到男女平等，中國女人的社會地位一點也不比西方女人差。說起來，這都得感謝共產黨。早在毛澤東時代，中國就流行著“女人能頂半邊天”的說法。新中國講究平等，反對地主對農民的壓迫，也反對男人對女人的壓迫。在共產黨的鼓勵下，中國女人和男人一樣，接受教育，加入生產活動。女人是男人財產的觀念因此被打破了。

改革開放以後，所謂的“女強人” 在中國更是處處可見。根據《中華女性網》二零零三年所提供的一項統計：中國的高級政府官員以及私營企業裏的高級主管或專業人員(如會計師，律師)，有百分之四十九點三是女性。

生詞用法

1	顶	頂	dǐng	to stand up to; to carry on the head; measure word for hat	婦女能頂半邊天。/這個工作很重，我怕他頂不住。/他頭上頂了一個球。/一頂帽子(màozi)

2	世纪	世紀	shìjì	century	二十一世紀/兩個世紀/經過了兩個世紀/上個世紀/下個世紀
3	妇女	婦女	fùnǚ	women	婦女地位/婦女代表
4	组织	組織	zǔzhī	to organize; organization	組織討論會/組織一個婦女活動/婦女組織/學生組織/黨組織
5	争取	爭取	zhēngqǔ	to fight for; to strive for	爭取權利/爭取平等的條件/爭取機會
6	权利	權利	quánlì	right (n.); interest	受教育的權利/女人的權利/ 你沒有權利這樣做。
7	缠	纏	chán	to tangle; to twine; to bind	這幾根繩子(shéngzi-string, cord)纏在一塊兒了。/這孩子真頑皮，把繩子纏在他頭上。/纏小腳的女人。
8	忍受	忍受	rěnshòu	to endure; to suffer; to bear	忍受壓力/忍受不好的條件/忍受不了/忍受不住
9	束缚	束縛	shùfú	to fetter; to constrain; bondage; rigid control	爸媽束縛不了她。/ 他被傳統觀念束縛了。/傳統的束縛/家庭的束縛
10	时代	時代	shídài	times; era; age	新時代/毛澤東時代/青年時代/文化大革命時代/時代廣場(guǎngchǎng)/時代雜志(zázhì)
11	娶	娶	qǔ	to marry a woman; to take to wife	娶了三個太太。/把她娶回家/娶她當太太
	一旦	一旦	yídàn	once; in case; now that	見語法
12	嫁	嫁	jià	(said of a woman) to marry; to marry off	她想嫁一個有錢人。/她嫁不出去。/他把女兒嫁給了一個律師。
	视为	視為	shìwéi	把/被...視為 (see grammar section)	見語法
13	财产	財產	cáichǎn	property; assets	個人財產/公司的財產/ 他有很多財產。
14	犯罪	犯罪	fànzuì	to commit a crime	犯了很重的罪。/打人是犯罪的事。
15	处罚	處罰	chǔfá	to punish; to penalize; punishment	處罰這個孩子。/這孩子被老師處罰。/這孩子受到了老師的處罰。/爸媽罰他三天不能看電視。

16	平等	平等	píngděng	equal; equality	男女平等/平等的機會/平等的關係/平等的地位/孩子和父母之間是平等的。
17	地位	地位	dìwèi	status; position (in a society, a family, an organization, etc.)	經濟地位/家庭地位/他在公司的地位很高，但在家裏沒什麼地位。
18	感谢	感謝	gănxiè	to thank; to acknowledge; thanks (n.)	感謝王小名給我們大家帶來這麼好聽的歌！/非常感謝你的幫助。/我對他有說不出的感謝。/我對他非常感謝。
	共产党	共產黨	Gòngchăn dăng	the Communist Party	他是一名共產黨員。
	毛泽东	毛澤東	Máo Zédōng	Mao Zedong	
19	讲究	講究	jiăngjiu	to be particular about; to pay great attention to	他不講究吃穿。/學習要講究方法。/吃東西要講究衛生。
20	反对	反對	fănduì	to oppose; to be against; to object to	他反對女兒嫁給那個農村人。/我不反對你的計劃。
21	压迫	壓迫	yāpò	to oppress; to repress; oppression	壓迫貧窮的人/壓迫別的國家/反對別人的壓迫/對婦女的壓迫
22	地主	地主	dìzhŭ	landlord; landowner	
23	农民	農民	nóngmín	farmer; peasant	
24	鼓励	鼓勵	gŭlì	to encourage; encouragement	熱情的鼓勵/鼓勵孩子開口說話/感謝你的鼓勵/在老師的鼓勵下，…
25	接受	接受	jiēshòu	to accept; to take; to receive	接受一個禮物(lĭwù)/接受教育/他的看法沒有被接受
26	教育	教育	jiàoyù	to educate; education	教育孩子/教育犯罪的人/大學教育/ 給孩子提供最好的教育。
27	生产	生產	shēngchăn	to produce; to manufacture; production	生產食品/加速生產/ 這東西是日本生產的。
28	打破	打破	dăpò	to break; to smash	把一個杯子打破了/打破沉默/打破傳統
29	女强人	女強人	nǚ qiángrén	able woman	她是一個女強人，是三個公司的經理。

30	处处	處處	chùchù	everywhere; in all respects	現在處處都能找到中國飯館。/ 他處處嚴格要求自己。
31	根据	根據	gēnjù	according to; bases; on the basis of	根據他的說法，.../ 你得有根據才能這麼說。
32	中华	中華	zhōnghuá	China; the Chinese nation	
33	女性	女性	nǚxìng	the female sex	
34	网	網	wǎng	net; internet	魚網/英特網/網球/他每天上網六個多小時。/ 他喜歡在網上買東西。
35	提供	提供	tígōng	to provide; to supply; to offer	提供幫助/提供機會/提供好的學習條件/ 學校給我們提供留學機會。
36	统计	統計	tǒngjì	to count up; statistics; census	一項統計 / 統計人口/ 根據統計，...。/你統計一下，有幾個人去，幾個人不去。
37	官员	官員	guānyuán	official (n.)	政府官員/外交官員—diplomatic official
	以及	以及	yǐjí	as well as; along with; and	見語法
38	私营	私營	sīyíng	privately-operated	私營公司/私營商店/私營企業/私立學校(private school)
39	企业	企業	qǐyè	enterprise; corporation	私營企業/國營企業/一家企業
40	主管	主管	zhǔguǎn	to be in charge of; the person in charge	他主管這個工作。/誰是你們公司的主管？
41	专业人员 專業人員		zhuānyè rényuán	professionals	他是一位電腦專業人員。
	如	如	rú	as; as if; such as	如你說的/如父親一樣 見語法
42	会计师	會計師	kuàijìshī	senior accountant; chartered accountant	

課文

第二部分

表面上看，目前中國的女性地位似乎不比男性差，然而，仔細想一想，五千多年來“重男輕女”的傳統觀念在短短的五六十年內真的完全改變了嗎？

為了控制人口增長，中國政府實行獨生子女政策。由於一家只能有一個孩子，不少婦女懷孕後急於知道孩子的性別，如果懷了女孩，馬上就墮胎。中國的男女比例曾經達到一百一十五比一百。這個問題，在農村比在城市嚴重得多。但在城市裏，更讓人傷腦筋的是女人往色情行業裏跳的問題。改革開放以前哪有什麼色情行業？但開放以後，“男人一有錢就變壞，女人一變壞就有錢”。高級領導、高級主管身邊開始出現所謂的“小秘”。談公事，談生意，也總少不了性感的女人陪著喝酒、唱歌。還有一些女人，為了物質享受，竟然願意做富商的“二奶”、“情人”。女人是不是真的頂了半邊天？看來還很難說。

生詞用法

	表面	表面	biǎomiàn	surface (see grammar for “表面上”)	見語法
43	目前	目前	mùqián	at present; at the moment	美國目前的經濟情況/ 她目前還沒有男朋友。/ 目前，她還沒有男朋友。
	然而	然而	rán’ér	however	見語法
44	仔细	仔細	zǐxì	careful; attentive; closely; carefully	仔細聽/仔細看/仔細找/仔細想一想/ 他是一個很仔細的人。
45	重男轻女 重男輕女		zhòngnán qīngnǚ	to value the male child only; to prefer sons to daughters	重男輕女的想法/ 他的父母重男輕女。

46	内	內	nèi	within; inside	國內/房子內/三天內/在一年內
47	控制	控制	kòngzhì	to control; to dominate; control (n.)	控制別人/受別人的控制/忍受政府的控制
48	增长	增長	zēngzhǎng	to increase; to grow; growth	增長知識/增長了很多/加速增長/人口的增長
49	实行	實行	shíxíng	to carry out; to implement	實行新政策/實行教育改革
50	独生子女	獨生子女	dúshēng zǐnǚ	the only child	獨生子女政策/他是獨生子。
51	政策	政策	zhèngcè	policy	改革政策/人口政策/教育政策/環境政策
	由于	由於	yóuyú	due to; because of; in that	由於老師的鼓勵，他進步很快。/由於下雨，他不能出去玩。 見語法
52	怀孕	懷孕	huáiyùn	to be or to become pregnant	她懷孕五個月了。/她懷了一個女孩子。/她想懷孕，懷不上。
53	急于	急於	jíyú	to be impatient to; to be eager to	急於回去/急於知道
54	性别	性別	xìngbié	gender (性 = sex)	男性/女性
55	堕胎	墮胎	duòtāi	to have an abortion; abortion	她懷孕以後決定墮胎。/她墮了三次胎。/她把孩子墮了。
56	比例	比例	bǐlì	proportion; ratio	男女比例/富人和窮人的比例/很高的比例/比例很低
57	曾经	曾經	céngjīng	ever; once; formerly	他曾經說過要幫我忙。/我曾經去過英國。/我不曾說過這樣的話。/我不曾去過日本。
58	达到	達到	dádào	to achieve; to reach (a number, a goal, or a standard)	達到某個年齡(niánlíng)/達到父母的要求/達到高級水平/達到標準(biāozhǔn)/達到目的(mùdì)/ 中國人口達到十三億了。
59	严重	嚴重	yánzhòng	critical; serious (said of problems or illnesses)	嚴重的問題/ 他病得很嚴重。
60	伤脑筋	傷腦筋	shāng nǎojīn	to cause sb. a headache; knotty; bothersome	這件事很讓人傷腦筋。/這是件傷腦筋的事。/ 她為孩子上大學傷腦筋。/別傷腦筋了，到時候總有辦法。

61	色情	色情	sèqíng	erotic; eroticism	色情小姐/色情行業/色情書/色情電影
62	行业	行業	hángyè	industry; profession; vocation	各行各業/色情行業/教育行業/服務行業
63	领导	領導	lǐngdǎo	to lead; leader	領導別的人/熱情的領導/公司領導/學校領導/國家領導
64	出现	出現	chūxiàn	to appear; to arise; to emerge	出現問題/ 等了他一個小時，他才出現。
65	小秘	小秘	xiǎomì	" little secretary;" i.e. a secretary who also acts as a mistress	這個主管有一個小秘。 (秘書 : secretary)
66	公事	公事	gōngshì	business errand; official business	他週末也得談公事。/ 你要把公事私事分開，在公司的時候別做私事。
67	性感	性感	xìnggǎn	sexy	他很性感。/性感的女孩子
68	陪	陪	péi	to accompany; to keep sb. company	陪病人/陪女朋友買東西/ 你陪我一塊兒去看電影吧！/三陪小姐
69	物质	物質	wùzhì/ (Taiwan: wùzhí)	material; substance	物質生活和精神生活/物質追求
70	竟然	竟然	jìngrán	unexpectedly; to ne's surprise	哎呀，我竟然把女朋友的生日忘了！/ 學了三年中文，你竟然連這麼簡單的字都不認識。
71	愿意	願意	yuànyì	to be willing to	他願意幫忙。/ 他不願意陪我。
72	富商	富商	fùshāng	富裕(fùyù = rich)的商人; rich businessman	他是香港富商。 / 富商就是富裕的商人。 /改革開放以後出現了很多富裕的商人。
73	二奶	二奶	èrnǎi	concubine; mistress	他有一個二奶。/她那麼年輕漂亮，怎麼願意做一個二奶?
74	情人	情人	qíngrén	lover; sweetheart	他太太不知道他在公司裏有個情人。/ 2 月 14 號是情人節。

句型和語法

- 一旦(“一旦” can be used in front of or after the subject to form a hypothetical sentence. It signifies that once the condition of the first clause is fulfilled, the event of the second clause is expected to follow. “就” is often used in the second clause in this pattern) .

  我一旦有了錢，一定給那些孤兒們捐一點。
  If I have money someday, I will definitely donate some to orphans.

  一旦我存夠了錢，我就要買一輛寶馬車。
  Once I save enough money, I'll buy a BMW.

  婦女們一旦爭取到權利，就不可能再忍受傳統的束縛。
  Once women strive for and achieve power, they will no longer be able to endure the restraints of traditional beliefs.

  你上了法學院(fǎxuéyuàn)以後，生活會有什麼不一樣嗎？
  (回答問題)=〉

- **B 被 (A) 看成 XX/被當成/被視為 (with “被” this is a passive pattern that means that the subject B is seen as XX by A. See also L1 把…當成/看成).**

  她嫁過去以後，就被視為先生家的財產了。
  Ever since she married into the man's family, she has been seen as her husband's property.

  地主們被共產黨看成壓迫農民的壞蛋(huàidàn)。
  Landlords were seen by the Communists as scoundrels who put pressure on farmers.

  她只是一個普通(pǔtōng)的婦女，但大家把她當成一個女強人。
  (也可以說)=>

- **說起來(“說起來” can be used at the beginning of a sentence or as a conjunction in between two sentences. It means “speaking of…” or “speaking of that.” See also L1 說起…)**

  說起來，會計師的工作不比律師的工作輕松。

Speaking of the work load of a CPA, it is not really lighter than the work of a lawyer.

過去，中國農民常受到地主的壓迫，說起來，這種情況各國的歷史上都出現過。
Speaking of the oppression of peasants by the landlords, such situations appear in the history of every country.

女人開始受教育，開始加入生產活動，說起來，這都得感謝共產黨。
Women started to receive education and to participate in manufacturing. Speaking of that, all of it is thanks to the Communist Party.

他們家還有嚴重的重男輕女觀念。這一點有點讓人傷腦筋。
(也可以說)=〉

- 在 **XX 的_____(之)下 (This pattern is used in front of a sentence phrase. Only a disyllabic nominalized verb may go in the blank. It means "under the _______of XX").**

在政府的控制下，人口的增長慢了下來。
Under the government's control, population growth slowed down.

在人民的爭取下，私營企業受到的束縛越來越少。
Under the pressure of popular objection, private enterprises now face fewer and fewer restrictions.
因為老師的鼓勵，他的中文越學越好。
(也可以說)=〉

- 更 **("更" can be used in front of verb phrases. "更" in the second clause shows that, in comparison to the first clause, the second clause is even more extreme and therefore requires no additional explanation).**

找不到工作我幫不了你，交不到女朋友你更別來找我。
I can't help you find a job, and you certainly shouldn't expect me to help you find a girlfriend.

中國女人的地位本來就不差，改革開放後，女強人更是處處可見。
Originally, the status of Chinese women was not bad. After the Reform and Opening, successful women are even more prevalent.

我沒給你打電話，更沒去宿舍找你。
I didn't call you, and I certainly would never look for you in your dormitory.

- **S 所+Verb+的+Noun (Use of "所" in this pattern is originally from classic Chinese, but it is commonly used in modern written Chinese. It can be translated as a relative pronoun such as "what," "which," or "that").**

  專業人員所告訴你的話，你都記住了嗎？
  Do you remember what the professionals told you?

  不幸地，墮胎是他們最後所作的選擇。
  Unfortunately, an abortion was the last thing that they would have chosen.

  你父親幹過哪幾種行業？
  (回答問題)=〉

- 以及 **("以及" is also a expression from classic Chinese that is more often used in written Chinese. It connects noun phrases and is used before the last of the items to be connected).**

  請你們把書，筆，以及其他要用的東西帶好。
  Please bring books, pens, and other things that you need.

  我曾經去過北京，上海，以及西安幾個城市。
  I have been to cities like Beijing, Shanghai, and Xi'an.

  你在中學的時候，最喜歡的課有哪些？
  (回答問題)=〉

- 如 **("如" is an expression from classic Chinese that means "to be like" or "such as." In spoken language "像" is more appropriate).**

  就如她所說的，姚明，麥可喬丹等球員，都成了大家眼中的英雄。
  Just as she said, basketball players such as Yao Ming and Michael Jordan all became heroes in everybody's eyes.

  專業人員如律師，會計師等，有百分之四十六是女性。
  Forty-six percent of professionals such as lawyers and CPAs are female.

  那些人可以算是歷史上的偉人呢？
  (回答問題)=〉

- **___分之___ (originally, "分" meant "to divide" . "三分之二" means two parts of a thing divided into three parts, such as the fraction "2/3" .Notice that when we say a percentage, we don't say "一百分之 xx" . Instead, we say "百分之 xx").**

  這個國家有百分之五的人口不認識字。
  Only five percent of the population of this country is illiterate.

  我賺的錢只有我妹妹賺的錢的四分之一。
  The money I make is only one fourth of the money my sister makes.

  你們學校的男女比例是多少？
  (回答問題)=〉

- **表面上…，(實際上)… ("表面上" literally means "on the surface" and indicates that something only appears to be true. It is usually used at the beginning of the first clause. "實際上," "其實," "但是," or "然而" usually follows in the second clause and indicates the reality that contrasts with the appearance).**

  表面上，他是一個愛家的男人，實際上，他在公司裏有個小秘。
  He seems to be a family man on the surface; however, he is actually having an affair with a secretary in the company (literal translation: "he has a secretary lover").

  他們表面上很談得來，其實互相看不起。
  Apparently they get along very well, but actually they look down on each other.

  這位同學看起來很高興，其實心裏很難過！
  (也可以說)=〉

- **然而 ("然而" is a conjunction more often used in written Chinese that means "however". We don't have to repeat the subject again in the clause after "然而.")**

  他做的算是高級官員的工作，然而，賺的錢卻沒有路上賣冰水的多。
  His job can be considered that of a high-ranking officer. However, he doesn't make as much money as those ice-drink vendors on the street.

獨生子女政策控制了人口的成長，然而，也帶來了不少社會問題。
The one-child policy controlled population growth. However, it also brought a lot of social problems.

美國真的已經是一個男女平等的社會了嗎？
(回答問題)=〉

- **Reduplication of a single-syllable adjective (When a reduplicated single-syllable adjective is used a) with "的" as a modifier, it has a stronger descriptive power and shows a personal [and usually positive] feeling; when a reduplicated form is used b) as a complement after 得, it gives the adjective greater strength and vividness).**

a) 那女孩有一雙大眼睛。(That girl has a pair of big eyes).
那女孩有一雙大大的眼睛。(That girl has a pair of lovely big eyes).

你看那些黃黃的花兒，多漂亮！
Look at those lovely yellow flowers. How beautiful they are.

短短的幾十年內，情況就改變了。
In as short as a few decades, the situation has changed.

b) 你最好走得遠遠的，再也不要回來。
You had better go as far as you can and never come back.

他的屁股(pìgu)被媽媽打得紅紅的。
His bottom turns so red after being beaten by his mother.

- **為了..., ... / ..., 是為了... ("為了" means "for the purpose of" . It needs to be used in the first clause. However, you can use "是為了" in the second clause. This shifts the focus of the sentence from the things someone does to the purpose of the actions).**

為了在這工作方面更專業，他下了班還去上課，學更新的東西。
In order to become more professional at work, he takes classes after work and learns new things.

我們急於知道孩子的性別，是為了方便準備孩子出生後要用的東西。
The reason we are eager to know the sex of the child is so that we can conveniently prepare the things the child will need.

你為什麼選擇這所大學呢？
(回答問題)=〉

- 由於 (**"由於" is more often seen in written Chinese and means "due to" or "owing to". It can be used in the first part of a sentence to introduce a cause. When used in the second clause, it needs to follow "是" . When we use the pattern "…是由於…" the focus of the information is the cause, while in the pattern "由於…, …" the focus is more on the result).**

由於父親的反對，他不準備到中國去訪問了。
Due to the objection of his father, he won't be visiting China any more.

中美兩國的關係越來越好是由於實行了新的外交政策。
The improvement of the Sino-American relationship is due to the practice of new diplomatic policies.

為什麼有那麼多的女性願意(yuànyì)往色情行業裏跳呢？
(回答問題)=〉

課堂活動

(一) 用課文裏學到的生詞和句型回答問題:

- 十九世紀的中國女人和現在的中國女人有什麼不同?
- "嫁"和"娶"有什麼不一樣?
- "女人能頂半邊天"是什麼意思?
- 為什麼課文裏說,中國的女人得感謝共產黨?
- 所謂的"女強人"是什麼?
- "重男輕女"是什麼意思,這樣的觀念在中國已經改變了嗎?
- 中國政府的獨生子女政策帶來什麼好處,壞處?
- 為什麼中國流行著"男人一有錢就變壞,女人一變壞就有錢"的說法?

(二)從不同的角度**(jiǎodù)**來討論:

- 城市裏該不該有色情行業呢?
  - 毛澤東
  - 女強人
  - 從農村來的漂亮性感女人
  - 高級男性主管
  - 傳統中國婦女
- 色情行業該不該合法化 (héfǎ huà)?
  - Las Vegas 的政府官員
  - 愛滋病(AIDS)組織
- 出現色情行業、小秘、以及二奶,這些和男女平等有關係嗎?
  - 有關係
  - 沒關係
- 中國實行應該實行獨生子女政策嗎?
  - 中國政府
  - 關心人權的美國人
  - 中國農民
  - 一個要兒子也想要女兒的女人

(三) 你的看法

- 所謂男女平等是什麼?你認為這個社會做到了男女平等嗎,為什麼?
- 如果你是男性,你會希望你的太太是個女強人嗎?為什麼?
- 如果可以選擇,你希望當男人還是女人?為什麼?
- 你認為很多女人做色情工作跟男女平等有關係嗎?

練習題

一. 詞彙練習：(選擇最合適的詞完成句子或段落)

(一) *(娶 嫁 纏 陪 頂)*

1. 你願意____給我嗎？結婚以後我一定讓你過富裕的生活。
2. ____個女強人有什麼不好？你想____人家，人家還不一定想____給你呢！
3. 奶奶，我不要你____我去買東西，走的太多，你那____過的小腳會受不了的。
4. 你看，那小狗把球______在頭上玩呢！

(二) *(根據 以及 由於 急於 曾經 目前)*

1. 我們應該____男女的比例來決定應該選一個男性領導還是女性領導。
2. 這件事你不要______決定，應該先問問一些專業人員後再決定。
3. 新時代的婦女在社會權利______家庭地位方面都提高了很多。
4. ______改革開放的影響，中國人的很多傳統觀念正在漸漸改變。
5. _____中國農村重男輕女的觀念還很嚴重，不過比上個世紀好多了。

(三)

1. *(墮胎 懷孕 忍受 接受 反對 性別 小秘 政策)*

小麗______了。這應該是件高興的事，可是小麗卻高興不起來，一直在為要不要_____傷腦筋。不是因為獨生子女_____或者孩子的_____，更不是因為她____不了孩子帶來的麻煩，而是因為小麗是一個富商的______，她知道，這個社會、甚至她的父母都不會______這個孩子。

2. *(處處 鼓勵 犯罪 權利 打破 處罰)*

在中國，雖然提供色情服務是一種______活動，但你______都可以找到色情小姐。有些人認為，雖然政府不應該______色情行業，但要是有人願意做，他們也有______這樣做，不應該受到______。

3. *(地主 生產 財產 壓迫 爭取 組織)*

以前每個農村都有幾個______。他們從來不參加______活動，卻有很多______。他們______農民，使農民的生活非常貧窮。後來，在共產黨的領導下，中國農民才慢慢______到了平等的權利和地位。

4. *(嚴重　束縛　仔細　如)*

請你______統計一下，在這幾個農村中，哪幾個經濟增長比較慢，看看他們經濟增長慢是不是因為傳統觀念的______，______：重男輕女、看不起生意人等等。

5. *(出現　講究　達到/達得到/達不到　實行)*

老王每天努力工作是為了給自己的孩子提供很好的物質條件。但他教育孩子卻一點都不_____方法，總以為_____最嚴格的教育方式就是好的。如果孩子______自己的要求，老王就很生氣，甚至還打孩子。

二.　語法練習：(用提供的句型或詞彙完成句子或者改寫句子)

1. A:大明對他太太真好，我希望我也能嫁一個那麼好的先生。
   B:____。
   (表面上…,實際上…)
2. 吃飯的時候你得控制一點，如果你胖起來了，就很難再瘦(shòu)下去了。*(一旦)*
3. 她是一個很傳統的女孩子，由於男朋友的鼓勵，她才穿上了那套性感的衣服。*(在… 下)*

三.　翻譯練習：(用提供的詞或句型翻譯下面的句子)

1.　被…看成/視為…　在…看來　一旦　然而

Some American people consider abortion a crime. Once one gets pregnant, you have to give birth to the baby. In the perspective of these people, the unborn baby has the right to live. However, some people oppose this opinion. They think that it is the pregnant woman who has the right to decide.

2.　由於　受到　要不然　話是沒錯　再說

A:　Because of the one child policy, the increase in the Chinese population is under control now. Otherwise, the huge population would strongly affect Chinese economic development.

B：You are right. But I don't think the government has the right to punish those families that have more than one child. Besides, the male and female ratio in China is now a very serious problem.

四.　作文：(從下邊幾個題目中, 選擇一個, 寫一篇不少於 500 字的作文。你至少要用六個所提供的句型或詞彙)

為了...，.../...是為了..	表面上	以及	然而	把/被...視為...
在…下(such as in 在政府的控制下）	所+Verb+的	急於	由於	這樣下去

1. 美國婦女的地位怎麼樣？談談你對男女平等的看法。
2. 很多女人不得不在色情行業工作，你認為這跟男女平等有關係嗎？為什麼？
3. 在你看來，色情行業應不應該合法化？
4. 請你介紹一下中國的獨生子女政策，你對這項政策有什麼看法？

第三課　孩子，我要你比我強

Let's warm-up with a review exercise!

Match the words in characters with Pinyin and English:

漢字	拼音	英文	哪兒學過
強			二年級
活潑			二年級
生氣			二年級
經濟			二年級
聰明			二年級
發現			二年級
嚴格			二年級
大聲			二年級
一生			第一課
值得			第一課
熱情			第一課
頑皮			第一課
使			第一課
忍受			第二課
傷腦筋			第二課
然而			第二課

拼音

1. cōngming	2. dàshēng	3. huópō	4. jīngjì
5. qiáng	6. rán'ér	7. rěnshòu	8. rèqíng
9. shāngnǎojīn	10. shēngqì	11. shǐ	12. wánpí
13. yángé	14. yīshēng	15. zhídé	16. fāxiàn

英文

a. to cause sb. a headache	b. angry	c. to make; to cause	d. naughty
e. smart	f. loud	g. lively	h. economy
i. strong	j. however	k. to endure	l. enthusiastic
m. strict	n. a lifetime	o. to be worth	p. to discover

聽力&口語

聽錄音回答問題

對話一

1.	2.	3.	4.	5.

生詞：出版，暢銷，讀者，家長，培養
複習：講究，教育，鼓勵，提供，傷腦筋，(希望，嚴格)

對話二

1.	2.	3.	4.	5.

生詞：笨，申請，名校，獎學金，免不了
複習：竟然，根本，傷腦筋，頑皮，(聰明，打籃球，用功，差)

對話三

1.	2.	3.	4.	5.

生詞：不打不成器，家教，補習，重視，嬌慣，競爭
激烈，逼，輕松，吃苦，討厭，孤僻
複習：卻，名校，竟然，教育，培養，交流，笨
(活潑，生氣，用功，方面)

根據對話一回答問題：

1. 老李的書出版了嗎？他的書是關於什麼的？
2. 你覺得他的書會賣得怎麼樣?為什麼? 你會買他的書嗎？

根據對話二回答問題：

1. 對話中的小明要上一所什麼樣的大學？這為什麼讓老李沒想到呢？男說話人老王對這件事有什麼看法呢？
2. 聽了老王的話以後，老李在教育自己的孩子方面會有什麼改變？

根據對話三回答問題：

1. 小麗的媽媽為什麼打她？
2. 小麗的爸爸和媽媽對教育小麗有什麼不同的看法？
3. 你覺得週末應該讓孩子學習嗎？

口語用法

1. 上次你說你的書要出版了，我在書店裏怎麼找都找不到！ 到底出版了沒？
("怎麼+Verb+都/也" is a pattern that can be translated as "no matter how hard one tries, still/just not …" . There can be two subjects in this pattern such as "我怎麼說他都不聽", which means "No matter what I said, he still wouldn't listen).

權力在女人的手上，男人們怎麼爭取都沒有用的。
Power is the hands of women. No matter how hard men try to gain power, their efforts are in vain.

他那傳統的老觀念，怎麼改也改不過來。
It is impossible to change his traditional beliefs.

(When"到底"is used in an interrogative sentence, it imparts a strong sense of impatience, anxiety, or eagerness).

昨天你說去，今天又說不去，你到底去不去？
Yesterday you said you would go, today you said that you won't go. Are you going or not?!

昨天那個給你打電話的人到底是誰？
Who exactly is the one who called you yesterday?

他到底跟你說了什麼？
What on earth did he tell you?

2. 嗯！你這個觀念很有意思，看來你的書真的值得看嘍。
("看來" means "it seems" or "it looks like" . It is similar to "我看", but "我看" leans more towards one's own subjective feeling, and can introduce one's suggestion; "看來" tends to introduce a judgment or estimation based on the information mentioned).

看來你並不相信我說的話。
It seems that you don't believe what I said.

太晚了，看來我們今天去不成了。
It is too late. It looks like we shouldn't go today.

A: 中國同意派乒乓球隊到美國訪問了！
B: 是嗎？看來中美兩國的關係要慢慢好起來了。

A: China agreed to send its Ping-Pong team to visit the US.
B: Really? It looks like the relationship between China and the U.S. will start to get better.

3. 你不能光看考試，我相信小明一定很聰明。
("光" can be an adverb used before a verb meaning "only, simply" in spoken Chinese. It is not used in front of a quantity).

我問她愛不愛我，她光笑不說話。
I asked her if she is in love, she simply smiled and said nothing.

他怎麼可以光吃不幹？太自私了！
How can he only eat but not work? That is too selfish.

4. 小孩子哪有不想玩的？頑皮、不用功是免不了的。
("免不了"means "hard to avoid; unavoidable". It is usually used before a verb phrase, or in the pattern of "…是免不了的". "難免" has the same meaning and function as "免不了", but less colloquial).

他的父親很重視他的考試。要是他沒考好，他的父親免不了會生氣。
His father attaches the most importance to his tests. If he doesn't test well, it's hard to avoid making his father angry.

小孩子什麼都不懂，做錯事是難免的。
The small child doesn't understand anything, so his mistakes are unavoidable.

5. 所以說嘛，孩子小時候笨不見得就真的笨。
("所以說嘛/呀" is used in a discourse meaning "that's the reason why" or "that's just the point" . Usually the speaker uses "所以說嘛/呀" after he knows the listener consents the points he mentioned earlier in the discourse).

A: 實行獨生子女政策以後，中國的人口成長得到了很好的控制。
B: 所以說嘛！共產黨政府也有它好的地方。人口問題不控制是不行的。
A: After carrying out the one-child policy, China's population growth is under very good control.
B: See, that's why we say there are things good about a communist government. The problem of population growth has to be controlled.

A: 看來老王開飯館真賺了不少錢呀！
B: 所以說嘛，我告訴你我們也該找個好地方開個飯館。
A: It seems that Lao Wang has earned a lot of money by running a restaurant.

B: That is why I told you that we should find a good place to run a restaurant, too.

6．哎，你怎麼能打孩子呢？別打別打！有話跟她好好說嘛！
(When you say "有話好好說" to someone, you ask him or her to calm down and have a peaceful conversation instead of initiating a quarrel or a fight).

別吵了！有話坐下來好好說清楚。
Stop fighting! Sit down and calmly talk things through.

你怎麼打人呢？有話好好說。
You can't hurt people. Speak nicely (to resolve the matter).

7．你看看，小麗她這次考試竟然只給我考了二十分。("給我" can be used in front of a verb phrase to show one's anger and indignation or to indicate one's commanding or threatening tone. In this sentence, it means, "How could this happen to me?!")

他怎麼能給我去幹色情行業！
How can he work in the sex industry! How could he do that to me!

我要帶你去見我的父母。你竟然給我穿得這麼性感。
I'm bringing you to see my parents. How could you dress so immodestly?

你想出去玩得先給我把功課做完。
If you want to play, you have to finish your homework first.

8．把我給氣死了！
("把我給氣死了" or "氣死我了" means "it really pissed me off").

今天小王把我給氣死了！他說來跟我一起複習數學，結果我在圖書館等了他三個小時他都沒來。
Today Xiao Wang really pissed me off. He said that he would join me to review math, but it turned out that I waited him for three hours at the library and he still didn't show up.

("給" can be used before the verb in a "把" or "被" sentence for stress. While using "給", "被" is often replaced by "讓" or "叫".)

她男朋友把她的水給喝了。
Her boyfriend drank all her water.

這孩子讓/叫他爸爸給慣壞了。
This kid's dad spoiled him rotten.

9. 二十分就二十分，你別那麼重視考試嘛！ ("XX 就 XX" means "it's okay" or "so be it!". "就" here indicates one's passive acceptance or resignation. Sometimes it indicates one's indifference).

當二奶就當二奶，我不怕別人笑我。
I'm fine with being a concubine. I don't care if people laugh at me.

受處罰就受處罰，誰讓我犯了罪呢？
I'm fine with taking the punishment. I have no one to blame for my crime.

A: 你想跟我一起旅行可以，但你得每天開車。
B: 開車就開車，我不怕每天開車。
A: You can travel with me, but then you have to drive every day.
B: That is fine. I am not afraid of driving every day.

A: 對不起，我把你的書丟了。
B; 丟了就丟了，別擔心。
A: I am sorry that I lost your book.
B: If it is lost, it is lost. Don't worry.

10．上不了名校有什麼大不了的? 我只要我們孩子高高興興地生活。
("有什麼大不了的" or "沒什麼大不了的" both mean, "It is not a big deal" and/or "it is nothing serious, alarming, or remarkable").

他只是給學校捐了一點錢，有什麼大不了的？
He just donated a little money to school. It's nothing remarkable.

你的手機只是沒電了，沒什麼大不了的問題。
Your cell phone is just out of battery, it is not a big deal.

11. 誰說我們小麗笨? 她還小.
("誰說" can be used in a rhetorical question to oppose an idea, meaning "says who?").

A: 美國的東西太貴了，很多東西我都等回到中國以後再買。
B: 誰說美國的東西貴？有的東西比在中國買便宜多了。
A: Everything in the U.S.A. is too expensive. There are many things I have to wait until I return to China to buy.

B: Who says American is expensive? There are a lot of things that are much cheaper here than in China.

誰說這家飯館的生意不好？你看， 顧客不是很多嗎？
Who said that this restaurant doesn't have a good business? Look, aren't there a lot of customers?

12．你這樣…，到時候她不愛說話，一個朋友也沒有，你會高興嗎？
("到時候 XX" is a transition of "到 XX 的時候." It can be translated as "then" or "when the time comes." It carries an assumption that a change will happen or the time will come).

我給你介紹女朋友你不要，到時候娶不到老婆可別哭。
You don't want me introduce potential girlfriends to you. Just don't cry when you can't find a wife.
你先別問。到時候就知道了。
Don't ask now. You will know when the time comes.

她沒有馬上同意，但到時候也不一定會反對。
She didn't agree right away, but she might not oppose it when the time comes.

口語練習：請用聽力對話裏學到的生詞和口語用法討論下面的問題：

怎麼+Verb+ 都/　到底 /　看來/　所以說嘛… /　光+Verb Phrase /　誰說… 有話好好說 /　給我+VP/　XX 就 XX /　什麼大不了 /　到時候

1. A— 你寫了一本關於培養孩子的書，但是賣得很不好。你希望你的朋友可以　　幫你。
   B —你的朋友希望你幫他，讓他的書成為暢銷書。但其實你不太關心他的書，也不是很想幫他。

2. A—你的兒子現在六年級，你想讓他補習，讓他為申請大學做準備。
   B—你覺得太太對孩子太嚴格了。你希望孩子輕松一點。

課文

第一部分

繼《哈佛女孩劉亦婷》贏得本年度暢銷書冠軍之後，《我家笨笨上劍橋》、《輕輕松松上哈佛》、《耶魯男孩》、《牛津圓夢》等書陸續跟著出版。這些書之所以會受歡迎，就是因為中國這些望子成龍，望女成鳳的家長們，個個都恨不得也能馬上培養出個"哈佛女孩"或"耶魯男孩"。

然而，在一片叫好聲中，有個五歲的青島小女孩，卻勇敢地站出來說"不"。這位小女孩的媽媽是《哈佛女孩劉亦婷》的熱情讀者。按照培養劉亦婷的模式，這位媽媽每天追著女兒給她讀名著聽，逼她學這個，逼她學那個。結果，原本性格活潑，頑皮開朗的小女孩，竟然變得孤僻，動不動就哭、就生氣。終於有一天，她再也忍受不了媽媽的教育方式，大聲喊："我討厭劉亦婷！我不要上哈佛！"

中國父母對子女教育的重視是無人能比的，然而，申請名校，拿獎學金，難道就等於一生的成功嗎？答案顯然是否定的，很多父母也都能認識到這一點。

生詞用法

	继	繼	jì	following	見語法
	哈佛	哈佛	Hāfó	Harvard University	
	刘亦婷	劉亦婷	Liú Yìtíng	name of a Harvard student from China	
1	赢	贏	yíng	to win; to beat in competition	我們球隊贏了三場球賽。/我們隊以三比一贏了他們隊。/贏得數學冠軍/他贏了三百萬。

2	本年度	本年度	běnniándù	this year; the current year	本學期/本班/本課/本年度計劃
3	畅销	暢銷	chàngxiāo	to sell in high volume; best-selling	這本書很暢銷。/這是本暢銷書。/中國電視機暢銷海內外。
4	冠军	冠軍	guànjūn	champion; championship; first place prize winner	冠軍杯/冠軍賽/乒乓球冠軍/全國冠軍/贏得世界冠軍
5	笨	笨	bèn	stupid; foolish; clumsy	笨方法/笨手笨腳/你的想法真笨。/笨死了！/笨蛋 (dàn)!
	剑桥	劍橋	Jiànqiáo	Cambridge; Cambridge University	
6	轻松	輕鬆	qīngsōng	to relax; relaxed; light; calm	輕松的音樂/輕松的工作/感到輕松/咱們輕松一下，別太累了。/這門課一點也不輕松。
	耶鲁	耶魯	Yēlǔ	Yale University	
	牛津	牛津	Niújīn	Oxford; Oxford University	
7	圆梦	圓夢	yuánmèng	to fulfill a dream or a goal	圓了當老師的夢。/沒有圓拿冠軍的夢。
8	陆续	陸續	lùxù	one after another; successively	客人陸續來了。/學生陸陸續續地走了進來。
9	出版	出版	chūbǎn	to come off the press; to publish (of books)	出版字典/出版書/這本書是兩千零三年出版的。/你的書出版了沒有？
10	望子成龙，望女成凤	望子成龍，望女成鳳	wàngzǐ chénglóng, wàngnǚ chéngfèng	to hope that sons and daughters will grow up to be successful	我的父母望子成龍。/ 哪一個父母不望子成龍呢？
11	家长	家長	jiāzhǎng	the parent or guardian of a child	家長會/嚴格的家長/家長和孩子的關係
	恨不得	恨不得	hènbùdé	to be very anxious to (do something); to itch to	恨不得飛回家/他恨不得馬上做完功課去踢足球。見語法
12	培养	培養	peíyǎng	to cultivate; to foster; to educate	培養孩子/培養一種觀念/培養一種習慣
13	一片	一片	yípiàn	a slice; a stretch (of land, water); a scene of (rejoicing, sound)	一片肉/一片草地/一大片水/一片哭聲/一片叫好聲
14	叫好	叫好	jiàohǎo	to cheer on; to commend; acclaim	向球隊叫好/這是一部大家都叫好的電影。

15	勇敢	勇敢	yǒnggǎn	brave; courageous	勇敢的精神/勇敢的孩子/去吧！去吧！你應該勇敢一點兒。
16	读者	讀者	dúzhě	reader (a person); readership	一本書的讀者/報紙的一位讀者
17	按照	按照	ànzhào	in accordance with; to follow (an instruction, regulation)	按照計劃/按照要求/按照實際情況/我會按照你介紹的方法做。
18	模式	模式	móshì	model; mode	培養模式/管理模式
19	名著	名著	míngzhù	famous book; masterpiece	世界名著/文學名著/一本名著/一部名著
20	逼	逼	bī	to compel; to force	逼孩子學習/逼媽媽給她買衣服/逼學生回答問題/別逼我！
	结果	結果	jiéguǒ	result; finally; as a result; as it turns out	見語法
	原本	原本	yuánběn	original; originally; formerly	見語法
21	性格	性格	xìnggé	disposition; personality; character (synonym: 個性)	安靜的性格/性格開放/他的性格和媽媽很像。
22	开朗	開朗	kāilǎng	(of a person) open; cheerful; extroverted	性格開朗/開朗的孩子/他性格很開朗。
23	孤僻	孤僻	gūpì	unsociable; eccentric (a negative usage); introverted	性格孤僻/孤僻的老人/這個人太孤僻了！
24	无法	無法	wúfǎ	unable; incapable (usually followed by two-syllable verb)	無法幫助/無法開口/無法忍受
	动不动就 動不動就		dòng-búdòng jiù	easily; often (to have certain reaction)	他動不動就感冒。/他動不動就生氣。見語法
25	方式	方式	fāngshì	way; method; style	領導方式/生活方式/工作方式/簡單的方式
26	喊	喊	hǎn	to shout; to yell; to cry out; to call a person	他大喊"幫幫我"。/他總是對父母大喊大叫。/我聽到外面有人喊你，你去看看。/我喊了他好幾聲，他都沒聽見。
27	讨厌	討厭	tǎoyàn	to dislike; to be disgusted with; to be fed up with	我討厭這個地方。/你這個人真討厭。/我討厭住在大城市。

28	重视	重視	zhòngshì	to attach importance to; to value highly	他很重視考試。/這個國家對教育很重視。/他的父母很重視孩子的培養。
29	无人能比	無人能比	wúrén-néngbǐ	incomparable; beyond comparison	父母對孩子的關心無人能比。/麥可喬丹是個無人能比的球員。
30	申请	申請	shēnqǐng	to apply	申請工作/申請大學
31	名校	名校	míngxiào	well-known schools	一所名校。
32	奖学金	獎學金	jiǎngxuéjīn	scholarship; fellowship	申請獎學金/得一萬元獎學金
	难道	難道	nándào	[a word to strength one's rhetorical intonation]	見語法
33	等于	等於	děngyú	to be equal to; to be equivalent to; to amount to	一加一等於二。/考試沒考好不等於沒學好。/他說了等於沒說，我還是不懂。
34	成功	成功	chénggōng	to succeed; successful; success;	這個計劃成功了。/他終於成功了。/他的成功是他努力的結果。/大家都為他的成功高興。/成功的企業/這個企業做得很成功。/他成功地追到了那個女孩子。
35	答案	答案	dá'àn	answer (n.); 答 = to answer	問題的答案/這題練習的答案是什麼？/你答對了，我答錯了。
36	显然	顯然	xiǎnrán	obvious; evident; obviously	很顯然，他的中文比你的好。/他的答案顯然是不對的。/她站著睡著了，顯然太累了。
37	否定	否定	foǔdìng	to negate; to deny; negative (肯定=to affirm; positive; surely (see also L7)	否定你的看法/別否定孩子的想法/他的答案是否定的。

課文

第二部分

但是，面對越來越激烈的社會競爭，家長們還是免不了要為孩子的教育傷腦筋，特別在經濟條件好起來以後，中國父母給孩子請家教的請家教，報補習班的報補習班。一到週末，孩子們又是學鋼琴，又是學畫畫的。父母們捨得為孩子花錢，也捨得為孩子花精力、花時間。為了孩子，哪怕天天吃苦也是值得的。

中國父母一向望子成龍、望女成鳳，而獨生子女政策更使父母把全部的希望集中在一個孩子身上。這些獨生子女所受到的壓力是那些在美國成長的孩子們難以想象的。但與此同時，獨生子女多多少少都會受到父母的嬌慣，而成為家中任性、霸道的"小皇帝"。一般外國人對中國孩子的印象是"聰明、用功"，但我們也越來越發現很多中國孩子缺乏獨立性和責任心，創造性和適應能力也沒有西方孩子那麼強。

時代在改變，中國人培養孩子的觀念和方式也在改變。"不打不成器"的傳統觀念在許多家長的眼裏已經不適用了，何況一家就這麼一個孩子，也捨不得打。但為了把子女往西方名校裏送，大多數家長還是選擇當嚴格的父母。

生詞用法

38	面对	面對	miànduì	to face; to confront	面對困難/面對問題/面對激烈的競爭/我的房子面對公園。
39	激烈	激烈	jīliè	intense; fierce; violent(ly)	激烈的球賽/激烈的競爭/激烈地討論問題/吵得很激烈
40	竞争	競爭	jìngzhēng	to compete; to vie for; competition	自由競爭/名校之間的競爭/申請大學的競爭很激烈/我要跟她競爭這個工作。/競爭得過/競爭不過
41	免不了	免不了	miǎn-bùliǎo	to be unavoidable; bound to be	如果你總是不講究衛生，你免不了會生病。/父母免不了為孩子的教育擔心。
42	家教	家教	jiājiào	private tutor	跟家教學習/請一名家教幫你。
43	报	報	bào	to register for/in	報補習班/報名參加球隊/向小王報名

44	补习班	補習班	bǔxíbān	cram school	上補習班/補習英文/你的數學需要補習。
45	钢琴	鋼琴	gāngqín	piano	彈(tán-to play)鋼琴/一架鋼琴
	舍得	捨得	shěde	to willingly expend; not begrudge	捨得花錢/捨不得花錢/不捨得花錢　見語法
46	精力	精力	jīnglì	energy; vigor	這麼晚還不睡，你的精力真好。/今天忙了一天，現在一點精力都沒有。
47	吃苦	吃苦	chīkǔ	to endure hardship	吃了很多苦/很能吃苦/吃不了苦/申請大學要吃很多苦
	一向	一向	yíxiàng	all along, as always (until the present)	見語法
48	全部	全部	quánbù	total; all	全部學生/全部精力/全部時間
49	集中	集中	jízhōng	to concentrate; to focus on	集中精力/集中大家的想法/集中你的注意力/外面太吵了，我不能集中精神學習。
50	压力	壓力	yālì	pressure	生活壓力/學習壓力/來自父母的壓力/他受不了這麼大的壓力。/老師給他的壓力太大了。
51	成长	成長	chéng-zhǎng	to grow up; growth	人口成長/經濟成長得很快。/關心孩子的成長。
	难以想象 難以想像		nányǐ-xiǎngxiàng	hard to conceive of ; unimaginable	難以想象的壓力 (見語法"難以")
52	与此同时 與此同時		yúcǐ-tóngshí	at the same time; meanwhile	美國人很喜歡中國生產的便宜東西，但與此同時，他們也反對從中國進口東西。
	多多少少		duōduō-shǎoshǎo	more or less	見語法
53	娇惯	嬌慣	jiāoguàn	to spoil; to pamper; pampering	別嬌慣這孩子。/這孩子被嬌慣壞了。/他把女朋友嬌慣壞了。/她從小受到父母的嬌慣。
54	任性	任性	rènxìng	capricious; willful; stubborn	任性的孩子/你別太任性了，你得替父母想想。
55	霸道	霸道	bàdào	overbearing; high-handed; bossy	霸道的孩子/他對同學很霸道。
56	皇帝	皇帝	huángdì	emperor	

57	印象	印象	yìnxiàng	impression	我對他的印象很好。/他給我留下了很深的印象。/我對這件事沒什麼印象。
58	缺乏	缺乏	quēfá	to lack; to be short of	缺乏乾淨的水/缺乏信心/缺乏朋友/缺乏能力
59	独立性	獨立性	dúlìxìng	independence; (性, as a suffix, means "nature")	獨立性很強/很獨立/很有獨立性/缺乏獨立性/美國是在哪一年獨立的？
60	责任	責任	zérèn	duty; responsibility (責任心/責任感: sense of responsibility)	很強的責任心 /我的責任很重。/他很有責任感。
61	创造性	創造性	chuàng-zàoxìng	creativity	創造性很強/很有創造性
62	适应	適應	shìyìng	to adapt to; to get with it; to fit in	適應新環境/適應新的方法/適應農村生活/他適應得很慢。
63	能力	能力	nénglì	ability; capacity for	工作能力/生產能力/適應能力/獨立能力/能力很強/很有能力
64	不打不成器		bùdǎ-bùchéngqì	"spare the rod, spoil the child"	不打不成器的傳統觀念 A: 你幹嗎打孩子？ B: 不打不成器啊！
65	适用	適用	shìyòng	to be applicable; suitable for use	你的學習方法對我不適用。/這樣的政策在中國不適用。
	何况	何況	hékuàng	much less; not to mention	見語法
66	大多数	大多數	dàduōshù	great majority; most	大多數學生/在大多數情況下
67	选择	選擇	xuǎnzé	to select; to choose; election; choice	選擇一輛車/ 我沒有選擇，只好這樣做。/學中文還是學日文，你得做個選擇。/

句型和語法

- **繼 ...(之) 後 ， ....("after (someone/something)" or "following (someone/something)" ; The subject of the first clause must have something in common with or an impact on the subject of the following phrase) .**

  繼李小龍(Bruce Lee) 之後，成龍 (Jacky Chen) 成了最受歡迎的功夫好手。
  After Bruce Lee, Jackie Chan became the most popular Kung Fu master.

  繼 Motorola 之後，Nokia，Samsung 等手機公司在中國的生意也發展了起來。
  Following Motorola, the business of cell phone companies in China like Nokia, Samsung, and others, started to pick up.

  十九，二十世紀的時候，移民(yímín)到美國的，主要是哪些國家的人？
  (回答問題)=〉

- **Subject+之所以... (就) 是因為... (By using "之所以", we place the result in the first clause and state the reason in the second clause following "是因為". "就" can be used with "是因為" for emphasis, meaning "the exact reason is...").**

  這本書之所以暢銷，是因為中國有太多望子成龍的家長們。
  The reason this book sold so well is that too many parents in China place all their hope in their kids.

  小張：他每天花那麼多時間打球，會不會影響他學習啊？
  小李：不打球怎麼行？學校之所以給他獎學金，就是因為他球打得好。
  Xiao Zhang: He spends so much time everyday playing ball. Isn't that going to impact his studies?
  Xiao Zhang: How could he not play? The reason the school gave him a scholarship is that he's such a good player.

  她是個女強人，你真要娶她嗎？
  (回答問題)=〉

- 恨不得 **+ Verb Phrase ("我恨不得" literately means "I hate that I can't...". But it is typically translated as "I am anxious to..." or "I am itching to..."**

There can be other subjects besides "我" for "恨不得". "恨不得" is followed by a verb phrase).

有些臺灣人，恨不得臺灣能馬上獨立，但有更多的中國人，恨不得馬上把臺灣拿下來。
There are some Taiwanese who are itching to declare independence, but there are even more Chinese who are itching to take control of Taiwan.

這位熱情的讀者，恨不得在一天內就把這幾本書都看完。
The passionate reader is anxious to finish all these books in a single day.

(完成句子)=〉他非常喜歡法國電影，
________________________________。

- **一片 XX 聲 ("片" is a measure word used for something flat, such as "一片餅乾", "一片麵包". When we say "一片 XX 聲", "片" is associated with the concept of "something that spreads out." It means "The sound/voice is all around").**

  車禍發生後，只聽到一片哭聲，誰都不想多說什麼。
  After a car crash occurs, you can hear only widespread weeping. Nobody wants to say anything.

  在一片叫好聲中，哈利波特(Hālì Bōtè)拿下了暢銷書冠軍。
  To great acclaim, *Harry Potter* became a number one best-seller.

  由於大家的反對，色情行業終於被踢出了這個城市。
  (也可以說)=〉

- **…，結果… ("結果" is used as a conjunction in a second clause; it can be translated as "as a result" or "as it turns out." The first clause is usually an action or a situation, not a cause leading clearly to an effect. "結果", meaning, "as a result" or "consequently," introduces the eventual status or result that the action or situation has developed into. Usually the eventual status or result is unhappy or not what the speaker expected).**

  我以為讓她上補習班會對她的學習有幫助，結果她卻越來越討厭上學。
  I had mistakenly believed that making her attend cram school would be beneficial to her studies, but as it turns out, she just increasingly hated going to class.

他申請了牛津，劍橋等幾所學校，結果，沒有一所學校要他。
He applied to Oxford, Cambridge, and other similar schools, but as it turns out, none of them accepted him.

(完成句子)=〉中國以為最少可以在兩千零四年的奧運拿到三十五面金牌(jīnpái)，________________________________。

- 原本 **(When we use "原本", we indicate that things are different from the original or earlier time. It is often used with "但是", "後來", "結果" etc.).**

他原本是個開朗的孩子，但後來變得有點孤僻。
He was originally a cheerful kid, but he later became somewhat unsociable.

我原本學的是圖書館學，結果沒當成圖書館員，竟然當了個中文老師。
I originally studied library science, but as it turns out I didn't become a librarian. Instead, I became a Chinese teacher.

你不是說七月要到中國去嗎？怎麼沒去呢？
(回答問題)=〉

- 動不動就 **("動不動就" is used in front of a verb phrase meaning "VP at every possible moment". "動不動就哭" means "to cry for any reason" ; "動不動就生氣" means "to easily get angry or offended").**

他的女朋友動不動就生氣，我真不懂他為什麼還那麼喜歡跟她在一起。
His girlfriend gets offended so easily. I really don't understand why he still likes being with her so much.

這家店賣的衣服，動不動就得上千塊錢，你最好還是到別家去買吧！
The clothes that this store sells often cost over $1,000. You'd better go shopping at a different store!

(完成句子)=〉這家公司生產的汽車雖然便宜，但
____________________。

- 難道 **("難道" can be placed in front of or after a subject to create a rhetorical phrase meaning the contrary of what is said).**

你說中國人愛錢，難道美國人就不愛嗎？
You say Chinese love money. Is it true that Americans don't?

她難道不知道她女兒不喜歡鋼琴也不喜歡畫畫兒嗎？為什麼一定要花錢逼女兒去學那些東西呢？
Could it be that he doesn't know his daughter doesn't like either the piano or painting? Why does he want to spend money to make her study those things?

(完成句子)=〉你給孩子這麼大的壓力，
________________________________。

- 認識到 **(to realize; to understand…)**

他雖然只有五歲，但已經能夠**認識到**申請名校的重要性。
Although he is only five-year-old, he can already understand the importance of applying to famous schools.

家長們漸漸**認識到**，要培養孩子的獨立性和責任感就不能太嬌慣孩子。
Parents gradually realize that, if they want to teach children independence and responsibility, they can't spoil their children too much.

(完成句子)=〉許多人慢慢認識到________________________________。

- 就 + 這麼/那麼 **("就" here implies a sense of there being only a few or of there being not enough of something).**

一家就這麼一個孩子，嬌慣是難免的。
There is only one child in each family. It is unavoidable that parents will spoil him or her.

一個月就賺那麼一點錢，自己生活都還不夠呢，哪夠交女朋友啊！
(He) makes so little. It's not even enough for him to support himself. How can it be enough to go out with a girlfriend?

你寫的就這麼短？不能多寫點嗎？
Is what you wrote as short as this? Can't you write more?

你不能就這麼走了。
You can't simply leave like this.

小王這學期上三門課。
=> (Insert "就" and "這麼" into the sentence and then translate it)

- **VP1 的 VP1，VP2 的 VP2 (This pattern is used to describe a perspective. In**

the perspective, subjects are each doing something. Verb Phrase 1 and Verb Phrase 2 are samples of the things they do).

這教室裏，看書的看書，睡覺的睡覺(shuìjiào)，沒有一個人關心老師在教些什麼。
In this classroom, some people are reading, some people are sleeping, and not even one person is paying attention to what the teacher is teaching.

一到週末，這些孩子們打球的打球，游泳的游泳(yóuyǒng)，每個人在運動(yùndòng)。
Once the weekend comes, some kids play ball, some swim – everyone is doing sports.

下了課以後，學生們都作些什麼呢？
(回答問題)=>

- 一到 **XX… ("一到" is used in the first clause, either in front of or after a time phrase, meaning "whenever it is XX" or "once it is XX").**

一到考試前一天晚上，他就睡不著覺。
Whenever it is the night before an exam, he can't sleep at all.

星期三一到，我們就去找律師談話。
Once Wednesday comes, we will talk to a lawyer.

他每天九點鐘一定給他女朋友打電話。
(也可以說)=〉

- 又是 **VP1** 又是 **VP2** 的 **(VP1 and VP2 are samples of a list of things the subject does).**

這幾個學生，又是唱歌，又是跳舞的，把晚會辦得非常熱鬧(rènào)。
These students are singing and also dancing. They made the evening party extremely lively.

這孩子又是哭又是吵的，我真是快要忍受不了了。
This child is always crying and making noise; I'm seriously about to lose it (literal translation: "I really am about to be unable to endure it").

除了補習數學(shùxué)，他還補習電腦(diànnǎo)，每天都忙得不得了。
(也可以說)=〉

- 捨得/ 捨不得 (**"捨得" means "be willing to expend", even though one is giving up things one cherishes. Both "不捨得" and "捨不得" mean the opposite. They are interchangeable. Structurally, when "不" occurs in front of "捨得", it negates "捨得", whereas in "捨不得", "不" functions as it does in the structure of "找得著/找不著").**

只要他的太太開口，再貴的東西他也捨得買。
All it takes is for his wife to ask and nothing is too expensive for him to be willing to buy.

這孩子這麼不聽話，你又捨不得罵(mà)，又捨不得打，難道不怕把他嬌慣壞了嗎？This child is so disobedient, but you found it too difficult to scold or spank him. Aren't you afraid you're spoiling him?

在中國住了兩個多月，我愛上了這兒的人，愛上了這兒的生活方式，現在要走了，我覺得太捨不得了。
I have lived in China for two months and I have fallen in love with the people and the way of life. Now that it is time to go, I'm not willing to leave.

為了培養孩子，要她花精力，要她花時間都行。
(也可以說)=〉

要她把新車借(jiè)給朋友開沒關係，但要她把新衣服借給朋友穿，她一定不願意。
(也可以說)=〉

- 哪怕+ **(… 再/有多)…也/都(no matter how…; even if…)**

為了把那個漂亮的女孩追到手，哪怕吃再多苦都是值得的。
To make that beautiful girl become my girlfriend, no matter how much suffering I have to go through, it is worthy it.

哪怕競爭有多激烈你也得試一試。
No matter how competitive it is, you should try.

哪怕不睡覺，我也要把這個問題想清楚。
I will think clearly about this problem even if it means I can't go to bed.

不管孩子有多任性，你也得逼他去補習。
(也可以說)=〉

- 難以(**"難以" occurs in front of a two-syllable verb, meaning "hard to." It is usually used only in written Chinese).**

 一個活潑、開朗的孩子，怎麼會變得那麼孤僻呢？真是讓人難以相信。
 How can an active, cheerful child become so introverted as this? It's hard to believe.

 對女人來說，來自傳統的壓力是一種難以擺脫的束縛。
 For women, the pressures of tradition are a bondage that is hard to get rid of.

 那麼多困難，他竟然成功了！我真是無法想象。
 (也可以說)=〉

- 一向 (**"一向" indicates that an act or situation has remained the same from a certain time in the past up to the time being discussed. You can't say "畢業以後我會一向給你寫信". Here you have to use "一直" instead).**

 這孩子一向非常獨立，做什麼事都不需要靠別人。
 This child has always been very independent; he doesn't need to rely on anyone to do things for him.

 中國父母對教育一向非常重視。
 Chinese parents have always considered education to be very important.

 孤兒院裏，找到個健康活潑(jiànkāng huópō) 的男孩一向都不容易。
 At the orphanage, it has always been difficult to find a healthy and out-going boy.

 從以前到現在，這家公司的生意都很好。
 (也可以說)=〉

- 多多少少 (**"多多少少" is used in front of a verb phrase, meaning "more or less" , "to some degree" ,or "somewhat").**

 沒上過大學，找工作時多多少少會吃點苦。
 If you haven't gone to college, you will more or less undergo hardship (literal translation: "eat bitter") when looking for jobs.

 考試以前，我多多少少有點緊張(jǐnzhāng)。
 Before a test, I'm somewhat nervous.

你對上個星期學的東西還有一點印象嗎？
(回答問題)=〉

- 何況 **("何況" occurs at the beginning of the second clause. When it is used to introduce a further reason, it is the same as "況且". However, "何況" can also be used rhetorically to indicate that what is stated in the second clause goes beyond what is mentioned in the first clause.)**

學鋼琴學畫畫什麼的都得花不少錢，何況**(or** 況且**)**還得花精力、花時間，我看還是算了吧！
Taking piano or painting lessons costs a lot of money, not to mention parents must be willing to expend time and energy. I think you have better forget it!

這孩子一向缺乏獨立性，何況**(or** 況且**)**適應能力也不太強。我們不應該讓他一個人去。
This child is always dependent, and besides that, he is not good at adapting (to new environments). We should not let him go alone.

這個題目聰明的學生都不一定會，何況那些笨學生呢？
Smart students might not necessarily know the answer to this question, not to mention the stupid students.

A: 你有辦法讓這霸道的小皇帝週末好好在家讀書嗎？
(完成句子)=〉 B: 要讓聽話的孩子週末不出去玩都很難，

____

課堂活動

(一) 用課文裹學到的生詞和句型回答問題：

- 劉亦婷是誰？她的書對中國社會有什麼影響？
- 青島的五歲小女孩為什麼討厭劉亦婷？
- 經濟條件好起來以後，中國孩子們的生活有什麼不同？
- “小皇帝”是什麼？
- 外國人對中國學生一般有什麼樣的印象？為什麼呢？
- “不打不成器”是什麼意思？現在的中國父母同意這樣的觀念嗎？

(二)從不同的角度(jiǎodù)來討論:

- 上美國名校值得嗎？
  - 歐洲人(Ōuzhōu rén)
  - 望子成龍的中 國父母
  - 比爾蓋茨 (Bǐěr Gàicí)
  - 小布什總統(Bùshí zǒngtǒng)
- 獨立性和創造性重要，還是用功聽話重要？
  - 望子成龍的中國父母
  - 開放的美國父母
  - 嚴格的中國老師
- 一個中國孩子和一個美國孩子的對話：
  - 中國孩子
  - 美國孩子

(三) 你的看法

- 下邊是兩對父母為他們的九歲孩子安排的時間表，你覺得哪個比較好？為什麼？如果你是他們的父母，你會怎麼安排？

	王小明的父母	李為的父母
1:00 – 2:00	做數學練習	照顧妹妹
2:00 – 3:00	做英文練習	看電視
3:00 – 4:00	跑步 或 游泳	賣檸檬汁 (níngméngzhī)
4:00 – 5:00	學鋼琴	和別的小朋友玩
5:00 - 6:00	學畫畫	做飯
6:00 - 7:00	吃飯，休息	吃飯，休息
7:00 – 8:00	看電視	洗碗(xǐwǎn)

練習題

一. 詞彙練習：(選擇最合適的詞完成句子或段落)

(一) *(贏 逼 喊 報 怕)*

1. 她很____蛇(shé-snake)，一看到蛇，她就大聲____。
2. 我太太喜歡跳舞，可是我不太會跳，所以她____我來____這個跳舞班，希望我學完以後可以常常跟她跳舞。
3. 知道自己的球隊____了冠軍以後，他們非常高興，大聲地____著學校的名字。

(二) *(責任/責任心/責任感　創造/創造性　獨立/獨立性)*

1. 雖然她很聰明，可是我討厭跟她做同屋，因為有的事情是她的________，可是她卻不管。
2. 他一點________都沒有，誰願意跟他一起做事。
3. 向別人學習很重要，可是你也得有________，不能什麼都照別人的方法做。
4. 我感謝父母給我________了這麼好的學習條件和發展機會。
5. 你得替孩子的將來想一想，要培養他的________，不能什麼事情都替他作決定。

(三) *(等於 何況 難道 按照 顯然 一向 恨不得 結果 原本)*

1. 上名校不_____一生的成功。大學生活和專業的選擇決定著將來的成功。
2. 你為什麼要逼我看這本暢銷書，______暢銷書就一定是好書？
3. 你不應該完全______他的模式來培養你的孩子，他培養孩子的模式對你的孩子不一定適用，________這兩個孩子的成長環境完全不一樣。
4. 很______，他非常嬌慣孩子。孩子要什麼，他______不會說"不"。
5. 為了讓他的書早點出版，他該休息的時候根本沒好好休息，________一天能工作四十八小時。________，突然生病，住進了醫院。
6. 小華______想請父母替他們照顧幾天孩子，可是一想到父母的身體越來越差，她又不好意思開口了。

(四)

1. *(多多少少　難以想象　無人能比　精力　成功　霸道)*

在我們學校，他彈鋼琴的水平可以說________。我想，他為鋼琴花的____、吃過的苦都是其他人________的。不過，小小年紀鋼琴就能達到這樣的水平，也使他________有一點驕傲，有時候甚至有一點______，似乎認為誰都得聽他的。

2. *(開朗　動不動　孤僻　霸道　免不了)*

A: 你和你先生性格都很活潑，怎麼你們的孩子卻這麼______，不喜歡說話？而且還________就哭。

B: 誰說我們孩子________？孩子在陌生人面前________會沉默一些，跟我們在一起的時候他有說有笑，______得很呢。

3. *(成長　喜歡　成功　討厭　勇敢　激烈)*

每個人的______中，都會經歷各種各樣的競爭。有的人很______競爭，而有的人卻認為有競爭才有進步。現在這個社會，各個行業競爭都非常______。只有______地面對競爭，才能適應競爭，贏得______。

4. *(任性　缺乏　能力　重視　重要　輕松)*

被父母嬌慣的孩子，常常______責任感，很______，想做什麼就做什麼， 獨立性也比較差，缺乏照顧自己的________。所以說，我們做家長的一定要______對孩子的培養，不能因為愛孩子就嬌慣孩子。

二. 口語表達練習：(用提供的句型或詞彙完成句子或者對話)

(有/沒什麼大不了的　　怎麼 verb 都 verb 不/沒…　有話好好說嘛
把…給氣死了　　X 就 X (as in“二十分就二十分”)

1. A: 怎麼辦，這次考試我沒考好。
   B: 別緊張。不就是一次考試嘛，___________。
2. 你快幫我看看這封信是什麼意思，我___________。
3. 你男朋友的電話你怎麼不接呢？不要再生氣了，___________!
4. 我花那麼多錢給他買的名著他一本都沒看，___________!
5. A: 我們一年只能給你一千塊獎學金。要是你願意接受,你下個星期就可以來上學。
   B: ___________, 雖然不多，總比沒有好。

三. 翻譯練習：(用提供的詞或句型翻譯下面的句子)

1. 繼…之後/ 動不動/ 恨不得/ 無人能比

   After her book became the number one best seller, her brother itched to publish a book on how to educate child. He often tells people: "My model of children education is incomparable".

2. 捨得/捨不得　又是…又是… 的

   Her parents were not reluctant to spend money on her. They hired a private tutor and sent her to a cram school.

3. 難道/ 結果

   A: Aren't you afraid that you are putting too much pressure on your child?
   B: My only hope is for my child. I need to be strict to her. My parents spoiled me too much, and as a result, I couldn't receive a scholarship and I couldn't go to a famous college. I have gone through a lot of hard times.

四. 作文：(從下邊幾個題目中, 選擇一個, 寫一篇不少於 500 字的作文。你至少要用六個所提供的句型或詞彙)

免不了/難免	哪怕...也...	與此同時	多多少少
一到...,就...	何況	等於	難道
繼...之後,...	結果	動不動就	恨不得
...之所以...是因為...	一向		

1. 如果我做父母...
2. 一個中國孩子的獨白(monologue)
3. 上名校等於一生的成功嗎？
4. 請談談你對中西方教育模式的看法

第四課 中國的民間團體與民間活動

Let's warm-up with a review exercise!

Match the words in characters with Pinyin and English:

漢字	拼音	英文	哪兒學過
發展			二年級
相信			二年級
世界			二年級
害怕			二年級
了解			二年級
嚴重			二年級
貧窮			第一課
無私			第一課
壓迫			第二課
提供			第二課
物質			第二課
官員			第二課
處罰			第二課
曾經			第二課
重視			第三課
贏			第三課

拼音

1. céngjīng	2. fāzhǎn	3. chǔfá	4. guānyuán
5. hàipà	6. liǎojiě	7. píngióng	8. shìjiè
9. tígōng	10. wúsī	11. wùzhì	12. xiāngxìn
13. yánzhòng	14. yāpò	15. yíng	16. zhòngshì

英文

a. ever	b. material	c. official (n.)	d. poor
e. selfless	f. serious	g. to be afraid	h. to believe
i. to develop	j. to oppress	k. to provide	l. to punish
m. to know; to understand	n. to value highly	o. to win	p. world

聽力&口語

聽錄音回答問題

對話一

1.	2.	3.	4.	5.

生詞：村民，艾滋病，感染，賣血，衛生
複習：色情行業，農村，捐，貧窮，賺錢，認為，領導，富裕
(差，發展，了解，嚴重，世界)

對話二

1.	2.	3.	4.	5.

生詞：治病，迷信，落後，避免，中醫
複習：勇敢，其實，觀念，願意，何況，陪
(厲害，相信，害怕，經驗，嚴重)

對話三

1.	2.	3.	4.	5.

生詞：總統，主席，選舉，環境，保護
民間，支持，限制，解決，改善，允許
複習：權利，認為，政策，重視，缺乏，責任，鼓勵，根本
組織，在…看來，(經驗，發展，同意，老百姓，靠)

根據對話一回答問題：

1. 對話中討論的這個農村發生了什麼事？怎麼發生的？
2. 說話人認為，對這件事政府應該做些什麼？

根據對話二回答問題：

1. 小華生病咳嗽(késòu), 她奶奶為什麼不讓她去看醫生？她為什麼不去醫院？

1. 小華的朋友小文給他什麼建議？

根據對話三回答問題：

1. 對話中談到什麼和臺灣政治有關的事？說話的人關心這些事嗎？有什麼問題是他更關心的？這個問題和政治家有什麼關係？
2. 對於上面談到的問題，說話人覺得政府現在做得怎麼樣？以前呢？

口語用法

1. 可不是嗎，政府現在很重視這個問題，正在想辦法幫助這些村民。
("可不是嗎" is like "exactly" or "that is right" in English when you agree strongly with someone).

A: 現在的年輕人跟我們那時候可真不一樣。
B: 可不是嗎，這些年輕人只知道追求物質享受。
A: Nowadays the young people are really different from what we were.
B: Absolutely, all they know is the pursuit of material pleasures.

2. 什麼跟什麼嘛！穿紅衣服能治病，這也太迷信了吧!
("什麼跟什麼嘛！" means, "How is that even relevant?" or, "What are you talking about?!" So does "哪跟哪啊！" They are used to show strong disagreement with what one has just heard).

A: 你別給孩子太大壓力，週末讓他輕松輕松吧!
B: 什麼跟什麼嘛！我只是買本名著讓他讀，哪給他什麼壓力了！
A: Don't put too much pressure on the child. Let him relax during the weekend!
B: What are you talking about? I just bought him a classic book to read. What kind of pressure did I put on him?

A: 我看小王是在追求你，你看他常常來找你。
B: 哪跟哪啊！我們只是在一起學習。
A: I think Little Wang is in love with you. He visits you quite often.
B: How is that even relevant? We just study together.

3．A: 可是. . .
B: 別可是了，趕快去看大夫吧。
(In a discourse, if one says "可是" or "但是" to continue making excuses to explain or defend oneself, before he/she finishes, the other person can use "別可是了" or "別但是了" to interrupt and disagree the first person).

A: 你已經看了一天書了，該出去走走，休息一下。
B: 可是…
A: 別可是了，去吧！
A: You have been reading for a whole day. It is time for you to go outside for a walk.
B: But…

A: No "buts", just go!

4. 不用謝，小華，我們倆還客氣什麼。
("xx 還客氣什麼" is an idiomatic phrase used to indicate that "xx" are very close and don't have to thank each other. If one responds to the other's thanks with "我們倆還客氣什麼," he is telling his friend that he values the friendship and it is his great pleasure to help."還" is used for emphasis).

A: 小文，非常感謝你今天幫忙，要不然，我真不知道該怎麼辦！
B: 哎呀，小文，你跟我還客氣什麼。
A: Xiao Wen, thank you so much for the big favor today. Without you, I would be really helpless!
B: Oh, Xiao Wen, don't mention it.

A: 我這次能得到這個工作都是因為小文，我得好好謝謝他。
B: 你們倆還客氣什麼， 都十幾年的好朋友了。
A: This time I got this job is because of Xiao Wen. I really have to thank him.
B: You don't have to do that. (Doing that will bring a distance between you two). You and Xiao Wen have been friends for more than ten years.

5. 誰當總統都一樣，我根本不關心. (Interrogative sentence + "都一樣" is a colloquial pattern which means no difference will be made regardless of the result. Sometimes you can add an adjective phrase after "一樣" if you want to be more specific).

A: 你應該好好用功，要不然你拿不到名校的獎學金。
B: 用功不用功都一樣，我知道我一定拿不到什麼獎學金。
A: You should study hard; otherwise you won't receive a scholarship to go to a famous college.
B: Working hard won't make a difference. I know for sure that I can't win any scholarship.

這孩子就是笨，你用什麼模式培養他都一樣。
This child is simply stupid. It won't matter what method you use to teach him.

A: 這個茄子 (qiézi) 你想讓我怎麼做著吃？
B: 怎麼做都一樣不好吃，我就不喜歡茄子。
A: How do you want me to cook this eggplant?
B: It won't be tasty no matter how it is cooked. I don't like eggplant.

6. 民間環境保護活動離不開政府的支持.

(“離不開” means, “Can’t do without” . It is often used to indicate a strong connection between two things).

現代生活離不開電腦。
Our modern lifestyle requires a computer.

我今天的成功離不開我父母的教育和支持。
My current success is inseparable from the education and support given to me by my parents.

7. 也就是說，如果政府不支持，不會有很多人參加的。
(“也就是說” means “in other words”, you can also say “換句話說”. It is used as a cohesive device in a discourse to continue explanation or to state the point a different way).

政府對經濟問題的重視，遠遠超過了對環保問題的重視。換句話說，對政府來說，經濟比環保重要。
The government devotes much more attention to the economy than to environmental protection. In other words, economy is more important to the government than environmental protection.

日本有百分之九十的一次性筷子是中國做的。也就是說， 日本人每天都在吃中國的樹。
90% of the disposable chopsticks used in Japan are made in China; in other words, Japanese are eating Chinese trees everyday.

口語練習：用聽力裏學到的生詞和口語用法討論下面的問題：

可不是嘛/　什麼跟什麼嘛！/　別可是了，…/
Question + 都一樣，/　…離不開…　/　也就是說，…

1. A— 你是中國的政府官員。你覺得中國農村的艾滋病問題沒有想象中的嚴重，你覺得中國政府可以控制得很好。
   B— 你是關心艾滋病問題的美國人。你覺得中國一定得讓美國幫忙解決艾滋病的問題。

2. A— 你生病了，得住院。但醫院只有四樓有房間，你不想住。
   B—你是 A 的太太，你覺得他應該住院。但是你不想到醫院去看他，因為你害怕看到血。

3. A— 你是政治家，你重視經濟問題。
   B—你是老百姓，你關心環保問題。

課文

第一部分

發展民間團體、組織民間活動在過去曾經被中國政府視為非法行為。除非政府批準，否則要發展民間團體簡直是不可能的。就算是現在，民主改革已經進行了幾十年，但民間團體要想順利發展，仍然得政府正式點頭同意。

法輪功組織的合法性在中國就是一個有爭議性的話題。這個宗教團體，既不屬於中國的傳統道教佛教，也和西方的基督教沒有什麼關係。很多人練法輪功是因為他們相信練法輪功可以治病，有一部分人甚至走火入魔，不吃不睡，生病也不去看醫生。由於法輪功組織的規模和影響力越來越大，一九九九年，中國國家主席江澤民以打破迷信、打倒李洪志為理由，限制法輪功組織的發展。

法輪功以外，一些其他的民間活動在發展時也曾受到各種各樣的壓力。有時候，這些壓力並不是來自共產黨，而是來自發展中國家不可避免的官僚作風以及老百姓落後保守的觀念。

生詞用法

1	民间	民間	mínjiān	folk (adj.); nongovernmental	民間音樂/民間故事/民間組織/民間活動
2	团体	團體	tuántǐ	organization; group	社會團體/民間團體/學生團體/團體冠軍/團體賽
3	非法	非法	fēifǎ	illegal; unlawful	非法出版物/非法聚會/非法組織
4	行为	行為	xíngwéi	action; behavior	非法行為/合法行為/無私的行為/官僚行為/保守行為/霸道的行為

	除非	除非	chúfēi	only if; only when; unless	除非你幫我，否則我不幫你。/除非你努力學習，要不然你一定考不上大學。 見語法
5	批准	批准	pīzhǔn	to approve; to sanction; to authorize	批準一個計劃/計劃已經被批準了。/他被批準為黨員。/我的申請得到了批準。
	否则	否則	fǒuzé	otherwise; or else	申請必須在二十四小時內進行，否則不能被批準。/你得注意衛生，否則會生病。 見語法
	简直	簡直	jiǎnzhí	simply; at all	這個美國人的中文簡直跟中國人的一樣好。/這個星期簡直沒有一個好天氣。 見語法
	就算…也/还/仍		jiùsuàn	even if	見語法
6	民主	民主	mínzhǔ	democratic democracy;	民主國家/民主政府/民主制度/我們主管做事很民主。
7	顺利	順利	shùnlì	smooth going; smoothly;	事情進行得很順利。/他的一生非常順利。/我們順利完成了這項計劃。/工作正在順利進行中。
8	仍然	仍然	réngrán	as usual; still (adv.)	他不工作以後仍然很忙。/他們的關係仍然不好。
9	正式	正式	zhèngshì	formal; official	正式的晚會/正式比賽/這件衣服太正式了。/我正式給你們介紹一下，這位是…。
10	点头	點頭	diǎntóu	to nod one's head; to signal one's agreement	他對我點頭打招呼。/他向我點點頭。/對我參加籃球賽的事，我媽媽點頭了。
11	法轮功	法輪功	fǎlúngōng	Falun Gong	
12	合法性	合法性	héfǎxìng	legitimacy (合法 = legal; lawful)	合法行為/合法組織/合法活動/合法財產/合法權利
13	争议	爭議	zhēngyì	controversy	有爭議的問題/他們在這個問題上有很大的爭議。/這是個爭議性很強的問題。/這個問題引起了很大的爭議。
14	话题	話題	huàtí	subject (of talk); topic	換話題/有爭議性的話題/有趣的話題
15	宗教	宗教	zōngjiào	religion	宗教改革/宗教自由/宗教音樂/宗教政策/宗教活動

16	属于	屬於	shǔyú	to belong to; to be part of; to be included in	這是屬於我的財產。/他希望有個屬於自己的家。/中國政府認為臺灣屬於中國。
17	道教	道教	Dàojiào	Taoism/Daoism	
18	佛教	佛教	Fójiào	Buddhism	
19	基督教	基督教	Jīdūjiào	Christianity	
20	练	練	liàn	to practice	他每天早上起來練功夫。/我每星期練唱三次。/他練法輪功。
21	治病	治病	zhìbìng	to treat disease; to cure illness	大夫把他的病治好了。/這種病沒法治。
22	走火入魔		zǒuhuǒ-rùmó	to have blind faith in; to be possessed by the Devil	他練功夫練得走火入魔，連覺都不睡了。/ 他信教信得走火入魔，連爸爸媽媽都不要了。
23	规模	規模	guīmó	scale; scope; extent	公司的規模/生產規模/這次活動的規模很大。/政府大規模地進行經濟改革。
24	影响力	影響力	yǐngxiǎng-lì	power of influence (力 can be a suffix meaning "power or ability", such as in 創造力，想象力，適應力)	很有影響力/中國經濟發展對世界有很大的影響力。/她在公司裏說話很有影響力。
25	主席	主席	zhǔxí	chairman	國家主席/足球聯盟主席/當主席
	江泽民	江澤民	Jiāng Zémín	name of former Chinese chairman	
26	迷信	迷信	míxìn	superstition; blind worship	迷信行為/迷信觀念/這是迷信，你別相信。/他迷信風水。
27	打倒	打倒	dădăo	to beat down	那五歲的小孩把這個大胖子給打倒了。/打倒迷信/這種說法已經被打倒了。
	李洪志	李洪志	Lǐ Hóngzhì	the founder of Falungong	
28	理由	理由	lǐyóu	reason	沒有理由不上課/他不批準的理由是什麼?
29	限制	限制	xiànzhì	to restrict; restriction	年齡限制/時間限制/限制說話時間。/政府限制私營企業的發展。/婦女的權利受到了限制。

30	避免	避免	bìmiǎn	to avoid; to prevent (something from happening)	避免車禍/避免麻煩/婚禮上應該避免穿黑色的衣服。/你最好避免在五點鐘走，五點車最多。
31	官僚	官僚	guānliáo	bureaucratic; bureaucracy;	官僚行為/這樣做太官僚了。/他在政府官僚裏待久了，做事特別慢。
32	作风	作風	zuòfēng	style; style of work; method of doing something	他的生活作風有問題。/ 這家公司改變了過去的作風。
33	落后	落後	luòhòu	to fall behind; backward; underdeveloped	落後的生活/~觀念/~條件/你現在比別的同學好，可是還得用功，要不然還可能會落後。
34	保守	保守	bǎoshǒu	conservative	保守的觀念/保守的行為/他作風很保守。/他穿得太保守。

課文

第二部分

高耀潔原本是河南中醫學院的教授。九十年代，在河南省幾個貧窮的農村，許多村民在別無選擇的情況下不得不靠賣血來賺錢養家。但農村的衛生條件很差，很多人因使用不乾淨的針頭而感染上了艾滋病。面對這些不幸的病人，高耀潔教授站出來，無私地給他們提供物質幫助，改善當地的衛生條件，並通過免費發送小手冊教村民怎樣防治艾滋病。

然而，高教授的行為卻受到了河南地方官員的反對。這些官員害怕中央政府發現當地的非法賣血活動，為了避免受到處罰，他們竟然限制高教授的活動，不允許她向村民發送艾滋病防治手冊。當時中央政府不了解情況的嚴重性，也不希望中國的艾滋病問題引起世界的注意，因此，一開始對高教授的活動采取不支持的態度。中央政府相信，只有靠政府才能解決問題。

同時，當地的村民對艾滋病完全不了解，他們以為這種病一定和色情行業有關係，當高耀潔把艾滋病防治手冊發送給他們的時候，他們只是害怕地往地上一扔。只有在經濟上得到高耀潔幫助的那些艾滋病孤兒，真心感謝高耀潔這位無私的老太太。二零零零年以後，中國政府漸漸對艾滋病問題重視起來了。二零零三年，高耀潔被中央電視臺選為"感動中國年度人物"。

中國政府並不是不允許發展民間組織或組織民間活動，但他們絕對不希望民間組織的影響力超過政府。這也許和臺灣的歷史經驗有關。七十年代，臺灣出現了一些環境保護組織，這些環保組織的重要成員，後來成立了一個反對黨，挑戰執政的國民黨政府。二零零零年，這個反對黨贏得了臺灣的總統選舉，取代了原來的政府。目前，中國最大的民間環保組織"自然之友"是在政府的支持下發展起來的，反對政府的可能性非常小。看來中國的民間組織要自由發展還有很長一段路要走。

生詞用法

	高耀洁	高耀潔	Gāo Yàojié	name of a female Chinese doctor	
	河南	河南	Hénán	name of a Chinese province	
37	中医	中醫	zhōngyī	Chinese medicine (西醫=western medicine)	
38	学院	學院	xuéyuàn	college (for a higher degree)	法學院/商學院/文學院/理學院/工學院
39	教授	教授	jiàoshòu	professor	
40	省	省	shěng	province	
41	村民	村民	cūnmín	villager	
42	别无选择 别無選擇		biéwú-xuǎnzé	to have no choice	你只能吃這個，你別無選擇。
43	血	血	xiě	blood	

44	养家	養家	yǎngjiā	to support the family (養 = to raise; to provide food)	他靠賣血養家。/ 中國的傳統是男人賺錢養家，女人在家照顧孩子。
45	卫生	衛生	wèishēng	hygienic; sanitary hygiene; sanitation;	衛生紙/衛生間/吃飯前不洗手不太衛生。/這個地方的人很不講究衛生。
46	使用	使用	shǐyòng	to use; usage	使用權/使用時間/使用方法
47	针头	針頭	zhēntóu	pinhead; needle tip; 打針= to give an injection	我擔心他給我打針的針頭不衛生。
48	感染	感染	gǎnrǎn	to infect, infection; to be infected with	他感染上了艾滋病。/他的笑聲感染了所有的人。
49	艾滋病	愛滋病	àizībìng	AIDS	
50	改善	改善	gǎishàn	to improve; to modify	改善環境衛生/改善生活/改善工作條件/中美關係得到了很大的改善
51	通过	通過	tōngguò	to pass; by means of	他通過了考試。/ 通過討論，大家同意給孤兒捐錢。/他總是通過看電視學中文。
52	免费	免費	miǎnfèi	free (of money)	這些書都是免費的，你隨便拿吧。/他這個出租車司機(sījī)竟然免費送我回家。
53	发送	發送	fāsòng	to dispatch (letters, etc.); to hand out	把防治手冊發送出去。/給大家發送禮物。
54	手册	手冊	shǒucè	handbook; manual; pamphlet	漢語語法手冊/艾滋病防治手冊/旅行安全手冊
55	防治	防治	fángzhì	prevention and cure	防治疾病(jíbìng - illness)/防治大水(flood)/防治職業病
56	中央	中央	zhōngyāng	center; middle; central	公園的中央有很多人在跳舞。/中央政府/中央電視臺(CCTV)/中央領導/中央公園
57	允许	允許	yǔnxǔ	to allow; to permit; permission	允許離開/允許你進來/得到父母的允許
58	引起	引起	yǐnqǐ	to cause; to arouse; to attract (notice)	引起麻煩/引起問題/引起興趣/引起爭議/引起政府的重視
59	因此	因此	yīncǐ	hence; therefore	中國在世界上的影響力越來越大，因此，學漢語的人也越來越多。/他昨天晚上沒回家，她

					父母因此很生氣。
60	采取	採取	cǎiqǔ	to adopt; to take (a method, a way, etc.)	采取這樣的做法/采取某種態度/采取你介紹的方式/采取某種政策。
61	支持	支持	zhīchí	to support; to back	互相支持/支持的態度/ 美國人的做法得到了英國人的支持，但法國人不想支持美國。
62	态度	態度	tàidu	attitude; manner	她對這件事持(chí - hold)反對態度。/ 我還不知道他對法輪功的態度。/這服務員的態度真差！
63	解决	解決	jiějué	to resolve (a problem); to solve	解決問題/解決困難/解決爭議
64	扔	扔	rēng	to throw; to toss; to throw away	把報紙扔在地上/把書扔出去/把問題扔給他。/把這個扔掉吧，沒用了。
65	电视台	電視臺	diànshìtái	TV station	
66	感动	感動	gǎndòng	to move someone's emotions; to feel touched (讓人感動的= touching)	他的話感動了我。/ 她無私的幫助把我感動得說不出話來。/你對我這麼關心，我非常感動。/這部電影很感動人(or 讓人感動)。
67	人物	人物	rénwù	figure; personage; character	重要的人物/歷史人物/英雄人物/電影裏的人物/小說人物
68	绝对	絕對	juéduì	absolute; absolutely	絕對的好男人/絕對的權利/你說話太絕對了。/你別害怕，這樣做絕對不會感染的。/我絕對沒有把這件事告訴過別人。
69	超过	超過	chāoguò	to exceed; to surpass	超過 30 個/你的漢語超過了三年級的水平。/印度(Yìndù)的人口快超過中國了。/老師說的超過了我的接受能力。
70	环境	環境	huánjìng	environment; surroundings	學習環境/生活環境/自然環境/社會環境/環境管理/環境政策
71	保护	保護	bǎohù	to protect ; to defend; protection	保護國家/保護環境/保護家人/他們把孩子保護得很好。 /孩子受到了很好的保護。

72	成员	成員	chéngyuán	member	成員國/一個民間組織的成員/一個聯盟的成員
73	成立	成立	chénglì	to found; to establish	成立一個國家/成立一個組織/成立一家公司/這所大學是什麼時候成立的？
74	反对党	反對黨	fǎnduìdǎng	opposition party	新政府受到了反對黨的挑戰。
75	挑战	挑戰	tiǎozhàn	to challenge; challenge	挑戰別的競爭者/接受挑戰/向同學挑戰/有挑戰性的工作
76	执政	執政	zhízhèng	to be in power; to be in office; to be at the helm of the state	執政黨(the party in power)/美國現在哪個黨執政？
77	国民党	國民黨	Guómín dǎng	KMT: Chiang Kai-shek's political party; nationalist party	
78	总统	總統	zǒngtǒng	president (of a country)	
79	选举	選舉	xuǎnjǔ	to elect; to select by vote; election	選舉總統/選舉人 or 選民 (voter)
80	取代	取代	qǔdài	to replace; to take over	很多工人被機器取代了。/CD 似乎已經取代了錄音帶，但也可能會被 mp3 取代。
81	自然	自然	zìrán	natural; nature	自然環境/自然博物館/自然保護/我跟他說話覺得很不自然。

句型和語法

- 被視為 (see 被看成 L2)

- 除非…否則…/ 除非…不然… **(Like "雖然" and "但是….", "除非" and "否則" or "不然" are usually used in pairs, though "除非" in the first clause used on its own can make a complete sentence that means "unless…." "否則" and "不然" are used in the beginning of the second clause, meaning "otherwise." "否則" is used more frequently in written Chinese. When they are not used in a pair with "除非", we usually have "得" (have to), "最好" (had better), "必須" (must), etc. in the first or second clause) .**

  除非有政府的批準，否則宗教團體是不能走上街頭進行什麼活動的。
  Unless they have government approval, religious organizations aren't allowed to demonstrate publicly (literal translation: "to walk on the street").

除非你可以改變你爸媽那傳統的觀念，不然，你最好還是別讓他們知道這件事。
Unless you can change your mom and dad's traditional ways of thinking, you'd better not let them know about that stuff.

一般的學生，都能申請到獎學金嗎？
(回答問題) =〉

- 簡直(**"簡直" is used as an adverb when a person states his judgment. An exaggeration or emphasis is usually implied. It may be translated as "simply" or "really") .**

  練功怎麼能練到不吃飯，不睡覺呢？你這樣做簡直就是走火入魔！
  How can you practice to the point of not eating or sleeping? Working like this means you're simply obsessed!

  這地方的衛生條件太差了！簡直讓人住不下去。
  The sanitary conditions of this place are too poor! It makes it simply impossible for people to live here.

  她那麼討厭美國人，你還在他面前說美國人好，你真是想讓她生氣!
  (也可以說) =〉

- 就算…也 **("就算" means "even if" or "even though." It indicates a supposition or concession and is often used in conjunction with "也" or "還是". It may occur after the subject) .**
  就算我父親不支持，我還是不會改變我的想法。
  Even if my dad is unsupportive, I still won't change my mind.

  你就算再說一百次，她也不會相信基督教真能給人治病。
  Even if you say so a hundred more times, she still won't believe that Christianity can cure people's illnesses.

  我給你五百塊錢，你幫我在公司裏多爭取一點權利好不好？
  (回答問題) =〉

- 就：法輪功組織的合法性在中國就是一個有爭議性的話題。**("就" is used here to stress the idea that the subject of the clause is a good case or example. In the text we talked about the restrictions on forming private organizations**

in China. The sentence below suggests that Falun Gong is a good example to demonstrate those restrictions).

A:我們有沒有從臺灣來的中文老師?
B: 有啊！張老師就是從臺灣來的.
A: Do we have any Chinese teachers from Taiwan?
B : Sure, Teacher Zhang (for example) is from Taiwan!

陳二：這本書要到哪兒去買呀?
王立：到處都有，學校的書店就有。
陳二：Where can I go to buy this book?
王立：You can buy it anywhere; the school bookstore, has it, for example.

小英：老一輩的人，觀念都很保守。
(完成句子) =〉 小文：誰說的?

____

- 以 A 為 B (**以 A 為 B means "take A as B" or "regard A as B."**)

普通話的發音以北京口音為標準(biāozhŭn)。
Mandarin Chinese takes the Beijing pronunciation as standard.

小張很聰明，獨立性和責任心都很強，他的父母總是以他為驕傲。
Little Zhang is very intelligent and has strong independence and responsibility. His parents always take a pride in him.

他把辦公室當成他的家，吃，睡，都在裏邊。
(也可以說) =〉

- 並+ 不 **or** 沒(**"並" is used before a negative form for an emphasis. It indicates that the fact is not as one thought or expected).**

中央政府並不支持當地的環境保護活動。
The central government does not support the local environmental-protection activities [as you thought].

這個話題並沒有引起太大的爭議。
This topic did not stir up as big a controversy as you thought it would.

(完成句子) =〉 我以為地方官員做好了防治的工作，沒想到____________

- **不是…而是… ("而" can be used in the second clause to indicate a contrary. As in the "不是…而是…" pattern, "而" indicates contrary information to presumptions the listener might have).**

  這些壓力並不是來自共產黨，而是來自發展中國家無可避免的官僚作風以及老百姓落後保守的觀念。
  The pressure doesn't come from the communist party. Instead, it comes from the unavoidable bureaucracy in developing countries and the backward and conservative notions of the people.

  這位教授是個美國人，但他不采取美國的上課方式而采取中國的。
  This professor is an American, but he doesn't adopt the American style of conducting class and instead uses the Chinese one.

  他信的不是佛教而是道教。你跟他談佛教的事他當然不懂。
  The religion he believes in isn't Buddhism, but Taoism. If you talk to him about Buddhism, of course he doesn't understand anything.
  上海是個落後的地方嗎？
  (回答問題) =〉

- **靠+ (來)+(VP)("靠" means "to rely on" or "to depend on.")**

  有不少村民靠賣血來賺錢。
  Many of the villagers depend on selling blood to make money.

  他靠環保團體的影響力贏得了總統選舉。
  He relied on the influence of environmental protection organizations to win the presidential election.

  靠著王大夫的經驗，一定可以把你的病治好的。
  [Because you are] depending on Dr. Wang's experience, your sickness will certainly be cured.

  你要成功得靠你自己。
  To be successful you must depend only on yourself.

  (回答問題) =〉 他是怎麼找到工作的？

- **(因 (為) /為了)… 而… ("而" can be used as a conjunction to indicate a reason or cause).**

他因為捐血而感染了艾滋病。
Due to blood donation, he became infected with AIDS.

江澤民說，他是為了打倒迷信而限制法輪功的發展。
Jiang Zemin said that in order to discredit superstitions, he restricts Falun Gong's development.

他因語言交流的困難而決定離開美國回到中國。
Because of difficulties communicating, he decided to leave U.S.A and go back to China.

他因為害怕，所以馬上把手冊往地上一扔
(也可以說) =〉

- 只有…才…(**"才" in this pattern is used to indicate a precondition, implying the verb phrase stated after "才" is not easy to accomplish).**

只有大家和政府一起努力，環境問題才有可能得到改善。
The environmental problems can only be improved if everybody works together with the government.

只有使用一次性的針頭才能避免感染。
Only by using disposable syringes can we avoid infection.

要是不改善衛生環境，就沒有辦法解決這個問題。
(也可以說) =〉

- 在…上 (**"在…上" is used as an adverbial phrase to specify a certain aspect of the situation).**

他雖然很有自己的想法，但在經濟上還不能完全獨立。
Although he has his own thoughts, he is not yet financially completely independent.

在解決艾滋病問題上，中國政府的態度已經越來越開放。
In terms of solving the AIDS problem, the Chinese government's attitude is increasingly open.

農村裏的生活條件雖然改善了許多，但很多人的觀念還是非常保守。
(也可以說) =〉

課堂活動

(一) 用課文裏學到的生詞和句型回答問題：

- 組織民間活動和犯罪有什麼關係？為什麼會有這樣的情況呢？
- 法輪功是個什麼樣的團體？為什麼這個話題有爭議性？
- 河南的小農村裏，為什麼會有那麼多村民得艾滋病？
- 中國早期的艾滋病的防治工作為什麼做得不成功？老百姓的態度又是怎麼樣呢？那時，政府為什麼不支持高耀潔的活動？後來呢？
- 臺灣的環保組織和政治有什麼關係？這對中國的民間組織活動有什麼影響？

(二)從不同的角度(jiǎodù)來討論:

- 該不該限制法輪功的發展？
  - 練法輪功的人
  - 江澤民
  - 生了病的貧窮農民
  - 反對中國政府的臺灣人
  - 堅持宗教自由的美國人
  - 支持政府的中國人
  - 醫生
- 對於保護環境和解決艾滋病的問題，發展中國家和發達國家哪個更有責任？
  - 發展中國家
  - 發達國家
- 高耀潔的做法對不對？
  - 河南省的地方官員
  - 艾滋孤兒
  - 常賣血的農民
  - 美國婦女聯盟

(三) 你的看法

- 很多中國人認為政府不能對民間的活動一點限制也沒有，你覺得呢？為什麼？
- 某些中國人認為，中國的問題要靠中國自己來解決，不需要世界其他國家來管，特別是美國。你覺得這些中國人為什麼會有這樣的想法呢？如果你要改變這種想法，你會怎麼跟他們說？

練習題

一・　詞彙練習：(選擇最合適的詞完成句子或段落)

(一) *(選舉 態度 感染 官僚 理由 解決 防治)*

1. 一旦______上了這種病，就很難治好。因此，我們一定要做好_____的工作。
2. 他說他沒有______相信共產黨政府的______作風比國民黨政府更嚴重。
3. 能不能______一個問題，最重要的絕對不是你的能力，而是你的______。
4. 誰贏得這次______，誰才能對黨的發展有最高的影響力。

(二) *(允許 批準 采取 發送 反對 感動 成立)*

1. 醫院已經______了我的申請，明天我就可以______新的方式來幫助病人了解艾滋病了。
2. 這家醫院不______我給捐血的村民_____免費的針頭，我真不知道該怎麼辦。
3. 雖然他太太一開始______他用自己的錢來保護環境，但後來還是被他的無私______了。
4. 我們_______了一個幫助艾滋病孤兒的組織，成員大都來自兒童福利團體和其他民間組織。

(三)

1. *(否則 迷信 避免 通過 支持 點頭 行為)*

老張是一個基督徒(Jīdūtú- a Christian)，而我一向認為基督教是一種______。因此，老張總是想______討論使我也接受基督教。每次跟老張聊天，我都試著______說起宗教這個話題，因為，一說起基督教，除非我______，同意他的看法，______他會一直說下去。除了討論以外，老張也想通過自己的________來影響我。

2. *(規模 成立 引起 發送 自然 限制 支持)*

中央電視臺的＿＿＿＿＿很大，在中國的影響力也很大。它是在政府的＿＿＿下＿＿＿的，多多少少會受到政府的控制。因此，中央電視臺所說的事，人們＿＿＿不會完全相信，有時還會＿＿＿＿一些爭議。

二・　語法和口語練習：(用提供的詞彙或句型改寫句子或完成句子和對話)

1. 他反對我練法輪功的理由是法輪功會讓人走火入魔。*(以...為...)*
2. 要使落後的農村發展起來，必須實行開放的經濟政策。*(離不開)*
3. A: 你想在家看電影 DVD，還是到電影院看電影？
   B: ＿＿＿＿＿＿＿＿＿＿＿＿＿＿＿，只要我們一起看就好。*(...都一樣)*
4. A: 我簡直不敢相信，她那麼年輕漂亮，怎麼嫁給那樣一個老教授？
   B: 是啊，＿＿＿＿＿＿＿＿＿＿＿＿＿＿＿＿＿＿＿＿。*(就算..., 也...)*
5. A: 我可以申請加入你們這個組織嗎？
   B: ＿＿＿＿＿＿＿＿＿＿＿＿＿＿＿＿＿＿＿＿＿＿＿＿。*(除非...，否則... or 只有...才...)*
6. A: 我聽說王教授信佛教。
   B:＿＿＿＿＿＿＿＿＿＿＿＿＿＿＿＿＿＿＿＿＿＿。*(不是...,而是...)*
7. A:＿＿＿＿＿＿＿＿＿＿＿＿＿＿＿＿＿＿＿＿＿＿＿＿＿。
   B: 可不是嗎！真讓人無法忍受。
8. A:＿＿＿＿＿＿＿＿＿＿＿＿＿＿＿＿＿＿＿＿＿＿＿＿＿。
   B: 什麼跟什麼嘛！

三・　綜合練習：讀下面的短文，並選擇合適的詞填空：

中國各大＿1＿中，＿2＿來自印度，＿3＿來自西方國家，只有＿4＿是在中國發展起來的。一千多年以前，有幾個皇帝非常支持佛教，因此佛教在中國的發展曾經很＿5＿。但基督教在中國發展卻受到了很多的＿6＿。過去，共產黨曾經害怕一些基督教組織通過宗教的影響力＿7＿政府，很多基督教活動都被視為非法活動。但現在在中國，基督教不但有合法地位，＿8＿幾乎＿9＿了佛教，成為影響力最大的宗教組織。

1. a.宗教 b.道教 c.基督教
2. a.佛教 b.道教 c.基督教
3. a.佛教 b.道教 c.基督教
4. a.佛教 b.道教 c.基督教
5. a.困難 b.順利 c.規模
6. a.支持 b.反對 c.限制
7. a.挑戰 b.執政 c.超過
8. a.但是 b.而且 c.而是
9. a.控制 b.挑戰 c.取代
10.

四· 翻譯練習:(用提供的詞或句型翻譯下面的句子)

1. 因(為)…而　　也就是說

   Because of foreign organizations' support, Falungong is becoming more and more influential. In other words, without the help from foreign countries, Falungong might just be a small organization.

2. 在…上　　靠　　並+Neg.

   Although he has been doing very well studying, I find that whenever he needs to make a decision, he still counts on his parents. In my perspective, this is a serious problem. However, his parents haven't yet realized this.

五· 作文:(從下邊幾個題目中,選擇一個,寫一篇不少於500字的作文。你至少要用四個所提供的句型或詞彙)

除非…否則	就算…也…	以A為B	離不開
不是…而是…	只有…才…	在…上	也就是說

1. 政府應不應該限制民間組織發展?
2. 對於保護環境和解決艾滋病的問題,發展中國家和發達國家哪個更有責任?
3. 說一說你知道的民間團體,這些團體給大家帶來什麼好處?壞處?

第五課 秘密

Let's warm-up with a review exercise!

Match the words in characters with Pinyin and English:

漢字	拼音	英文	哪兒學過
擔心			二年級
敢			二年級
原因			二年級
太極拳			二年級
到處			二年級
孫女			二年級
外套			二年級
突然			第一課
沉默			第一課
卻			第一課
終於			第一課
陪			第二課
仔細			第二課
打破			第二課
引起			第四課

拼音

1. chénmò	2. dānxīn	3. dàochù	4. dǎpò
5. gǎn	6. péi	7. què	8. sūnnǚ
9. tàijíquán	10. tūrán	11. yǐnqǐ	12. yuányīn
13. zhōngyú	14. zǐxì	15. wàitào	

英文

a. careful	b. coat; jacket	c. everywhere	d. finally
e. granddaughter	f. reason	g. silent	h. sudden
i. Tai-chi	j. to accompany	k. to break	l. to cause
m. to dare to	n. to worry	o. yet, but	

聽力&口語

聽錄音回答問題

對話一

1.	2.	3.	4.	5.

生詞：岳母，下崗，妻子，退休，單位，織，悶
複習：年紀，老太太，(無聊，孫子/孫女，熱鬧，老頭，太極拳，一邊…，一邊…)

對話二

1.	2.	3.	4.	5.

生詞：逃犯，禿頂，個子，果然，抓，躲
複習：頭發，竟然，突然，按照，(擔心，敢，老頭，警察 jǐngchá)

對話三

1.	2.	3.	4.	5.

生詞：皺眉頭，發呆，心事，嘆氣，不三不四，時髦，迫不及待
色鬼，馬虎，胡思亂想，警告，教訓，估計
複習：禿頂，絕對，解決，簡直，性感，主管，陪，忍受，年紀，
保護，支持，娶，教授，傳統，嚴格，責任心，作風，(丟)

根據對話一回答問題：

1. 對話中，提到誰不工作了嗎？是不是因為做得不好，公司不要她了？她那幾個年輕同事的情況跟她一樣嗎？
2. 老太太要賣毛衣嗎？為什麼她不喜歡在家裏打毛衣，要到公園裏去打呢？

根據對話二回答問題：

1. 兩個說話人是做什麼的？他們在公園裏做什麼？
2. 他們要找的人有什麼特點？他們打算怎麼抓他？

根據對話三回答問題：

1. 哥哥怎麼知道妹妹可能有麻煩？
2. 妹妹的麻煩事是什麼？她哥哥知道以後說什麼？他想怎麼幫妹妹？
3. 妹妹覺得應該怎麼辦？哥哥覺得妹妹的主意怎麼樣？

口語用法

1. A: 不是我媽，是我妻子她媽，我岳母。
   B: 噢，是你岳母

(“噢” is a modal particle used to express how one now has the correct information after being wrong or confused at the outset. It is pronounced like “aw” in “law” with a soft lengthened a rising-falling tone or falling tone. The Pinyin is “o”. The character can be “喔” or “哦”).

A: 你為什麼那麼著急？晚會八點才開始。
B: 噢，我以為六點就開始了。
A: Why are you in such a hurry? The party won’t start till 8:00pm.
B: Oh, I thought it starts at 6:00pm.

A: 很奇怪，我給那些村民發送艾滋病防治手冊的時候，他們都把它扔在地上，好像很害怕的樣子。
B: 你不知道，這些村民以為艾滋病一定跟色情行業有關係。
A: 哦。
A: How strange. When I distributed the AIDS prevention and control handbooks to those villagers, they all threw them on the ground, seeming as if scared.
B: You don’t understand. These villagers think AIDS is always associated with prostitution.
A: Oh, I see.

2. 她都已經 50 多歲了，現在不工作，算是退休，不算是下崗。

(“都” can be used in a pattern of “都…了” meaning “already”. It implies that the speaker thinks it is too late, too long, too old, too much, etc. It conveys a strong personal view. This pattern is often followed by a rhetorical question. “都…了” can be used in conjunction with “已經”. “都” is usually pronounced lightly).

你都已經買了三套這樣的衣服了，怎麼還買？
You’ve already bought three sets of these kinds of clothes, why are you still buying it?

我都告訴過你不要迷信了，你竟然還信法輪功信得走火入魔！
I already told you before not to be superstitious. How can you still believe in Falun Gong to the point of being obsessed?

3. …，要說下崗嘛，他們單位裹…，他們才算是下崗。

(“要說” means “as to, as for” in a conversation. It can be followed by a word, a phrase or sentence to introduce another topic or an aspect related to the previous topic. The comment on the topic is stated in the following clause. “要說” can be used with “嘛” as well. “嘛”is a modal particle used to indicate a pause within a sentence to draw attention).

城市裏的人已經有了一些環境保護的觀念，要說農村人嘛，他們還需要一些時間。
People in the city already have some concept of environmental protection, but as to people living in rural areas, they still need time to learn.

他籃球打得很好，要說足球嘛，他弟弟比他強多了。
He is very good at basketball, but as for soccer,his younger brother is much better at it.

他的性格是很開朗，但要說他的智商高嘛，我真看不出來。
He does have a pleasant and outgoing personality, but as for a high IQ, I really can’t tell.

4. 又不是賣毛衣賺錢，織那麼多毛衣，給誰穿啊？
(By using “又” in front of 不 or 沒, the following interrogative sentence becomes rhetorical question. The speaker indicates that because of such a fact, the conclusion can only follow).

只要每天高高興興的，貧窮一點又有什麼關係？
As long as you are happy everyday, where’s the harm in being poor?

你又沒有天生殘疾什麼的，幹嗎住在福利院裏，不出去工作？
Are you born with a defect or what? Why do you live in the charity home and not go out and work?

申請這個大學的競爭又不激烈，你根本不需要緊張。
The competitiveness of applying to this university isn’t intense anyway. I don’t think you need to be nervous.

5. 我不是告訴過你嗎，他是個禿頂的瘦老頭。
(“我不是告訴過你” means “didn’t I tell you?” You may insert a sentence between “我不是告訴過你” and “嗎”. When you say it, you indicate the displeasure aroused by not having listened to you earlier).

我不是告訴過你你贏不了他的嗎？可你還要跟他比！

Haven't I told you that you can't beat him? But you still wanted to compete with him.

我不是告訴過你這個組織的合法性還有爭議嗎？你為什麼還要加入呢？
Didn't I tell you that there is still some controversy over the legitimacy of this organization? Why do you still want to join it?

6．他是逃犯，我們是警察，我們幹嗎躲啊？ ("幹嗎" (also written as 幹嘛) is a colloquial way to say "why." It is used in front of a verb or at the end of the sentence. When you use "幹嗎", you are not only asking for the reason, you are also indicating that you disagree with the thing you are questioning. It is similar to "幹什麼", especially when used at the end of the sentence. "幹什麼" means "what are/is you/[subject] doing?").

你不支持他的臺獨想法，幹嗎選他當總統呢？
You don't support his pro-independence ideas, so why did you give him your vote for president?

那些農民幹嗎靠賣血賺錢呢?
What are those peasants doing selling their blood for money?

你幹嗎在我的桌子上學習？
Why are you studying on my desk?

去公園，穿那麼正式幹什麼？
You are going to the park. What are you doing for dressing up so formally like that?

7．走，現在就去抓他去。
("走" at the beginning of the sentence is part of an imperative structure meaning "Let's go; come on". We can use "吧" after "走" to soften the tone).

走，我們喝酒去！
Come on, let's get some drink.

走，我們去買那本暢銷書去！
Let's go buy the best-selling book.

走吧，該去取行李了。
Let's go. It's time we should get the luggage.

8．別急，我們先躲著。

("別急" means "no hurry", "hold on", or "don't worry", depending on the context. In this sample sentence, it means "hold on". The speaker suggests that they should hide a little longer before taking any action).

A: 哎呀，我得趕快去發送這些手冊。
B: 別急，你不是說是八點嗎？你還有二十分鐘呢。
A: Oh, I have to go and distribute these handbooks as soon as possible.
B: No hurry. Didn't you say it's 8 o'clock? You still have twenty minutes.

A: 我現在把雞蛋放進去？
B: 別急，等油再熱一點。
A: Do I put the egg in now?
B: Hold on, wait till the oil is a little bit hotter.

A: 我爸爸反對我加入學校的足球隊。怎麼辦？
B: 別急，我們找機會跟他好好談談。

A: My dad was opposed to me joining the school's football team. What can I do?
B: Don't worry. We can find a chance to have a talk with him.

9. 什麼？這老東西！簡直不想活了？
("東西" means "stuff", but when you say a person or an animal is "XX東西", you are cursing them. Saying "sb不是東西", "sb不是好東西" or "sb是什麼東西" are all cursing. "這老東西" is used to curse old people).

你是什麼東西！
Who do you think you are?

小李真不是個東西。我幫他那麼多次，他這次竟然不願意幫我。
Xiao Li is such a jerk. I helped him so many times, and this time he surprisingly was unwilling to help me.

10. 太過分了，這個老色鬼，你可要小心，不能馬虎啊。
("太過分了" means "goes too far". It is used to show one's anger when something has gone wrong and far beyond what he or she can endure.)

他們為什麼不批準我的申請？真是太過分了！
Why didn't they approve my application? They've gone too far!

太過分了！你怎麼能用那種態度跟父母說話？
I can't stand it! How can you speak to your parents with that kind of attitude?

11．現在他只是對你說些不三不四的話，以後很可能就對你動手動腳什麼的。
("什麼的" can be used after a noun phrase or a verb phrase to mean "anything like that").

這個孩子缺乏獨立性。每次出去不是生病就是丟東西什麼的。
This child isn't very independent. Each time he is away from home, he will get sick, or lose his stuff or something like that.

你別給我皺眉頭什麼的。笑一個！
Don't frown or do anything like that. (It will upset me). Smile!

你看，那個禿頂的老頭兒會不會是逃犯什麼的？
Do you think the bald, old guy could be an escaped convict or something like that?

12．你不能再忍受下去了。
("Verb+下去" is used to indicate the continuation of the action. If there is an object of the verb, the object will be introduced in the first part of the sentence. "得" and "不" can be used between the verb and "下去" to form a potential complement structure).

該怎麼處罰他，大家爭議太多，討論不下去了。
There is too much controversy regarding the punishment for him; the discussion can't be continued.

這孩子不但笨，而且對成績一點也不在乎，我實在輔導不下去了。
This child is not only stupid, but also does not care at all about his grades. I really can't keep tutoring him.

這麼吵，你怎麼看得下去？
It's so noisy, how can you continue reading?

口語練習：請用聽力對話裏學到的生詞和口語用法討論下面的問題：

噢！ / 都…了/　　要說…嘛/　　我不是告訴過你(…)嗎？/　　幹嗎/ …什麼的
走，(我們)+VP+去！/ 別急/　太過分了！/　不是什麼好東西/ VP+下去

1. A—你是單位主管，你得讓一個四十五歲的工人知道他明天得下崗。
   B—你是得下崗的工人。你希望主管能改變決定。

2. 你們是對話二裏的警察，你們討論要怎麼樣抓到逃犯。

3. A—你是對話三裏的妹妹，你要告訴老板關於老張的事。
   B—你是老板，老張是你的好朋友。你和他一樣是個色鬼。

課文

第一部分

“不早了，睡吧！你已經坐在被窩兒裏發呆老半天了”。

“我沒發呆。” 妻子淡淡地回了一句，卻仍舊靠著床頭，不打算躺下來。“我只是在擔心媽...”

傍晚時，岳母來過，看起來有什麼心事的樣子。

“沒事，就來看看小孫女。”

估計岳母想和女兒說些什麼，卻又不願意讓我聽到，於是，我拿了張報紙，進了臥室。

“媽是不是跟你說了什麼？”我知道妻子在等著我問她。

“唉！”她嘆了口氣。“媽說她不敢去公園了，怕再碰上那個老頭。她也真是的，待在家裏看看電視、織織毛衣，不就挺好的，去什麼公園嘛！”妻子埋怨起岳母來了。

“家裏待著悶嘛！要不，那麼多人寧可少拿錢，在單位多留幾年，也不願意退休或下崗。媽到公園裏沒什麼不好，那兒空氣好，活動的人也多，她每天到那兒走走，做做運動，對身體好。”我說。

“話是沒錯，但上公園去，幹嗎打扮得那麼時髦？你沒看她今天身上的那件外套？五十幾歲的人了，那種顏色也穿得出去！”

“過去你老埋怨她穿著太馬虎，現在又嫌她打扮得太時髦...”

“你懂什麼！過去爸在世，媽打扮年輕一點是應該的，可現在，她穿成那個樣，會引起誤會，人家也會說閑話的。那老頭...。”

“好了好了，別想那麼多了。你媽是個老實人，沒人會說她閑話。你別那麼在乎。睡吧！”

生詞用法

1	秘密	秘密	mìmi	secret; confidential	心中的一個秘密/開了一個秘密會議/秘密計劃/秘密活動/秘密選舉/秘密地做了這件事。
2	被窝	被窩	bèiwō	comfort of the blanket or quilt	她每天早上醒來以後都要在被窩裏看一會兒書再起來。/這被窩太舒服了，真讓人不願起來。
3	发呆	發呆	fādāi	to stare blankly; to daze off	他不說話，坐在那裏發呆。/他發了半天呆。/你吃飯啊!發什麼呆啊?
4	妻子	妻子	qīzi	wife	
5	淡淡	淡淡	dàndàn	light; slight; lightly, slightly	淡淡的顏色/淡淡的味道/淡淡地笑了一下/他看都沒看我，淡淡地說了聲“沒事”就走了。
6	回	回	huí	to respond	回信/回電話
7	仍旧	仍舊	réngjiù	still; yet	他仍舊住在老房子裏。/問題仍舊沒有解決。/等了三天，他的妻子仍舊沒有回來。
8	靠	靠	kào	to lean against	靠在墻上/靠著墻站著/靠著樹睡著了。
9	床头	床頭	chuángtóu	headboard; the head of a bed	靠著床頭看書/你的衣服在床頭
10	躺	躺	tǎng	to lie (down); to recline	躺在床上/請躺下來/在床上躺著/躺著看書對你的眼睛不好。
11	傍晚	傍晚	bàngwǎn	early evening; dusk	
12	岳母	岳母	yuèmǔ	mother-in-law (wife’s mother)	

13	心事	心事	xīnshì	sth. weighing on one's mind; a load on one's mind	你看起來好像有心事。/我把我的心事告訴了媽媽。
14	估计	估計	gūjì	to estimate; to evaluate; estimation	我估計做完這個工作需要三天。/我估計他今天不來了。/我估計了一下，下學期上這門課的學生會超過二十人。/你的估計不對。
	于是	於是	yúshì	thereupon; consequently	買完東西時間還早，於是我去了一下公園。 見語法
15	卧室	臥室	wòshì	bedroom	一間臥室
16	叹气	歎氣	tànqì	to sigh	她長長地嘆了一口氣。/別嘆氣，你把你的好運都嘆沒了。
17	碰上	碰上	pèngshàng	to encounter; (碰 = to touch; to bump)	我在商店裏碰上了一個老朋友。/我從來沒碰上過這樣的事。/他碰了我一下。/我的頭碰到門上了。
18	待	待	dāi	to stay for a period of time	待在家裏。/在家待著！別出去。/他要在北京待三天。
19	织	織	zhī	to knit; to weave	織毛衣/這件衣服是用絲(sī: silk)織的。
20	埋怨	埋怨	mányuàn	to complain; to blame	互相埋怨/埋怨別人/學生們喜歡埋怨老師給的功課太多。/老李埋怨我沒把事情跟她說清楚。
21	闷	悶	mèn	boring; stuffy; suffocative (mēn)	連一個說話的人都沒有，真是悶死我了。/這工作太悶，我幹不下去了！/ 請把窗戶打開，屋子裏太悶(mēn)了。
	宁可	寧可	nìngkě	would rather	見語法
22	单位	單位	dānwèi	unit (as an organization, department, division, section, etc)	我們單位/工作單位/單位領導
23	退休	退休	tuìxiū	to retire	退休年齡/退休生活/退休計劃/退休金
24	下岗	下崗	xiàgǎng	to be laid-off from a unit	單位讓他下崗了，現在他正在找工作。

25	空气	空氣	kōngqì	air; atmosphere	清新的空氣/緊張的空氣
26	打扮	打扮	dǎbàn	to dress up	她今天打扮得很漂亮。/我們參加的是個正式的晚會，你得打扮打扮。/我不喜歡你今天的打扮。
27	时髦	時髦	shímáo	stylish; fashionable	時髦女性/時髦人物/這種打扮不時髦了。
28	穿着	穿著	chuānzhuó	apparel; what one wears	穿著時髦/爸爸不在乎穿著。/她穿著講究。
29	马虎	馬虎	mǎhu	too casual; careless	工作馬虎/他穿得太馬虎了！/你這功課寫得太馬虎了，回去再寫一次！/他做事情很馬虎，不是忘這個，就是忘那個。
30	嫌	嫌	xián	to dislike someone or something for; to mind that	嫌麻煩/大家嫌她太霸道。/他嫌我做菜不好吃。
31	在世	在世	zàishì	to be alive	他在世的時候/我父親去世了，我母親還在世。
32	误会	誤會	wùhuì	to misunderstand; misunderstanding	你誤會我了，我不是那個意思。/他們兩個之間有些誤會。
33	闲话	閒話	xiánhuà	chitchat; gossip	我們沒談什麼重要的事，只是說了一會兒閑話。/不要說別人的閑話。/他說了你的閑話。
36	老实	老實	lǎoshi	honest, frank	他是個老實人，從來不說假(jiǎ)話。/他這個人很老實，別人說什麼，他都信。/老實說，我不喜歡他。
37	在乎	在乎	zàihu	to care about; to mind	她很在乎別人的看法。/只要學得好就行，別太在乎考試結果。

課文

第二部分

我關了燈，妻還說了些什麼，我已聽不清了。正當我迷迷糊糊要入睡時，卻突然讓妻給推了一下。

“怎麼啦？”

“你說那老頭會不會是個逃犯？”

“逃犯？怎麼會？你媽不是說他在打太極拳嗎？你別胡思亂想了！”

“不是逃犯也一定是個老色鬼，反正不是什麼好東西。你明天陪我到公園去，把那老頭給找出來，警告他幾句，讓他別再來煩我媽了。”

“好，好，好，我答應你。睡吧！”

第二天早上，我們來到了公園。公園裏空氣很清新，到處都是鍛煉身體的中老年人。我們隨著音樂聲，找到了打太極拳的人群。

我們耐心地等著，過了一會兒，打太極拳的人群慢慢散開了

“媽說是個高個兒、禿頂的老頭，我們到那邊看看”。

“那老色鬼果然在這兒。”儘管公園裏打太極拳的人不少，妻還是一眼就認出了岳母所說的那個老頭。

“我去把他叫過來！”妻子一副迫不及待的樣子。

妻急匆匆地走了幾步，卻突然回過頭來。

“怎麼啦？”我問。

“媽也來了。真是的。”我這時才看到，岳母正坐在打太極拳的人群旁邊，笑盈盈地打著毛衣呢。妻皺起了眉頭。

“別急”，我安慰妻子，“這樣吧，我們先躲到那棵樹後邊，仔細觀察一會兒。要是那老頭有什麼不三不四的言行，我們就過去把他抓住，當面給他點教訓。”妻子默默地點了點頭。

打太極拳的人群慢慢散開了。那老頭帶著溫和的微笑，來到岳母面前。“你來了啊！”

“嗯。”岳母站了起來，把織了一半多的毛衣放在老頭胸前比了比。“我大致估計了一下，沒想到正好。”聽到這句話，我簡直傻了。

兩位老人在長椅上默默地坐了幾分鐘，終於，老頭打破了沉默：“你和你女兒談了？”

岳母搖搖頭，長長地嘆了口氣：“哎！讓我怎麼開口...”

生詞用法

38	迷迷糊糊		mímihúhu	in a daze; muddled	我睡得迷迷糊糊的，他把我叫了起來。/他這個人常常迷迷糊糊的，不是忘了這個就是忘了那個。
39	入睡	入睡	rùshuì	to fall asleep	我躺下以後半天才能入睡。
40	推	推	tuī	to push	推門/推了他一下。
41	逃犯	逃犯	táofàn	escaped criminal; fugitive	一名逃犯/警察抓逃犯
42	胡思亂想	胡思亂想	húsī luànxiǎng	to let one's mind wander; to let one's imagination run wild; to have fantasies	先生回來晚了，她就開始擔心，開始胡思亂想。/你別胡思亂想，他怎麼可能是逃犯呢？

43	色鬼	色鬼	sèguǐ	lady-killer; pervert	他是個色鬼，見了漂亮女孩子就走不動了。
	反正	反正	fǎnzhèng	anyway; in any case	見語法
44	警告	警告	jǐnggào	to warn; to caution; warning;	醫生警告病人不要喝酒。/ 老師警告我不能再遲到了。/ 你警告他幾句就行了，別真打他。/如果那時他聽了爸媽的警告就不會出事了。
45	煩	煩	fán	to bother; annoying; vexed	我被這些小孩煩了一整天。/你真煩！/我覺得很煩。我想出去走走。
46	答應	答應	dāying	to agree to; to consent to	他答應嫁給我了。/ 他答應了我的要求。
47	清新	清新	qīngxīn	pure and fresh; fresh	清新的空氣/清新的早晨(zǎochén)/覺得很清新/清新的感覺
48	鍛煉	鍛煉	duànliàn	to exercise; to workout;exercise (n.)	鍛煉身體/鍛煉適應能力/ 缺乏鍛煉
49	隨	隨	suí	to follow	請隨我來。/ 他隨學校領導一起訪問北京大學。
50	人群	人群	rénqún	a crowd of people	在公園裏可以看到打太極拳的人群，跳舞的人群，甚至還有唱卡拉 ok 的人群。
51	耐心	耐心	nàixīn	patience; patiently	耐心等著/耐心觀察/耐心聽我講故事/他對我沒耐心。/教育孩子得有耐心。
52	高個兒	高個兒	gāogèr	a tall person; 個兒/個子 = height of a person	那個高個兒是誰？/他個子不高。
53	禿頂	禿頂	tūdǐng	bald; bald-headed	他禿頂了。/他是一個禿頂的中年人。/他的頭禿得很厲害。
	果然	果然	guǒrán	as expected	見語法
	儘管	儘管	jǐnguǎn	even though; in spite of	見語法
54	認	認	rèn	to recognize	這麼久不見，我都快認不出你來了。/ 他雖然戴了假發，但一開口說話還是被認了出來。

55	副	副	fù	a measure word; a; a pair of	一副眼鏡/一副笑臉/一副…的樣子
56	迫不及待 迫不及待		pòbùjídài	to be too impatient to wait	暑假(shǔjià - summer vacation)一到，他就迫不及待地飛回家看他的女朋友。/再過兩個星期我就可以買車了，我真是迫不及待！
57	急匆匆	急匆匆	jí-cōngcōng	in a hurry	他急匆匆地離開了，好像發生了什麼事。/ 他急匆匆地來，急匆匆的走，跟我說話的時間不到三分鐘。
58	回頭	回頭	huítóu	to turn one's head; to look back; later	往前走，別回頭。/ 回頭再聊，我現在得去工作。/回頭見(see you later)。
59	笑盈盈	笑盈盈	xiào-yíngyíng	smilingly	老頭兒笑盈盈地走了過來。/岳母笑盈盈地坐在那兒打毛衣。/王教授總是笑盈盈的。
60	皺眉頭	皺眉頭	zhòu-méitóu	to frown	一聽到這事，他就皺起眉頭來。/他向我皺了一下眉頭。
61	安慰	安慰	ānwèi	to comfort; to console; comfort	說幾句安慰她的話。/ 我沒有獲得獎學金，很難過，他打電話安慰我。/ 她只能從母親那兒得到安慰。
62	躲	躲	duǒ	to hide; to dodge; to avoid	快躲起來，別讓他看見我們。/ 他在房間裏躲著不願意見人。/ 小孩子喜歡躲在床下。/ 我很生氣，把書扔向他的頭，可是他躲過了。
63	觀察	觀察	guānchá	to observe; to watch; observation	觀察別的人怎麼做。/觀察一下再開口。
64	不三不四		bùsānbúsì	improper	她交了一群不三不四的朋友，又吸煙又喝酒的。/你穿的這是什麼衣服? 不男不女，不三不四的！/他總愛說些不三不四的話，真讓人聽不下去。
65	言行	言行	yánxíng	words and deeds	父母的一言一行都對孩子有很大的影響。/ 從他的言行，看不出他是個逃犯。
66	抓	抓	zhuā	to seize; to grab	警察(jǐngchá)抓小偷(xiǎotōu)/你抓好，別放手/他被抓住，逃不掉了。

67	當面	當面	dāngmiàn	to sb.'s face; in sb's presence	這件事咱們當面說清楚。/售貨員找的錢，你得當面點清楚，走出店外發現少找了就晚了。
68	教訓	教訓	jiàoxun	to teach sb. a lesson; a lesson	給那老色鬼一點教訓/ 教訓教訓那色鬼。/他把過去的教訓告訴我, 讓我避免發生同樣的事情。
69	默默地	默默地	mòmòdi	quietly; silently	他聽了我的話，默默地點點頭。/她默默地幫助別人。/媽媽總是默默地把我需要的東西都準備好。
70	散開	散開	sànkāi	to disperse; to scatter	人群散開了。/孩子們散開了。散開點，散開點！你們都擠(jǐ)在一塊兒怎麼打太極拳？
71	溫和	溫和	wēnhé	gentle; mild; moderate	溫和的性格/溫和的態度/溫和的微笑/溫和的天氣
72	微笑	微笑	wēixiào	to smile; smile	甜甜地(tiántiánde)微笑/他對我微笑了一下。/ 他的微笑讓人很舒服。
73	胸	胸	xiōng	chest	
74	大致	大致	dàzhì	roughly; on the whole; approximately	大致相同/他大致同意我們的計劃。/我大致估計了一下, …
75	正好	正好	zhènghǎo	exactly right; coincidently right (adj.)	這件衣服對你大小正好。
76	傻	傻	shǎ	stupid; stupefied; muddleheaded; silly	聽到他的話，我傻了，不知道該說什麼。/爸媽一看到他的成績，簡直傻了。/他傻等了我一個小時，也不知道打個電話。
77	搖頭	搖頭	yáotóu	to shake one's head	聽了他的話，爸爸點頭同意了，但媽媽搖了搖頭。

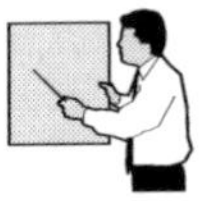

句型和語法

- 於是 (**"於是" means "therefore," "thereupon," "hence" or "as a result." It is used to link sentences. "於是" introduces a natural outcome of the previous event but does not necessarily indicate a strong cause and effect relationship).**

買完東西，時間還早，於是，我就到公園裏坐了一會兒。
After shopping, it was still early so I went to the park to sit for a while.

岳母看起來有心事又不願告訴我，於是，我也不多問，低頭進了臥室。
My mother-in-law looked like she had a lot on her mind but wouldn't tell me what, so I didn't ask her and just entered the room without a word.

私營企業發展起來後，國有企業簡直沒有生意可做，於是，這些員工們早退休的早退休，沒能退休的，整天擔心會下崗。

After private enterprises began to develop, government-owned companies simply ran out of business; hence the employees who could retire early did so, and those who couldn't worried all day about getting fired.

(完成句子) =>這些村民賣血時，用的全是不乾淨的針頭，於是

____

- **V 什麼(O)嘛！ ("V 什麼(O)嘛" is a colloquial pattern we use to indicate a complaint. The speaker doesn't think what was done or suggested was unnecessary or irrational).**

在家織毛衣不是很好嗎？去什麼公園嘛！
What's wrong with knitting a sweater at home? Why would you go to the park!

知道她不來，我買什麼酒嘛！
If I had known she wasn't coming, why would I have bought alcohol?

A: 我們喝點酒吧？
B: 你一會兒就要開車，喝什麼酒嘛？
A: Let's drink some beer?
B: You will be driving soon, how can you?

(完成句子) =>

1. 你看他，只有小學畢業就能賺那麼多錢	a. 你唱什麼歌嘛！
2. 那兒沒有一個人懂音樂，	b. 你準備什麼嘛！
3. 明天根本沒有考試，	c. 開什麼車嘛！
4. 那個商店離這裏很近，	d. 我還念什麼書嘛！

- **寧可 A 也（不）B ("寧可" means "rather". When you use this pattern, you mean "to make B (not) happen, I would rather compromise and reluctantly tolerate A." "寧可" introduces the preferred choice in a comparison between two dissatisfactory items or actions).**

這本書太好了，我寧可不睡覺也要把它看完。
This book is too good. I would rather not sleep so I can finish it.

父母寧可自己吃各種各樣的苦，也不要孩子的生活比別人差。
Parents would go though all kinds of hardships themselves rather than allow their child to live a worse life than others.

我寧可死也不要過不自由的生活。
Give me liberty or give me death.

(Without the use of "也", what stated after "寧可" is the preferred choice).

不給我自由，我寧可死。(There is also a saying known as: 不自由毋寧死 Bú zìyóu, wú nìng sǐ)
Give me liberty or give me death.

如果你一邊幫我，一邊埋怨，那我寧可自己幹。
If you keep complaining while you help me, then I would rather do it by myself.

小文：你的工作那麼好，為什麼不做了呢？
小許：離我家太遠了。我寧可少賺一點錢，找個離家近一點的。
小文：Your job is so good. Why aren't you doing it now?
小許：It's too far from home. I would rather make a little less money and find a job closer to home.

Harvard 大學和 UCLA 都接受了你的申請。你會念哪一所呢？為什麼？

Harvard	$$$$$	東岸	爸媽最希望你念的
UCLA	$$$	西岸	女朋友決定去念的

小張：雖然我喜歡東岸。但我女朋友在西岸，我寧可不去東岸也不要和女朋友分開。

小王： 我和你不一樣，哈佛那麼有名，我寧可讓女朋友生氣也要念哈佛，不念 UCLA.
(完成句子) => 小李：哈佛太貴了，____________________________。

- **…, …又… ("又" can indicate a speaker's displeasure when he thinks that the latter action taken by someone contradicts his earlier action).**

  你不是說獨生子女政策對人口的控制有很大的好處嗎？現在怎麼又反對起這個政策來了？
  Didn't you say that the one child policy had a beneficial effect on population control? Why are you opposing the policy now?

  他說他捨得買，結果又不願意付錢。
  He said he was willing to buy, but ultimately unwilling to pay.

  (完成句子) => 以前你總埋怨媽穿得太馬虎，現在媽穿得時髦一點，
  ____。

- **會…的 /不會…的 (We use "會…的" to assure the listener something will happen or "不會…的" to assure the listener something will not happen).**

  爸去世了，媽還每天打扮得那麼時髦。別人會說她閑話的。
  Dad passed away, but mom still dresses up so fashionably. Other people will surely gossip about her.

  相信我， 她不會是個逃犯的。
  Believe me, there's no way she's an escaped convict.

  再等等，他會來的。
  Just wait a little longer. He will certainly come.

  Finish the following dialogue or sentences with the above pattern:
  A: 你相信個宗教是有好處，但別走火入魔啊！
  (完成句子) => B: 媽， 你別擔心，____________________________。

  (完成句子）=〉 這次的考試不太難，只要你好好準備
  ________________。

- **好了好了！("好了好了" is used in a discourse, meaning, "ok, ok", "all right", "that is enough" with a sense of yielding or compromise. It also implies that**

the speaker hopes the listener can stop the conversation or stop what he or she has been doing).

A: …
B: 好了好了，不說了，快躺下來睡吧，
All right. Stop talking. You should lie down and sleep.

A: …, 你說，她打扮得那麼時髦幹嗎？
B: 她為什麼不能打扮得時髦一點？
A: 她先生不是才去世嗎？
B: 好了好了，別說人閑話了。
A: …, you say, why did she dress up so stylishly?
B: Why can't she dress up a bit fashionably?
A: Didn't her husband just pass away?
B: Come on. Stop gossiping.

- 怎麼啦？**("怎麼啦" is used in a discourse to show the speaker's concerns when he or she feels there is something wrong with the listener).**

A: 怎麼啦？你是不是不舒服？
B: 沒事。我只是心情(xīnqíng)不太好。
A: What's up? Are you sick?
B: I'm fine. I'm just in a bad mood.

A: 怎麼啦？你嫌這菜做的不好，吃不下去嗎？
B: 你誤會了。菜很好，我是怕胖，不敢多吃。
A: What's wrong? You don't like the cooking and cannot take it?
B: No. You misunderstood it. The cooking is great. I'm afraid of gaining weight and dare not to eat too much.

- **不+VP…也(一定)+VP。(The pattern "不是…也是" shows the confidence of the speaker, who implies that things wouldn't go far from his or her estimation. Things mentioned after "不" carry a stronger degree of significance than things mentioned after "也". The pattern "不是…就是" implies that there are no other options or possibilities.)**

那老頭不是逃犯也是個老色鬼。
That old guy would either be an escaped criminal or a pervert.

爸爸一旦知道這事，不打你也會好好教訓你一頓。

Once father knows about it, he would give you a lecture even if he doesn't beat you.

這種官僚作風，不讓老百姓埋怨也讓老百姓皺眉頭。
Even if people do not complain about the bureaucratic way of doing things like this they would frown.

她那件毛衣一定是織給那老頭或者他女兒。
(也可以說) =>

- 反正 (**"反正" means "anyhow, in any case". It is used as an adverb to indicate determination or certainty, and implies that the decision or the outcome will not be changed anyway).**

我不管他是下崗還是退休，反正他就是沒了工作！
I don't care he was laid off or he retired. He is out of work anyway.

你們願意到公園鍛煉身體你們就去吧！我反正是要待在家裏。
Go exercise in the park as you wish. I will stay home anyway.

反正，他是個老實人，你不用擔心他會做不三不四的事。
Anyway, he is an honest man. You don't have to worry that he would do wicked things.

別哭了，別哭了，反正事情已經發生了，哭也沒有用。
Don't cry. It happened already, crying is useless anyway.

(完成句子) =>A: 你打扮得那麼漂亮幹嗎？

- 果然 (**"果然" is a cohesive device used as an adverb or a conjunction in the second clause, meaning "as expected").**

A: 我跟你說的那部電影你看了嗎？
B: 看了。你說得沒錯，果然是部好電影。
A: Did you see the movie I told you to watch?
B: Yep. You were completely right. Just like you said, it was really a good movie.

叫你早點起來你不早點起來，你看，現在果然趕不上(gǎnbushàng)校車了吧！
I told you to get up earlier but you didn't. Look, sure enough you're going to miss the bus!

（完成句子）=> 以前就聽人說上海的女孩都很漂亮，到了上海以後，

______________________________________。

（完成句子）=> 我估計他能申請上好大學，後來

______________________。

- 儘管 (**"儘管" is more often used in written Chinese, meaning "although" or "despite." It works in conjunction with the cohesive adverbs "但是", "還是" or "卻").**

儘管別的國家都反對，英國和美國還是決定要打伊拉克。
Even though other countries are opposed, England and the United States are still determined to attack Iraq.

儘管他嘴上不說，但心裏卻對這件事非常不高興。
Even though he didn't say anything, he felt extremely unhappy about these things on the inside.

(回答問題) =>該跟誰結婚？

	語言	學歷	收入	外表	女朋友
小李	中文，不太流利的英文	研究生	$$	☺☺☺	以前有過三個
艾瑞克	英文，法文，日文	中學	$$$$$	☹	從來沒有交過女朋友

跟小李結婚好嗎？為什麼？
跟艾瑞克結婚好嗎？為什麼？

____。

- 一副 xx 的樣子 (**"樣子" means "appearance." "副" is like a measure word for "樣子". When we say "一副 xx 的樣子", we indicate that the subject appears to be xx; like "看起來", "看樣子" means: "it looks like...")**

他說起話來一副老師的樣子。
He talks like a teacher.

看樣子，他病得不輕。= 他(一副)病得不輕的樣子。
It looks like he is very ill.

他看起來很有經驗。
(也可以說) =>

- 這樣吧！(**"這樣吧" is used in a discourse for a suggestion or an idea made towards resolving a problem. It can be translated as "How about this…").**

A：這孩子這學期成績退步(tuìbù)了，英文考得這麼壞，明年怎麼考大學呢！
B：我也挺擔心的，這樣吧，我們找個家教到家裏來給他補習英文，你看怎麼樣？
A：This child's English has worsened this semester; she did so badly on her English tests. How can she take the college entrance exams next year?
B：I'm very worried too. What about this: let's find a tutor to come to the house to tutor her in English. What do you think?

A: 這個工作我申請兩次了，都沒有被批準。我看我這一生是沒有希望了。
B: 你別胡思亂想。這樣吧，你把申請信改一改，然後找個官員幫幫忙…
A: I applied twice for this job, but both times I was not approved. As I see it my life is hopeless.
B: Don't have wild thinking like that. How about this? You change the application letter a little bit, then find an officer to help you …

A: 打太極拳的那群人早就散開了，你讓我現在上哪兒去找那禿頂的老頭呢？
(完成句子) =>B: 這樣吧，__________________

- 帶著 (**"帶著" means "to carry". However, when used in literature, the objects of "帶著" do not necessarily have anything to do with "to carry". We simply use "with" to translate "帶著" in these sentences).**

老頭兒帶著溫和的微笑，向長椅走了過去。
With a gentle smile, the old man walked toward the bench.

那逃犯帶著緊張的心情, 給警察打了電話。
With a nervous state of mind, the escaped convict called the police.

她的臉上帶著兩行淚(lèi), 什麼都沒說，就靜靜地躺下了。
With two streams of tears down her face, she didn't say anything and just quietly lay down.

課堂活動

(一) 用課文裏學到的生詞和句型回答問題：

	可用的生詞：
1. 作者的妻子為什麼睡不著？	心事 嘆氣 碰上 色鬼
2. 作者的妻子對她的母親有什麼樣的埋怨？	幹嗎 打扮 嫌 時髦 說閑話 馬虎
3. 作者和妻子為什麼要到公園去？他們到的時候，發現了什麼？	煩 警告 躲 不三不四 抓 教訓 太極拳 溫和 笑盈盈 胸 量

(二)角色扮演(role play)

- 課文裏的岳母決定讓老頭跟女兒見面好好談談，如果你是他們，你會怎麼說？
  - 岳母
  - 老頭
  - 女兒

- 你在一個婚姻介紹所工作。你會把下面哪位先生介紹給哪位女士？為什麼？

	婚史	職業	子女	長處	短處
陳先生 38	結婚十一年，兩年前太太因病過世	出租汽車司機	兩男一女，10 歲，9 歲，3 歲	對女人專情負責	工作時間長
胡先生 35	結婚兩個星期，三天前離婚	電影明星	無	帥，身材好，總是能讓女人笑	愛花錢
董先生 32	結過三次婚，最長四年，最短一年半	大學教授	子：13 歲 女：3 歲	有學問 會做飯	有麻煩的父母

	婚史	職業	子女	長處	短處
王小姐 42	結婚七年，十年前因有新的男朋友離婚	醫生	兩女：18歲，16歲	漂亮 浪漫 重視子女教育	腿有問題，不能跑步 不做家事
李小姐 19	結婚兩個月，一星期前因先生有別的女朋友離婚	服務員	子：一個月(婚前懷孕)	溫柔 身材好	不懂得照顧孩子 高中沒畢業
何小姐 29	結過三次婚。最長六個月，最短四天	商業主管	無	有學問， 高收入，不需要別人照顧	不好看 不喜歡小孩

(三) 你的看法

- 課文裏的岳母為什麼不敢把秘密告訴女兒呢？如果你是她，你會怎麼做？如果你是女兒，你會怎麼做？
- 中老年人再婚找對象時會有哪些顧慮(gùlǜ-concerns)？女人再婚比男人再婚難嗎？
- 在中國人的傳統觀念裏，父母老了能和子女住在一起是件好事。你覺得這樣做有什麼好處和壞處？你結婚以後願意和父母住在一起嗎？你老的時候會希望和子女住在一起嗎？

練習題

一：詞彙練習：(選擇最合適的詞完成句子或段落)

(一)　*(躲 躺 煩 嫌 推 隨 靠)*

1. 他昨天喝多了酒，回來以後，一直覺得迷迷糊糊的，在床上____了一天才好起來。
2. 大家都在忙著準備開晚會，打掃衛生的打掃衛生，買東西的買東西，你卻____在自己的房間裏上網，太過分了吧？
3. 妻子給他織的毛衣他總是_____不時髦，讓他妻子很____。
4. 請你_____著大家往前走，看到一棵大樹，再走幾步就能看到廁所。
5. 我站得累死了，想____在他身上休息一會兒，可他馬上就把我____開了。

(二)

1. *(埋怨 警告 耐心 在乎 大致上)*

妻子常常_________先生做事情缺乏______，不夠仔細，什麼事情都是________滿意就行了，根本不追求最好的結果，而先生卻一點也不______妻子說什麼，想怎麼做還怎麼做。我看他們之間會發生問題的。

2. *(急匆匆 笑盈盈 穿著 打扮 皺著眉頭 觀察)*

今天下午我坐在公園的長椅上_____來來去去的人群。有些人_____很隨便，大概只為了鍛煉身體方便；有些人______得很正式，______地趕向車站，像是有什麼重要的事。讓我生氣的是：有個漂亮的女孩從我身邊走過，我________地向她打招呼，她卻把我當成色鬼，_________走開了。

二：語法和口語練習：(選擇詞語完成句子，或用提供的句型完成對話)

1. 我估計那件外套是那個禿頂高個兒的，人群散開的時候，________________。*(果然)*
2. 你岳母跟誰談戀愛都行，__________________________。*(反正)*
3. A: 週末的時候，你一般做些什麼？
   B: ____。*(…什麼的)*

4. A: 我哪有時間看朋友？我每天忙著給我的小孫女織毛衣呢！
   B: 大熱天的， 你______________，你孫女才不會穿呢！(V 什麼(O)嘛)
5. A: 咱們兒子這會兒在房間裏這麼安靜，一定是在上網。
   B: 不會吧？
   A:____。
   (不+VP… 也(一定)+VP, …)
6. A: 對不起，我不能跟你們出去玩，我得學習。
   B:____。
   (use "*又*" *to response, such as in "又不是賣毛衣賺錢，織那麼多毛衣給誰穿？)*

三：綜合練習：讀下面的短文，並選擇合適的詞填空：

我躺在臥室裏看電視，聽到先生在書房一次又一次重重地 1______，於是走過去看他怎麼了。他坐在那兒皺著眉頭 2______，竟然沒有注意到我進來了。問他是不是有 3______，他搖搖頭。我 4______他在為工作上的事煩，又不願意讓我擔心。我 5______地在他旁邊坐了一會兒，不知道該怎麼 6______他，只好告訴他早點睡覺，聽到他 7______地答應了一聲，我就先去睡覺，可是躺在被窩裏卻一直胡思亂想，久久不能 8______。

1. a. 發呆　b. 嘆氣　c. 搖頭
2. a. 發呆　b. 煩　c. 警告
3. a. 閑話　b. 埋怨　c.心事
4. a. 估計　b. 安慰　c.誤會
5. a. 淡淡　b. 默默　c.匆匆
6. a. 在乎　b.埋怨　c.安慰
7. a. 默默　b.淡淡　c.匆匆
8. a. 入睡　b.睡覺　c. 迷迷糊糊

四：閱讀練習：

害怕再婚的女人

我和丈夫原來感情一直很好，但不知道怎麼回事，他就和比他小十幾歲的秘書發生了關係。我雖然捨不得那段感情，但還是忍著痛和他離了婚。離婚後，親戚 朋友不斷地給我介紹對象，前前後後見過幾個，可那些人都是沒見幾次面就動手動腳的，嚇得我再也不敢再跟他們見面了。我有一個女兒，我得替我女兒想想，她今年 12 歲，剛上中學，我怕如果嫁了個不好的男人，害了我女兒怎麼辦？這樣過了大約兩年多的時間，我都沒敢再找對象。

半年前，我參加了一次大學同學會，見到了很多十多年沒見面的老同學，跟大家一起懷念大學生活，感到很興奮。在同學會上我與一位叫阿強的老同學談得比較多。他剛離婚不久，知道了我也是離過婚的，很自然地就談了起來。他開朗的性格給我留下了很深的印象。同學會後不久，有一天，我突然接到了阿強的電話，問我有沒有興趣去看一個畫展，他還請我帶著孩子一起去，他說他想孩子也會喜歡的。在畫展中，他拉著我女兒的手，耐心地給她介紹每一幅畫，也笑盈盈的和我交換看法，我們一起過了輕松愉快的一天。我看得出來，他對女兒好，而女兒也願意接受他。在那以後，我和阿強的關係一天比一天近，但我的擔心也一天比一天重。雖然阿強現在對我這麼好，可我原來的丈夫當初對我也很不錯的呀，我怎麼才能知道他是真心的呢？

嚇 (xià)：to frighten, to be frightened
害(hài)：to cause something unfavorable to happen to someone
畫展(huàzhǎn)：art exhibition

根據上文，判斷對錯(True or False)：
1．離婚的時候，作者還是對她的丈夫有感情。
2．親戚給作者介紹的男人，對她的女兒動手動腳，讓她很害怕。
3．作者第一次見到阿強是在她離婚兩年以後。
4．作者的女兒不太能接受媽媽交新男朋友的事實。
5．從文中可以看出經歷過離婚後，作者似乎對婚姻(hūnyīn-marriage)缺乏信心了。

五：翻譯練習(請用提供的詞彙或句型翻譯下面的句子)

1.　　寧可…也/真是的(see L1)/ 幹嗎/…嘛/

A: Many people would rather receive lower pay to stay in the work force (unit) for a few more years than retire early.

B: These people really don't know what they are doing. Why do they like working so much?

A: (You know), it is because it is too boring to stay at home all the time.

2.　　一眼就…/ 於是/ 迫不及待/ 簡直

My wife recognized the pervert at first sight; therefore, she didn't wait another minute to break the silence. I was almost stunned when I saw her run over to threaten him. I heard her say: "I am warning you now. Don't you ever bother my mother again. If I hear more gossip about you and my mother, I will teach you a lesson."

3.　　儘管/ 帶著/ 會…的

Although he has a gentle smile on his face now, after the crowd disperses, (believe me), he will hide behind the trees and start to frown.

六．作文：(從下邊幾個題目中, 選擇一個, 寫一篇不少於 500 字的作文。你至少要用六個所提供的句型或詞彙)

verb 下去 (as in 你不能再忍受下去了)	寧可	...，要說...嘛,...	會...的
不是 A,也(一定)是 B	於是	A 嫌 B...	果然
儘管...，但是/還...	幹嗎	一副...的樣子	反正

1.從某個角度看，我們課文的故事還沒有結束， 請你給這個故事一個結尾 (jíeweǐ-ending) (Please continue writing the text story using the first person as the son-in-law of the story.)
2.給媽媽的一封信---請你替故事裏的女兒給媽媽寫一封信。
3.“讓我怎麼開口？”--- 媽媽的獨白(monologue)。
4. 中老年人談戀愛或者再婚常常會碰到什麼問題？中國社會跟美國社會對這樣的事態度一樣嗎？請用我們課文的故事做例子來討論。

第六課 遲來的幸福

Let's warm-up with a review exercise!

Match the words in characters with Pinyin and English:

漢字	拼音	英文	哪兒學過
小心			二年級
興奮			二年級
好奇			二年級
離婚			二年級
認真			二年級
親戚			二年級
實行			第二課
屬於			第二課
獨立			第三課
環境			第四課
避免			第四課
否則			第四課
扔			第四課
估計			第五課
於是			第五課

拼音

1. bìmiǎn	2. dúlì	3. fǒuzé	4. gūjì
5. hàoqí	6. huánjìng	7. líhūn	8. qīnqi
9. rènzhēn	10. rēng	11. shíxíng	12. shǔyú
13. xiǎoxīn	14. xīngfèn	15. yúshì	

英文

a. careful	b. to be excited	c. thereupon	d. to estimate
e. curious	f. environment	g. to divorce	h. relative (n.)
i. serious	j. to throw	k. to carry out	l. to belong to
m. to avoid	n. independent	o. otherwise	

聽力&口語

聽錄音回答問題

對話一

1.	2.	3.	4.	5.

生詞：邀請，推銷，伴兒，幸福，婚姻

複習：絕對，禿頂，根據，觀察，傷腦筋，嫁，大多數，反正，享受
退休，擔心，人家，幹嗎，(離婚，商店)

對話二

1.	2.	3.	4.	5.

生詞：毛病，領養，拋棄，智商，冒險，正常

複習：前頭：活潑，似乎，懷孕，仔細，寧可，多多少少，觀察，
(安靜，認真，小心，可愛，過分，決定)

對話三

1.	2.	3.	4.	5.

生詞：聚會，單身，默契，羨慕，分手，後悔，求婚，冷靜，真正
來不及/來得及，孤單，豐富

複習：碰見/碰上，爭取，發呆，胡思亂想，懷孕，幸福，一副…的樣子
仍然，人家，突然，願意，驕傲

根據對話一回答問題：

1. 對話裏的媽媽做了什麼事讓女兒不高興？
2. 媽媽為什麼要那麼做呢？女兒有什麼不一樣的想法？

根據對話二回答問題：

6. 這個對話很可能發生在哪兒？說話的兩個人是什麼關係？他們為什麼要到那個地方？
7. 他們看到的頭兩個孩子怎麼樣？他們想把這兩個孩子帶回家，還是要另外看別的孩子？說話的兩個人有什麼不同的意見？

根據對話三回答問題：

1. 女說話人阿華昨天晚上做了什麼？什麼事讓她回來以後心裏不太舒服？
2. 阿華跟前男朋友是怎麼分手的？當初她希望自己嫁給他嗎？現在呢？她目前過得幸福嗎？
3. 男說話人覺得阿華和前男朋友分手是誰的錯?為什麼？

口語用法

1. 我邀請他來吃個飯也是為你好啊！
(“也是為你好啊” means “is for your own good”. “也” and “啊” are used to ease up the tension. A similar expression is “也是為你想啊!” meaning “it is on the concern of you.”)

A: 你不要管我是不是在胡思亂想。
B: 我讓你別胡思亂想，也是為你好啊！
A: It’s not your business whether or not I have wild thinking.
B: It is for your own good that I told you to cease your wild thinking.

A: 這兒又髒(zāng)又熱。你幹嗎要我躲在這兒。
B: 別埋怨了。我要你躲起來，也是為你想啊！
A: This place is dirty and hot. Why do you want me hide here?
B: Don’t complain. I asked you to hide for your own good.

2. 我總不能把你推銷給十八歲的年輕人吧！
(“總” can mean “anyway”, “after all.” It points out the most essential aspect of a matter. “吧” makes the sentence less affirmative).

派一個警察不夠，派二十個總找得到那個色鬼吧！
If sending one policeman is not enough, sending 20 should make it possible to find the pervert after all, don’t you think?

你要參加的是個正式的會，總得打扮打扮，不能穿得那麼馬虎吧！
The meeting you’re going to attend is formal. You should dress up a little bit, anyway—don’t wear such casual clothes!

(“吧” is often used at the end of an imperative sentence to give a softer or a consulting tone).
你走著去吧，別開車了！
Walk there. Don’t drive!

3. 這個不行，那個也不行，…
(“這個也不行，那個也不行，…” is used in a discourse to express a complaint. It can be translated as “this doesn't work, nor does that one” or “there seems to be nothing you will be pleased with”. It is either followed by a question, a negative comment, or a conclusion.

這個也不行，那個也不行，我看你今年找不到什麼合適的工作了。
This one is not ok, that one is not ok…I think you won't be able to find a suitable job this year.

今天不行，明天也不行，你到底什麼時候才要開始鍛煉身體？
Today is no good, neither is tomorrow. When on earth are you going to start your exercise?

這麼做也不行，那麼做也不行，你太迷信了。
This way doesn't work, neither does that way. You are just too superstitious.

你這個不吃，那個也不吃，到時候病了怎麼辦？
You eat nothing. What can we do if you get sick?

4. 看樣子很活潑啊！
("看樣子" means "It looks like" or "It seems" based on one's estimation. It is used colloquially).

這個學生上課的時候不是發呆就是睡覺，看樣子他不喜歡這門課。
This student either daydreams or sleeps in class. It seems that he doesn't really like this class.

已經一年了你的腿還沒有恢復，看樣子很難恢復了。
It has been a whole year but your leg still hasn't healed. Looks like it will be hard for it to be restored.

5．不管怎麼樣，我們都得領養個男孩子
("不管怎麼樣"means "no matter what", "anyway", or "by all means". It is used in spoken language to indicate that under any circumstances, the result will remain the same).

不管怎麼樣，我去公園時不敢再打扮得那麼時髦了。我真害怕那些閑話。
No matter what, when I go to the park I don't dare dress fashionably. I am really scared of those gossips.

我知道我的老板不會支持我。但不管怎麼樣，我都要爭取我的權利。
I know my boss won't support me, but no matter what, I will fight for my rights.

6．我也不知道怎麼搞的
("不知道怎麼搞的" can be translated as "I have no idea…", or "somehow…", or " who knows how it happened". It is used in spoken language and is followed by the matter that puzzles or bothers the speaker).

不知道怎麼搞的，我昨天還好好的，今天就突然生病了。
I have no idea how this happened. I was great yesterday, but today I got sick all of a sudden.

這個旅館的房間乾淨也安靜，可是不知道怎麼搞的，我就是睡不好。
The room of this hotel is clean and quiet. I don't know why, but I just can't sleep well.

7. 但說實話，你真的覺得幸福嗎？
("說實話" means "to be honest; to tell the truth". It is used to express one's personal feeling or opinion. In this sense, you can also say "說心裏話" or "說實在話". However, "說實話" can also mean "Tell me the truth". In this case, it can't be replaced by "說心裏話", or "說實在話").

說心裏話(or說實在話/說實話)，現代社會競爭這麼激烈。娶個女強人做太太也不錯。至少可以減少經濟壓力。
To be honest, nowadays the competition in society is really intense. It's not so bad marrying a career woman. At least she can alleviate some financial pressure.

說實話，是不是你在鼓勵這些非政府組織挑戰政府？
Tell me the truth, was it you who encouraged these nongovernmental organizations to challenge the government?

口語練習：請用聽力對話中學到的生詞和口語用法討論下面的問題：

…也是為你好啊！/　總…吧！/　哪有(你/人)這麼+VP的/　看樣子…
怎麼能這樣呢？/　不管怎麼樣/　我也不知道怎麼搞的/　說實話…
這+(S)+不+VP, 那+(S)+也不VP…(as in 這個不行，那個也不行)

1. A—你已經四十歲了，還沒有結婚，但你不喜歡你的媽媽不停地給你介紹對象。B—你的孩子已經四十歲了，還沒有結婚，你很擔心，很希望幫他找到對象。
2. A—你想到孤兒院領養一個健康的男孩子。B—你在孤兒院工作，想把一個有殘疾的女孩子推銷給A。
3. A—你後悔和以前的女朋友/男朋友分手，你給她/他打電話，希望恢復從前的關係。B—你已經結婚了，希望以前的男朋友/女朋友別再煩你。

課文

第一部分

年輕的時候，琳達沒認真想過結婚的事。過了四十，對於婚姻，不但她自己不敢想，親戚朋友們聚會時，也都似乎很有默契地避免談起這個話題。沒有人願意不小心傷了一個四十多歲還嫁不出去的女人！

琳達有工作，有房子，但她也有無限的寂寞。

“肯尼，如果當初你不顧父母的反對，娶我做妻子，你說，我們會不會幸福？”肯尼是個成功的律師。十年前，他聽從父母的勸告跟琳達分手後，選擇和一個同是韓裔的女人結了婚，但他和琳達還一直保持著朋友關係。

“就算我想娶你，你也不會想嫁給我的，對不對？你有屬於你的天空。”

肯尼說的也許沒錯。琳達一向非常獨立，從來不羨慕別人結婚，對她來說，結不結婚無所謂，她不需要一個男人來照顧她，更不希望有個男人來擁有她，限制她的生活。也許，這才是肯尼當時下決心分手的真正原因。然而，琳達也不想一個人孤孤單單過一輩子，她需要有個伴兒。

她想要個孩子。

四十歲了，就算能夠通過現代醫學手段進行人工受孕，她也屬於懷孕的高危險群。琳達不想冒這個險。若孩子天生有毛病什麼的，對她，對孩子來說，都不會好過，到那時，後悔就來不及了。

"領養吧！"琳達冷靜地告訴自己。

生詞用法

1	迟	遲	chí	late; delayed	你來得太遲了，大家早走了。/他昨天遲來了半個小時。/他起得太晚，一定又得遲到了。
2	幸福	幸福	xìngfú	happy, happiness	幸福的家庭/幸福的婚姻生活/過得很幸福/得到了幸福/追求幸福/關心孩子的幸福
	琳达	琳達	líndá	Linda	
	对于	對於	duìyú	to; for; with regard to	見語法
3	婚姻	婚姻	hūnyīn	marriage	一段婚姻/合法婚姻/婚姻生活/美好的婚姻生活
4	聚会	聚會	jùhuì	to gather; gathering; get-together	一場聚會
5	默契	默契	mòqì	tacit understanding; privity; unvoiced pact]	這些球員之間的默契很好。/這對夫妻很有默契，不必開口就知道對方心裏想什麼。
6	伤	傷	shāng	to hurt; to injure, wound; injury	傷了他的心/傷得很重/受了很重的傷
7	无限	無限	wúxiàn	unlimited; infinite	無限的責任/無限的時間
8	寂寞	寂寞	jìmò (Taiwan: jímò)	lonely, lonesome; loneliness	寂寞的生活/心裏很寂寞/他是個寂寞的男人。/他一到晚上就覺得特別寂寞。
	肯尼	肯尼	kěnní	Kenny	
9	当初	當初	dāngchū	in the first place; at the beginning	你當初是怎麼說的？現在怎麼都變了？/當初我打算待兩年就回去，沒想到一直待到現在。
10	不顾	不顧	búgù	to disregard; in spite of	不顧個人的安全/不顧一切地離開家/他不顧家人的反對，一個人去了中國。/為了留在美國，他連國內的妻兒都不顧了。 見語法
11	听从	聽從	tīngcóng	to obey; to listen to	聽從父母的意見/聽從官員們的安排/聽從老一輩的勸告

12	劝告	勸告	quàngào	to advise; to exhort; exhortation	他不顧朋友的勸告喝了酒還開車。/她勸我別生氣。
13	分手	分手	fēnshǒu	to split up; to say good-bye	我們在車站分手後，她回上海，我到北京。/他女朋友要和他分手，讓他很難過。
14	韩裔	韓裔	hányì	Korean-descendant (裔: descendant; offspring)	亞裔/華裔/他是一個韓裔美國人。
15	保持	保持	bǎochí	to keep; to preserve	保持安靜/保持關係/保持衛生/保持冷靜/保持聯系
16	天空	天空	tiānkōng	the sky; the heavens	
17	羡慕	羨慕	xiànmù	to envy; to admire	我羨慕你的好運。/我羨慕你有一個幸福的婚姻。/你可以免費上大學，真讓人羨慕。
18	无所谓	無所謂	wúsuǒwèi	to be indifferent; not matter	無所謂的態度/好吃不好吃無所謂，只要能吃飽就行。/你跟誰出去對我來說無所謂。
19	拥有	擁有	yōngyǒu/ (Taiwan: yǒngyǒu)	to own; to possess	擁有很多財產/擁有一個幸福的家庭/擁有一所漂亮的大房子
20	决心	決心	juéxīn	determination; resolution; (下決心 = make up one's mind)	下決心/下定決心/找到好工作的決心/我決心天天早起。/我下決心每天起床後鍛煉身體。/我有決心在三點以前做完功課。/他的決心很大。
21	真正	真正	zhēnzhèng	genuine; really	真正的朋友/真正的愛情/他沒有真正負起責任。
22	孤单	孤單	gūdān	alone; all by oneself; lonely	孤單的時候/孤單的日子/他感到孤單無助。/他過著孤孤單單的生活。
23	一辈子	一輩子	yíbèizi	as long as one lives; ; lifetime; a lifetime of	我一輩子都會記著你。/他吃了一輩子的苦。/我希望下輩子還做你的妻子。/你一定是上輩子作了好事，才能娶到這麼好的太太。
24	伴儿	伴兒	bànr	company; companion; partner	玩伴兒/老伴兒/旅遊的伴兒/找一個伴兒/咱們倆做伴兒。
25	能够	能夠	nénggòu	to be able to; to be capable of	他能夠說八種外語。/這一次我們一定能夠贏得冠軍。

26	医学	醫學	yīxué	medical science	
27	手段	手段	shǒuduàn	means; measure; artifice	醫學手段/執政手段/教學手段
28	人工	人工	réngōng	artificial；man-made; artificially	人工河/人工湖(hú)/采取人工的方式影響天氣
29	受孕	受孕	shòuyùn	to become pregnant	自然受孕/人工受孕
30	群	群	qún	group; measure word “a group of” “a herd of”	人群/羊群/魚群/高危險群/一群人/一群牛
31	冒险	冒險	màoxiǎn	to take a risk; at the risk of; risky	他喜歡冒險/他冒了很大的險。/他冒著犯罪的危險幫助他的朋友。/這樣做太冒險了。/他是個冒險家。
	若	若	ruò	if	見語法
32	天生	天生	tiānshēng	innate; inborn; inherent	他天生就這麼聰明。/他天生是個音樂家。/他有天生的殘疾。
33	毛病	毛病	máobìng	illness; breakdown; defect	他腦子(nǎozi)有點毛病，有時候說話都說不清楚。/他的車出了點小毛病。/他這人的毛病就是不管在哪兒都喜歡大聲說話。
34	后悔	後悔	hòuhuǐ	to regret	他後悔沒有聽父母的勸告。/我後悔今天沒有多穿一些衣服。/他覺得很後悔。
35	来不及	來不及	láibùjí	there’s not enough time (to do sth) 來得及=there’s still time to do sth	我來不及吃早飯就得去上課了。/你跑得快一點還來得及坐這班公共汽車。
36	领养	領養	lǐngyǎng	to adopt (children)	領養一個孩子/他不是親生的，是領養的。
37	冷静	冷靜	lěngjìng	to be calm; calm	保持冷靜/頭腦冷靜/你冷靜點！/我冷靜不下來/他做事很冷靜。

課文

第二部分

但領養也沒有那麼簡單。美國的領養機構條件很嚴格，手續也非常複雜。她一個單身女人，無法讓孩子擁有正常的家庭生活，除非她能給孩子找到個父親，否則要領養個美國孩子不那麼容易。於是琳達開始找中介公司，希望能領養個中國孩子。

“資料上的這個孩子叫秋雲，今年五歲。身體，智商什麼的都挺好，你看看這張照片。”

“看起來挺活潑，挺可愛的。但你仔細看她的眼睛，好像有點毛病啊？”

“我估計就是因為她的眼睛有毛病，才讓她父母給拋棄的。中國重男輕女的觀念一直存在，加上政府實行獨生子女政策，你知道，孤兒院裏的孩子，不是女嬰，就是天生有殘疾的。秋雲雖然眼睛有毛病，但不影響看東西。”

中介公司像是在推銷秋雲似的，想盡辦法說服琳達領養這個孩子。

“秋雲的遭遇十分特別。她一生下來，就被父母扔在醫院的廁所裏。醫院把她送到了派出所，派出所又把她轉到兒童福利院，後來，她還讓天津日報社領養了一陣子。”

“噢，天津日報社怎麼領養孩子呢？”

“他們以集體的名義領養秋雲，由記者們捐款，一起負責給她提供吃穿用的東西，並輪流接秋雲回家，讓她感受家庭生活。”

琳達覺得日報社"領養"秋雲的方法實在是太可笑了。她一下子覺得對秋雲有了份責任感，她相信自己可以為秋雲提供一個更好的生活。她決定領養秋雲。

坐上飛機，琳達來到了中國天津。面對陌生的環境，她並不害怕，只覺得興奮，好奇。"秋雲！"等終於抱著孩子時，她感覺如此滿足。

有了秋雲之後，琳達的日子忙了起來，也豐富了許多。她開始學中文，每逢星期天，還帶秋雲去中文學校。

"琳達，下星期帶秋雲來我們家坐坐，我教你中文。"邀請她的是小強尼的父親，比她小七歲，兩年前離了婚。

琳達帶著秋雲，去了小強尼家一次，兩次，三次…。四年以後，小強尼的父親向琳達求婚，四十六歲的琳達，高興地點了頭。

生詞用法

38	机构	機構	jīgòu	institution; organization	管理機構/政府機構/教育機構/領養機構
39	手续	手續	shǒuxù	procedure; formalities	辦手續/簽證手續/領養手續/法律手續
40	复杂	複雜	fùzá	complicated; complex; sophisticated	複雜的想法/複雜的手續/情況複雜/這個問題很複雜，用幾句話很難說清楚。
41	单身	單身	dānshēn	unmarried; single	他還是單身。/單身生活不見得就寂寞。
42	正常	正常	zhèngcháng	normal; regular; normally	正常的關係/情況很正常/恢復正常生活/大雪讓我們這幾天沒辦法正常上課。
43	中介	仲介	zhōngjiè	agency	婚姻中介/房屋中介/中介公司
44	资料	資料	zīliào	data, document	一份研究資料/查資料

	秋云	秋雲	qiūyún	name of a girl	
46	智商	智商	zhìshāng	IQ(intelligence quotient)	她那麼聰明,智商一定很高。/他想領養一個智商正常的孩子。
47	抛弃	拋棄	pāoqì	to abandon; to discard	拋棄財產/把孩子拋棄在大街上。/他為了留在美國，拋棄了國內的妻子和女兒。/他仍然沒有完全拋棄傳統的保守觀念。
	存在	存在	cúnzài	to exist; being; existence	工作中還存在不少問題。/農村還存在重男輕女的觀念。/這種不平等現象哪兒都存在。/法輪功的存在/官僚主義的存在/沒有人注意到他的存在。 見語法
48	孤儿院	孤兒院	gū'éryuàn	orphanage	一家孤兒院
49	女婴	女嬰	nǚyīng	baby girl (嬰兒= infant; baby)	
50	残疾	殘疾	cánjí	deformity, handicap	殘疾人士 (rénshi)。/他的手有天生的殘疾。/他的眼睛天生有殘疾。
51	推销	推銷	tuīxiāo	to try to sell; to market	推銷東西/把這東西推銷出去/向他推銷這些商品/一名推銷員
52	说服	說服	shuōfú/ shuìfú	to persuade; to convince	我說服他不喝酒了。/我說服不了他。/他本來想隨便穿件衣服就行了，但後來還是被我說服了，好好打扮了一下。
53	遭遇	遭遇	zāoyù	to encounter (unhappy thing); misfortune	遭遇不幸/遭遇車禍/遭遇危險/不幸的遭遇/一樣的遭遇
54	十分	十分	shífēn	very; fully	十分高興/十分容易/對他不幸的遭遇，我感到十分難過。/不管我說什麼，他都十分相信。
55	派出所	派出所	paìchūsuǒ	local police station	
56	儿童	兒童	értóng	children	兒童教育/兒童節/兒童電影/兒童出版物/十歲以下的兒童免費看電影。
57	福利院	福利院	fúlìyuàn	charity home (福利 = welfare; benefit)	兒童福利院/老年福利院/社會福利/這家公司的福利很好。
	天津	天津	Tiānjīn	name of a city in China	

58	报社	報社	bàoshè	newspaper office	日報社/黨報社/晚報社
59	一阵子	一陣子	yízhènzi	a period of time	這孩子常常會哭一陣子才起床。/這一陣子我特別想她。/你的病不要緊，過一陣子自然就會好的。
60	集体	集體	jítǐ	collective; team	集體財產/集體福利/集體觀念/集體宿舍/女人們集體走上街頭抗議。/以集體名義寫了一封信。
61	名义	名義	míngyì	the name of; 以…的名義= in the name of; (名義上 = nominal; in name)	以個人名義捐錢/以集體名義領養/名義負責人/名義校長/名義上，他是這孩子的父親，但他從沒照顧過這孩子。/名義上他們結婚了，其實他們一直分開住。
	由	由	yóu	by; through	見語法
62	记者	記者	jìzhě	journalist; reporter	一名記者/日報社記者/電視臺記者
63	捐款	捐款	juānkuǎn	to donate money; to contribute money; monetary contribution	給孤兒們捐款/這一回的捐款一共只有二百零三塊錢。
64	负责	負責	fùzé	to be responsible for; to be in charge of; responsible	對游客的安全負責/他負責學校的對外交流工作。/負起照顧孩子的責任/負責的領導
65	轮流	輪流	lúnliú	to take turns	輪流工作/輪流做飯/他們夫妻倆輪流送孩子上學。/今天輪到你接孩子了。
66	感受	感受	gǎnshòu	to feel ; to experience; experience (n.); feelings	我想感受一下總統的生活。/ 你應該去感受感受中國人過年的熱鬧。/幸福的感受/被拋棄的感受
67	实在	實在	shízai	indeed; really; honestly	你能幫我，實在太好了。/他說什麼，我實在聽不懂。
68	可笑	可笑	kěxiào	funny; silly; ridiculous	這個故事很可笑/ 她從來不幫朋友，卻總埋怨朋友不幫她，太可笑了。/這種可笑的做法我當然反對。

69	抱	抱	bào	to carry; to hold with both arms; to embrace	抱小孩/他一看見爸爸，就跑過去抱住他的腿。/我覺得好難過，你抱抱我。
70	如此		rúcǐ	as so; like this(as in 如此高興\如此興奮)	情況已經如此了，後悔也沒用。/ 他一直很霸道，結婚以後也如此。/ 如此重要的問題，你一定要問清楚。/看到孩子幸福的微笑，他感到如此滿足。
71	满足	滿足	mǎnzú	to feel content; to meet with; to satisfy, (讓人滿足/令人滿足= satisfying)	感到滿足/有了房子，也有了孩子，他覺得很滿足。/這樣的生活讓人滿足。/老師不能滿足你這個可笑的要求。/政府要滿足老百姓的生活需要。
72	丰富	豐富	fēngfù	to enrich; abundant; plentiful	書豐富了我們的生活。/旅遊可以豐富你的知識。/他的想象力很豐富。/他的生活很豐富，每天下班後，不是聚會，就是運動，看電影。
73	每逢	每逢	měiféng	on every occasion; when	每逢我們遇到困難，他總是耐心地幫我們。/每逢下雨，她就遲到。
74	邀请	邀請	yāoqǐng	to invite; invitation	小李邀請我們去他家吃飯。/你收到小李的邀請了嗎？
	强尼	強尼	Qiángní	Johnny	
75	求婚	求婚	qiúhūn	to propose (a marriage)	向…求婚/跟…求婚

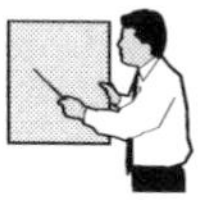

句型和語法

- 對於 and 對

(“對於”and “對” both are prepositions, introducing the topic or the aim of an action. In this sense, they are interchangeable. “對於” is more formal and “對” is more often used in spoken language.)

For example:

對(於)數學，我實在是沒有什麼興趣。
I really don’t have any interests in math.

對(於)這個問題，我們討論了三天三夜。
We had a discussion on the matter for three days and three nights.

他母親對(於)給福利院捐款的事非常支持。
His mother very much supports making donations to the charity home.

對(於)那些複雜的領養手續，他一點也不懂。
He does not understand at all those complicated adopting procedures.

A: 你是不是後悔進行人工受孕了?
(完成句子) =>B: 誰說的? 對於______________

(“對”can also mean “towards, to”. It can take an indirect object. “對於”can’t be used in this way).
For example:

他對我總是很好。
He is always very nice to me.

她對我說了一些不三不四的話。
She said something inappropriate to me.

我的房間對著公園。
My room faces the park.

- 不顧 **(to disregard, not heed, not pay attention to)**

他不顧政府的警告，到處向老百姓發送防治艾滋病的手冊。
Disregarding the government’s warnings, he handed out AIDS prevention and treatment brochures to people everywhere.

你怎麼能說走就走，不顧我的死活?
How can you leave like this, not caring whether I live or die?

他是個很有責任感的人，就算非常危險，他還是會想盡辦法完成工作。
(也可以說) =>

- **…, 加上…. (“加上” means “plus, beside, in addition”. It introduces additional reason or evidence before making an argument, a suggestion, or a conclusion).**

他的智商很高，加上一直都很用功，所以總是拿第一。
His IQ is high; in addition, he has worked hard all alone, so he always wins first place.

小李遲到了十五分鐘，加上根本沒把該準備的資料準備好，你說，老板怎麼可能對他印象好呢？
Little Li was 15 minutes late; besides, he didn't prepare at all the data he was supposed to prepare. How can the boss have a good impression on him?

A: 你怎麼突然決定回美國？
(回答問題) =>B:

- 若 **("若" is more often used in written Chinese, meaning "if." It occurs in the first clause in front of the verb phrase or at the beginning of the sentence)..**

那個推銷員若不是那麼可愛，這東西我也不會買。
If the salesperson hadn't been so lovely, I wouldn't have bought these things.

秋雲當初若沒有被送到福利院去，今天就不會被日報社以集體的名義領養。
If Qiu Yun hadn't originally been sent to the charity house, today she wouldn't have been adopted under the newspaper group's collective name.

如果他不那麼好奇，也許就不用冒這個險。
(也可以說) =>

- 存在 **("存在" means "to exist," "there exists," The sentence structure of** 存在 **when it's used as a verb, it's similar to "有" ("there is," or "there are"); however, it can also be used as a noun, meaning "existence.")**

人工受孕存在著一定程度的危險。
There exists a certain degree of risk in artificial insemination.

重男輕女的觀念，在保守的農村裏還是一直存在。
The concept of placing more importance on males than on females still exists in conservative areas of the countryside.

迷信觀念的存在影響農村的經濟發展。

The existence of superstitious ideas impairs the economic development of the rural areas.

這一對夫妻的婚姻有各種各樣的問題。
(也可以說) =>

- **(像(是)…似的 ("的" occurs at the end of sentence, meaning "as if" or "to be like." It can be used with or without "像" or "像是").**

記者們像是不了解殘疾人的痛苦似的，問起問題來又興奮又好奇。
The reporters seemed not to understand the pain of the suffering people; as the questioning began, they were excited and curious.

她**(像是)**把這領養來的孩子看成親生孩子似的，恨不得能為他提供一輩子的幸福。
She sees the adopted child as her own, and yearns to provide for him a lifetime of happiness.

你都結了婚了，怎麼還一副單身的樣子，一點責任感都沒有！
(也可以說) =>

- **Verb + 盡 +(xx) (When "盡" occurs between a verb and an object, it means "to do X a lot or completely" or "xx has been done to a great extent."**

為了讓孤兒們有個更好的生活，兒童福利院想盡辦法找人捐錢或領養。
In order to give the orphans better lives, the child welfare center thought of all the ways it could to get people to donate money or adopt.

妻子跟他說盡了好話，就是希望他能和她一起過個正常生活，別再冒險了。
His wife told him over and over, simply hoping that they could live a normal life, and not keep taking risks.

這些下崗的中年人，處處找不到工作，真可說是吃盡了苦頭。
These laid-off middle-aged workers can't find a job anywhere; you could really say they've had their fill of misery.

這個逃犯<u>什麼壞事都做了</u>，但在宗教的幫助下變成一個溫和，有愛心的人。

(也可以說) =>

- 以 **(Like "用", "以" is used to indicate the means by which an action is performed. However, it is usually used in written Chinese. "來" can be used in conjunction with "以" to introduce the purpose of the "以..." phrase. See also L4 "以...為...").**

  同學們以集體的名義給老師送了一束(shù)花。
  Some classmates sent a bunch of flowers to the professor collectively, under the name of the whole class.

  十多年前許多人就開始以電腦寫作(來)取代傳統的紙筆寫作。
  Ten-plus years ago, many people began using computers to write, replacing traditional writing instruments like pen and paper.

  如果不能自然受孕，也許可以試試用人工的方式要個孩子。
  (也可以說) =>

- 由 **(The use of "由" is a kind of passive structure. We can translate it as "by." It introduces an agent which has a responsibility for or authority over the activities being mentioned).**

  明天我們開一個晚會，買東西的事由你負責，打掃衛生由我負責。
  Tomorrow we are going to shoot a party. You are responsible for shopping and I am responsible for cleaning.

  這是一項由政府計劃的艾滋病防治工作，計劃雖好，但在實行的時候，還是難免受官僚作風的影響。
  This AIDS prevention and treatment project was planned by the government. Though it was planned well, when it was carried out it was hard to avoid being influenced by the bureaucrats' way of doing things.

  這份資料是由王先生的中介機構提供的,若有什麼問題，請你找他們，別找我。
  This piece of data was furnished by Mr. Wang's agency, so if there are any problems, please go to him, and don't ask me.

  在他們家， 太太帶孩子，先生賺錢
  (也可以說) =>

- **實在是 (like "真是", "實在" or "實在是", meaning "really". It functions as an adverb to emphasize personal feeling or personal judgment).**

  你這個人實在是太討厭了！
  You are really annoying!

  你能夠找到這麼好的一個伴兒，實在讓我羨慕啊！
  You were able to find such as great company like this. (It) really makes me jealous.

  對於這個陌生的環境，他又興奮，又好奇。=> (Insert 實在 into the sentence)

- **每逢… ("每逢"occurs in the beginning of the sentence, meaning "every time when it is X")**

  中國人有句話說"每逢佳節倍思親(Měiféng jiājié bèi sīqīn)。"意思是一到了傳統節日，就特別容易想念自己的親人。
  The Chinese have an expression that says "whenever it's a *jiājié*, one thinks about the family with particular affection." This means that when a traditional holiday arrives, you're particularly prone to miss your family.

  在臺灣，每逢選舉，馬路的兩旁就會出現大大小小的廣告(guǎnggào)。
  In Taiwan, every time there are elections, advertisements of all sizes appear on both sides o the street.

  只要有考試，他總是特別緊張
  (也可以說) =>

課堂活動

(一) 用課文裏學到的生詞和句型回答問題:

- 琳達的朋友為什麼總是不願意談起和婚姻有關的話題? (聚會, 避免, 默契, 傷, 寂寞, 孤單)
- 琳達以前的男朋友是什麼樣的人? 為什麼她沒有嫁給他? 他們還是朋友嗎? (不顧, 屬於, 一向, 擁有, 限制, 保持)
- 琳達為什麼不想通過醫學手段進行人工受孕? (危險, 冒險, 若, 毛病, 後悔)
- 為什麼琳達不領養美國孩子而要領養中國孩子呢? (機構, 單身, 正常, 除非, 中介)
- 琳達領養的孩子有過什麼特別的遭遇? 中介公司為什麼想推銷這孩子? (殘疾, 估計, 想盡辦法, 扔, 福利院, 記者, 輪流, 可笑)
- 琳達和小強尼的父親是怎麼認識的? 琳達會嫁給她嗎? (豐富, 邀請, 求婚, 點頭)

(二)從不同的角度來討論:

- "讓美國人領養中國孩子? "
  - 中國人小張同意
  - 中國人小王反對
  - 美國人大為同意
  - 美國人琳達反對

- "再生一個? "——小王第一個孩子天生有殘疾, 他想再生一個, 可是妻子覺得這個孩子已經很不幸了, 應該給孩子全部的愛, 不想再生。請分角色討論如何解決這個問題。

- 一個五十多歲的單身女士決定要通過人工受孕生一個孩子。有人覺得這種做法很自私, 有人覺得這是她的權利, 你有什麼看法?

(三) 你的看法

- 有些認為學生時代應該用功念書, 不應該交男女朋友, 有些人認為, 有了好工作, 再談戀愛比較實際, 然而, 也有人認為學生時代的愛情才是真正的愛情, 三十歲以後只有所謂的"結婚條件"沒有所謂的戀愛, 你的看法呢?

練習題

一．詞彙練習：(選擇最合適的詞完成句子或段落)

(一)*(後悔　說服　推銷　保持　拋棄)*

1. 他本來是不想當醫生的，後來被爸媽__________，下決心考醫學院了。
2. 這個孩子智商不太正常，也有其它一些天生的毛病。我估計就是因為這樣，她才被父母_______的。
3. 我真_______把秘密告訴他那個大嘴巴(zuǐba)。現在所有人都知道我離婚了。
4. 這兒的環境總是_________得乾乾淨淨的，讓人感覺真舒服。
5. 你怎麼把我當成商品到處___________？我根本不需要你給我介紹對象。

(二)*(羨慕　寂寞　分手　單身)*

和女朋友_______以後，他一直________，但他從來不_________結了婚的人，也從來不感到________。對他來說，婚姻像是一種束縛，他寧可一個人過自由的生活。

(三)*(來不及　來得及　無所謂　一陣子　一輩子)*

你冷靜一點，這件事很重要，說不定會影響你_____________。時間還早，別怕____________，我們可以再等_____________，兩三個星期後再做決定也____________。

(四)*(手續　手段　勸告　邀請)*

上一次我_________他到家裏來，就告訴過他，進入老人福利院需要一定的條件，申請的__________也有點複雜，最好耐心一點，按照要求一步一步來。沒想到他完全不聽從我的__________，采取這種可笑的__________，結果，當然是沒有被接受。

(五) *(遭遇　輪流　滿意　滿足)*

他的父母在一次車禍中________了不幸。從此以後，親戚們________照顧他。有的給他買衣服，有的給他買書。他在生活方面的需要，都可以________。可是精神方面呢？

二. 口語練習：(選擇詞語完成句子，或用提供的句型完成對話)

為你好　看樣子　一下子　說實話　好了好了　不管怎麼樣　不知道怎麼搞的

(Multiple answers for some of the blanks are possible)

1. 其他幾天我都好好的，但_________，每逢星期一，我就覺得生活特沒意思。
2. 我們勸你別冒險進行人工受孕也是_______，如果孩子有殘疾，你會後悔的。
3. 每次我們討論婚姻生活時，他都保持沉默，__________在這方面他不願意跟大家交流。
4. 你真厲害,__________就說服了你的父母，讓你請那麼多朋友到家裏聚會。
5. 離了婚，一個人過，當然比每天兩個人吵著過好，可是__________，寂寞的時候卻有點懷念那種吵來吵去的日子。
6. A:人家都有孫子，__________，你都得給我生個孫子。
   B:__________，我知道了，回頭我有時間再跟我老婆討論討論吧。

三. 閱讀練習

九月初，我們社區的週末中文學校又開學了。這是一所福利性的學校，學生大多數是附近的華人孩子。今年校長派我教一年級的小孩子。說真的，教慣了大學生，現在要面對這些頑皮不懂事的小孩子，我心裏還真有點害怕。

開學第一天，我注意到有三四個孩子長著張中國臉，卻由白人父母帶著。我心裏想，麻煩來了，這些被領養的孩子怎麼能聽得懂我用中文上課？而且，他們對中國，一定沒什麼了解。怎麼辦？這樣吧，讓他們試兩次，如果不行，就叫他們別來了，去找家教吧。我這樣想。

上課前，那幾位白人家長熱情地走過來跟我聊天。通過交談，我了解到領養中國孩子的手續比我想象的複雜了很多。為了對這些孤兒負責，中國的領養機構要求申請領養的家庭先寫一份報告，介紹一下領養家庭的經濟、居住、職業等情況，並且要提供很多資料。若得到批準，收到"來華領養通知書"，才能去中國辦領養手續。

這幾個家長還告訴我，領養了中國孩子以後，"中國"對他們來說更近了。為了讓孩子了解和感受中國文化，每年春節，他們都要給孩子買中國傳統的衣服，中秋節也一定要吃月餅，有的父母還學習做中國菜。當地領養中國孩子的家庭也常常聚會，一起交流培養孩子的經驗。

我問他們為什麼要領養孩子。他們說，年輕的時候追求自由和成功，不願意因婚姻或懷孕而影響工作。等成功了，年齡也大了，這時候，她們寧可領養一個需要愛的孤兒，也不願意冒險給這個世界增加一個殘疾孩子。

他們的話，他們的精神，深深地感動了我。我自己剛才的想法實在太自私了。要上課了，我高高興興地走進教室。該用什麼態度面對這些孩子呢？我想我已經找到答案了。

根據上文判斷(True/False)：

1. 作者的職業是小學老師，對教小孩子很有經驗。
2. 作者一開始認為，被領養的孩子又頑皮又不懂事，讓他有點害怕。
3. 要收到來華領養通知書，通常得先寫申請報告，提供很多資料。
4. 這幾個白人之所以領養中國孩子，是因為他們很喜歡中國文化。
5. 了解這幾個白人父母領養中國孤兒的原因以後，作者認為他們最好去請家教。

四．翻譯練習：(用提供的詞或句型翻譯下面的句子)

1. 不顧　像是…似的　進行

She disregarded the warning of the agent, and seemed determined to take the risk to have artificial insemination. It is really ridiculous.

2. 原來　由　如此

I thought he was adopted by a journalist but then I found out that he was taken care of in turns by the employees of the newspaper company. I have never encountered something so strange.

3. 一向　存在　每逢

There has been a great untold understanding between them all along. Whenever there is a gathering, they always avoid talking about their past misfortune.

4. 若　V+盡+O　並 or 並且　以

If he didn't have a strong sense of responsibility, he wouldn't have tried every single way to provide data to the police (station) as well as donated money in the name of his mother to help handicapped people enjoy a happy life.

五．作文：(從下邊幾個題目中, 選擇一個, 寫一篇不少於 500 字的作文。你至少要用四個所提供的句型或詞彙)

實在是	（像）…似的	存在	…，加上…
verb+盡	由 such as in (買東西由他負責)	不顧	每逢…

1. “再生一個？”
   ——小王第一個孩子天生有殘疾，他想再生一個，可是妻子覺得這個孩子已經很不幸了，應該給孩子全部的愛，不想再生。請談談你的看法。
2. 一個五十多歲的單身女士決定要通過人工受孕生一個孩子。有人覺得這種做法很自私，有人覺得這是她的權利，你有什麼看法？
3. 有的中國人覺得讓外國人來領養中國孩子讓中國政府丟臉，請寫下你的看法？

第七課　美國夢

Let's warm-up with a review exercise!

Match the words in characters with Pinyin and English:

漢字	拼音	英文	哪兒學過
商量			二年級
著急			二年級
吸毒			二年級
留學			二年級
派			第一課
墮胎			第二課
開朗			第三課
何況			第三課
恨不得			第三課
難道			第三課
養家			第三課
安慰			第五課
發呆			第五課
嘆氣			第五課
拋棄			第五課
手續			第六課

拼音

1. ānwèi	2. duòtāi	3. fādāi	4. hékuàng
5. hènbùdé	6. zháojí	7. kāilǎng	8. liúxué
9. nándào	10. pài	11. pāoqì	12. shāngliang
13. shǒuxù	14. tànqì	15. xīdú	16. yǎngjiā

英文

a. to use drug	b. to abandon	c. abortion	d. cheerful;optimistic
e. to comfort	f. worried	g. to discuss	h. to itch to
i. let alone	j. procedure	k. to send	l. to sigh
m. to stare blankly	n. to study abroad	o. to support the family	p. [a rhetorical emphasis]

聽力&口語

聽錄音回答問題

對話一

1.	2.	3.	4.	5.

生詞：夢，碩士，錄取，簽證，成績

複習：安靜，吵，獎學金，申請，競爭，激烈，(酒吧，旅遊，來不及)

對話二

1.	2.	3.	4.	5.

生詞：合資，培訓，偶爾，出差，管理，瞞

複習：嫌，環境，值得，態度，派，過分，(經驗，照相機)

對話三

1.	2.	3.	4.	5.

生詞：可惜，放棄，考慮，夢想，既然，重擔
　　　節省，可憐，殘酷，暫時，通訊，網絡

複習：政策，銀行，照顧，專業，壓力，羨慕，(順利，頭疼，恭喜 gōngxǐ)

根據對話一回答問題：

1. 小文的朋友昨天晚上為什麼沒睡好？小文呢？他睡得好嗎？
2. 小文昨晚的夢裏，發生了什麼事？
3. 小文是大幾的學生？他大學畢業後有什麼打算？他在大學的學習怎麼樣？他上研究生院的機會大嗎？

根據對話二回答問題：

1. 小劉為什麼要換工作？他要到一家什麼樣的公司工作？
2. 小劉進了新公司以後，可以馬上開始正式工作嗎？
3. 小劉以後得因工作經常去日本嗎？對於他的新工作，他太太是什麼態度？

根據對話三回答問題：

1. 大為家裏的經濟情況怎麼樣？為什麼他被耶魯(Yēlǔ)大學錄取了，還感到頭疼呢？安妮覺得大為可以怎麼做？大為對安妮的主意有什麼看法？
2. 安妮覺得大為應該念什麼專業？為什麼？大為同意嗎？

口語用法

1. 你現在才大學三年級，用不著想念碩士的事啊？(“用不著” means “unnecessary; do not need to”).

這些東西已經用不著了，你收起來吧。
These things are unnecessary now. Why don’t you put them away?

這考試一點也不難，你用不著緊張。
This exam is not hard at all. You don’t need to be nervous.

這是我自己的事，用不著你管！
This is my own business. It’s unnecessary for you to interfere.

2. 希望如此 (I hope so)

A: 別擔心，他的病過兩天就會好的。
B: 希望如此。
A: Don’t worry. He will get well in a few days.
B: I hope so.

A: 你試試人工受孕吧，說不定下個月就懷上了！
B: 希望如此。
A: Why don’t you try artificial insemination? Maybe you will get pregnant next month.
B: I hope so

3. 怎麼回事？**(**What’s wrong? What is the matter? What happened?)

你到底怎麼回事？開口說話啊！
What’s wrong with you? Talk to me!

都過了三年多了，我到現在還沒搞清楚這是怎麼回事。
It has been three years, but I still haven’t figured out what happened.

不是說好了大家輪流打掃的嗎？他怎麼回事？為什麼不幹呢？
Don’t we have a deal that we take turns cleaning? What is the matter with him? Why doesn’t he do it?

4. 哪裏哪裏，日本公司的管理經驗永遠值得我們學習。("哪裏" or "哪裏，哪裏" is a humble expression to use when given a compliment, which can be translated as "not at all." Literally, it means "where?" – This suggests that you couldn't possibly have been worthy of the compliment. In a similar sense, "哪裏" or "哪" can be used in front of a verb phrase to emphasize a negation.)

A: 你那兩個孩子真是又活潑又可愛。
B: 哪裏，哪裏，頑皮得很呢！
Your two children are really lively and cute.
Not at all. They are extremely naughty.

A: 你看，那女孩漂亮吧！
B: 哪 (裏) 漂亮啊！我看你的眼睛有問題。
Look, isn't that girl beautiful?
Are you kidding? I think your eyesight need to be examined.

你這哪(裏)是在幫我。你是在給我找麻煩嘛！
You are not helping me at all by doing this. You are making trouble for me.

5. 你還需要培訓啊？你的經驗已經挺豐富了。(For Beijing people， "挺" is probably used more often than "很" in front of adjectives. "挺好，挺好" means "quite good" or "great").

他在中國的時候，朋友挺多的，怎麼到了美國來，變得這麼孤僻？
He had quite a few friends when he was in China, so how did he become so unsociable when he came to the U.S?

他看樣子好像挺不高興的。
He looks quite unhappy.

那老頭挺溫和的，應該不會做出什麼不三不四的事來。
The old man is quite gentle. I don't think he would do anything inappropriate.

6. 要是申請到就好了，可惜沒有。("可惜" means "what a pity/ what a waste/ unfortunately").

差一點就可以說服他簽字了，真可惜！
I almost convinced him to sign it. It's really a pity.

這孩子智商還可以，可惜就是眼睛有點小毛病。
This child's IQ is ok, but unfortunately, he has a little problem with his eyes.

別扔，這東西還可以用，扔了就可惜了。
Don’t throw it away. This thing still has some good use. Throwing away is wasteful.

7. 既然考上了，就應該去. (“既然” is used in the first sentence clause before or after the subject to bring up an existing fact and the acceptance of it. It can be translated as “since”. “就”, “那麼”, “則” are often used in the following clause to indicate the inference or conclusion. “既然…就/那麼/則” can be translated as “since…., ….then.”)

既然你讓我多吃一點，我就不客氣了!
Since you asked me to eat some more, I will gladly help myself. .

你既然答應領養那個孩子，就得好好負起照顧他的責任。
Since you agreed to adopt that child, you should carry on the responsibility to take good care of him.

(Sometimes the inference or conclusion in the second clause can be expressed by a question or a rhetorical question).

既然決定已經不能改變了，後悔有什麼用呢？
Since the decision cannot be reversed now, what can regretting do?

既然你不相信我，幹嗎還問我？
If you don’t believe me, why did you bother to ask?

8.　不怎麼樣 (not especially good, not very good, so so).

A: 昨天的考試考得怎麼樣？
B: 不怎麼樣。有六十分就不錯了。
A: How did you do in the exam yesterday?
B: Not especially good. I’ll feel lucky if I score more than 60.

他的第一段婚姻過得不太幸福，第二段婚姻好像也不怎麼樣。
His first marriage wasn’t very happy. His second marriage didn’t seem especially good, either.

口語練習：請用聽力對話裏學到的生詞和口語用法討論下面的問題：

用不著/　希望如此/　怎麼回事？/　哪裏+ Verb Phrase/　可惜
不怎麼樣/　既然/　A(adj/verb)是A，可是…

1) A—你學中國歷史，但你想到美國留學。
   B—你覺得 A 留在中國念研究生比較好。

2) A—你是對話二裏的小劉，下星期你就要到日本接受培訓了，你今天得告訴太太你換工作了
   B- 你是小劉的太太。

3) A 和 B — 你們是男女朋友。你們都被某所名校錄取，也都被某所不怎麼樣的大學錄取了，但是 A 申請到了名校的獎學金，B 沒有。你們討論一下應該怎麼辦。

課文

第一部分

“桌上有你一封信，信封上寫的是英文。昨天來的”

“昨天就來了，你怎麼沒早告訴我？肯定是美國來的。”

“…”

“太好了！太好了！終於有所美國名校錄取我了！每月還給我八百美金的獎學金！小華，我終於可以去美國了！”

“什麼？你還一直在申請到美國留學？前幾年你申請的十幾所學校都把你拒絕了，我以為你早放棄了，根本不知道你還瞞著我在繼續申請。”

“這一次不一樣。我跟個家教補習了一年英文，我 GRE 成績比上一次高多了。”

“啊？你還花錢雇了家教！你竟然從來沒跟我商量過？英英就要上學了，我每天都非常節省，恨不得一塊錢當兩塊錢花，想給英英買雙好運動鞋都考慮老半天，你竟然還有錢去請家教。”

“不請沒辦法啊！小華，留學一直是我的夢想。現在我的留學夢終於要圓了，我可以去美國了，難道你不為我高興嗎？”

“我當然為你高興，但你走了，我和英英呢？”

這麼多年了，張華還常常回憶起那天何文拿到美國大學通知書的情景，每逢此時，她就忍不住掉眼淚。當時英英只有五歲，這些年來，她一個單身母親，被迫挑起了生活的所有重擔，賺錢養家，輔導孩子學習，陪孩子參加各種各樣的活動。每當累了的時候，張華是多麼希望何文在身邊給她一個肩膀靠一靠啊！ 開始她安慰自己這一切都是暫時的，可是這麼多年過去了，何文在哪兒呢？

何文再也沒有回來。他在美國讀了個商業管理學碩士，但畢業時，正好碰上經濟不景氣，工作不到半年就被解雇了。後來認識了一個洋女人，結了婚，弄了張綠卡在美國待了下來。很快，他和那洋女人也有了孩子。

英英八歲的時候，張華就在離婚協議書上簽了字，但她沒敢告訴英英，只告訴她，爸爸在美國"出差"。那時的英英，還是個天真頑皮，充滿幻想的小姑娘，張華怎麼忍心讓她幼小的心靈受到傷害？

生詞用法

1	肯定	肯定	kěndìng	definitely; certainly; definite; surely; (to affirm: see also Lesson 3 for 否定)	別擔心，他肯定不會知道的。/肯定的答案/他去不去，我還不肯定。/父母肯定了他的進步。/他的做法得到了父母的肯定。
2	录取	錄取	lùqǔ	to admit students (application); to recruit	錄取新學生/錄取新職員/他申請了五所學校，但一所也沒錄取他。/小林被法學院錄取了。

3	拒绝	拒絕	jùjué	to refuse, to turn down; rejection	拒絕你的要求/拒絕了她的申請/拒絕了那個色鬼的邀請/他拒絕回答我的問題。/他的拒絕讓我很難過。/我的要求遭到了他的拒絕。
4	放弃	放棄	fàngqì	to give up; to quit	放棄一個機會/放棄選舉權/放棄獎學金/他放棄了原本的想法。/我不得不放棄了那段感情。
5	瞒	瞞	mán	to hide the truth from a person	他瞞著父母去參加聚會。/別瞞我了，我已經知道了。/你是不是有什麼事情瞞著我？
6	成绩	成績	chéngjì/ (Taiwan: chéngjī)	grade; score; achievement	我這學期的中文成績很好。/她做主管以後，在福利改革方面，有很大的成績。
7	雇	雇	gù	to hire	他雇人幫他打掃衛生。/他雇家教教孩子英文。
8	节省	節省	jiéshěng	to economize; to use sparingly; to save; frugal	我們要節省時間。/(節)省下一定的生活費來幫助孤兒。/他生活節省。/她在穿著方面很節省。
9	考虑	考慮	kǎolǜ	to consider; to think over	你考慮考慮他的話。/我考慮一下再告訴你我的決定。/我給你三天的時間考慮。/他們正在考慮搬回北京住。
10	梦想	夢想	mèngxiǎng	to dream; to vainly hope; an earnest wish	我夢想有一天我的中文能和中國人一樣好。/孩子能上名校一直是他父母的夢想。
11	回忆	回憶	huíyì	to recall; to look back upon; to reminisce; memoirs	我常常回憶小時候的生活。/美好的回憶/對父親的回憶
12	通知	通知	tōngzhī	to inform; to notify; notice (n.)	老師通知大家星期五要考試。/那所學校通知他他被錄取了。/我收到通知了。/你看到我的通知書了嗎？
13	情景	情景	qíngjǐng	scene; circumstances	想起上一次朋友聚會的情景。/回憶起小時候和父母在公園玩的情景。

14	忍不住	忍不住	rěnbúzhù	can't help but do sth.	聽了我的話，他忍不住大笑起來。/老板不聽我的勸告，我忍不住和他吵了起來。/這個菜真好吃，我忍不住又吃了一盤(pán)。
15	掉	掉	diào	to drop; to fall; to shed	先生，您掉東西了。/他從樹上掉了下來。/一想到去世了的兒子，她就掉眼淚。
16	眼泪	眼淚	yǎnlèi	tears	流眼淚/掉眼淚/擦(cā: to wipe off) 眼淚
17	被迫	被迫	bèipò	to be forced to; to be compelled to	我被迫答應了孩子的要求。/因為付不起房租(fángzū)，我們被迫搬家。/我來上中文課是被迫的，其實我更喜歡日文。
18	挑	挑	tiāo	1) to shoulder 2) to choose; to pick	挑起責任/挑起養家的重擔/挑水/挑一個好日子。/他總是挑最髒(zāng)最累的工作做。
19	重担	重擔	zhòngdàn	heavy burden; heavy responsibility	工作的重擔/生活的重擔/妻子挑起了教育孩子的重擔。
20	辅导	輔導	fǔdǎo	to tutor; to coach; tutoring	輔導孩子學習/輔導學生的發音/當輔導老師。/他為我做了三次課後輔導。
21	肩膀	肩膀	jiānbǎng	shoulder(n.)	
22	一切	一切	yíqiè	everything; all	我喜歡這裏的一切。/你為我做的一切，我永遠記在心上。/一切困難都會過去的。
23	暂时	暫時	zànshí	temporary; for the time being	暫時的安排/暫時的需要/暫時的現象/你在這裏暫時等一下，我馬上就來。/目前的困難是暫時的，很快就過去了。
24	商业	商業	shāngyè	commerce ; trade; commercial	商業城市/商業電影/商業機構/商業區/商業統計/商業中心
25	管理	管理	guǎnlǐ	to manage, to supervise; management	管理這家公司/管理一所學校/商業管理/企業管理
26	硕士	碩士	shuòshì	Master's degree(M.A.)	碩士研究生/碩士畢業

27	不景气	不景氣	bùjǐngqì	Financial depression; recession of (economy; market)	商業不景氣/房子的市場不景氣。/前幾年的經濟不太景氣。
28	解雇	解雇	jiěgù	to fire someone; to lay off	他這個月解雇了三個職員。/老板把那個老色鬼解雇了。/他因為常常遲到而被解雇了。
29	洋女人	洋女人	yángnǚren	foreign woman(洋= foreign; ocean)	洋人/洋房/洋鬼子
30	弄	弄	nòng	to get; to fetch	她把孩子弄哭了。/你的話把我弄糊涂(hútu)了。/這些問題我還沒弄清楚。/我去弄點吃的。/你這是從哪兒弄來的?
31	协议	協議	xiéyì	an agreement	口頭協議/書面協議/在協議書上簽字
32	签	簽	qiān	to sign	簽字/簽名/簽協議/簽一份協議書
33	出差	出差	chūchāi	to go on a business trip	他到美國出差去了。/他上個月出了三次差。/她出差了三個月。
34	天真	天真	tiānzhēn	naïve; childlike innocence	天真活潑的小孩/天真的想法/你太天真了，這種事不可能發生。
35	充满	充滿	chōngmǎn	to be full of, brimming with	教室裏充滿了學生的笑聲。/空氣中充滿了花香。/你的明天充滿了希望。
36	幻想	幻想	huànxiǎng	to fancy; illusion	我常幻想大學畢業以後的生活。/他每天腦子裏充滿了幻想。
37	姑娘	姑娘	gūniang	unmarried girl, young lady	農村姑娘/小姑娘，你叫什麼名字?/他娶了一個漂亮的姑娘。
38	忍心	忍心	rěnxīn	to have the heart to	他不忍心拒絕孩子的要求。/醫生總是不忍心看病人受苦。/你忍心在孩子生病的時候出差?
39	幼小	幼小	yòuxiǎo	immature; infantile	幼小的孩子
40	心灵	心靈	xīnlíng	soul; heart	無私的心靈 / 幼小的心靈
41	伤害	傷害	shānghài	to hurt; to harm; harm; hurt	傷害孩子/傷害身體/傷害心靈/心靈的傷害

課文

第二部分

兩年後，張華瞞不下去了，終於將這個殘酷的事實告訴了英英。

“爸爸不會回來了。他和一個美國女人結婚了。”

英英哭了。她撲向張華的懷裏，大聲喊：“為什麼?為什麼爸爸不要我們了？”“他怎麼可以這麼狠心，他怎麼可以拋棄我們？”“我那麼崇拜他，那麼想他，他怎麼可以一點都不在乎我？”

“爸爸不是不在乎你，也許，他太慚愧，覺得沒有臉回來看你。”

不管張華怎麼解釋，何文那自私的決定，對英英的心靈已造成了深深的傷害。有一陣子，她變得孤僻，不愛說話，讓張華十分著急。儘管在朋友與老師的幫助下，英英慢慢地重新開朗起來了，但她心裏怎麼也擺脫不掉被拋棄的感覺，她知道，她這一輩子都不會原諒爸爸。

沒有爸爸的英英，更加好強，也更加努力。她不願讓別人看不起自己，她事事都要拿第一。

二零零零年，英英二十歲，清華電子工程系畢業，在一家中美合資通訊公司工作。

“何英，公司計劃派你到美國接受六個月的培訓，那兒網絡技術發達，你去學習學習。你先考慮一下，如果同意，我會盡快請人事處替你辦好簽證手續。”

英英做夢也沒有想到，她自己有一天也會踏上美國的土地。她捨不得媽媽，但這是一個難得的機會，何況只有六個月。

“英英，你爸也在洛杉磯，既然你到那兒受培訓，說不定...”

“媽！你不要跟我提他，我根本不想看到他。我想不通你為什麼到現在仍然忘不了他。這麼多年來，我們母女沒有他，不也過得好好的嗎？我有個無私，偉大的母親，我不需要爸爸。”

英英早就忘了爸爸長什麼樣子。洛杉磯的華人不少，她曾和許多看起來和爸爸年紀差不多的人擦肩而過，偶爾也會多看這些人幾眼，偶爾也會發呆，想想這些人為什麼待在美國，想想他們可能擁有什麼樣的故事。

這一天，她和同事又來到常去的那家中國飯館。遠遠地，她看見店門關著，門前聚著一小群人，似乎在議論著什麼，有人搖頭有人嘆氣。好奇地走近一點，英英聽到：

“可憐哪！十幾年的廚師都幹了，再怎麼地，也不該自殺啊！”

“當初他到美國來，還拿了獎學金呢！”

“可惜呀，和個洋女人搞在一塊兒。”

“為的是從洋女人身上拿到張綠卡吧！”

“可不是嘛！那洋女人又吸毒又墮胎的...”

英英沒有聽下去，頭也不回地快步離開了。

生詞用法

42	残酷	殘酷	cánkù	cruel; brutal	殘酷的人/殘酷的傷害/殘酷的行為/殘酷的競爭/你這樣對你的孩子，太殘酷了。
	将	將	jiāng	a written usage that means 1) = 會：will (auxiliary verb) 2)= 把: as in 把書給我	見語法
43	事实	事實	shìshí	fact; truth (事實上= in fact; as a matter of fact)	你說的和我聽到的不一樣，請告訴我事實。/事實上，他並沒有按照你說的做。/我不能接受這樣的事實。
44	扑	撲	pū	to throw oneself onto; to pounce on	老虎向小羊撲去。/這個小孩子向媽媽撲去。/他撲向媽媽的懷裏。/他撲倒在地上。/日本相撲(sumo)運動員
45	怀里	懷裏	huáilǐ	bosom	躺在媽媽懷裏/把孩子抱在懷裏
46	狠心	狠心	hěnxīn	to make up one's mind cruelly; cruel; cruel-hearted; heartless;	爸爸狠下心，重重地打了他三下。/做生意的人，心得狠一點，要不然賺不了什麼錢。/離婚的時候，他對妻子非常狠心，一點財產都不給她。/他狠心地拋棄了兒女。
47	崇拜	崇拜	chóngbài	to adore; to idolize; to worship	對大自然的崇拜/我崇拜那個教授。/她把毛澤東當神(shén)一樣崇拜。/我最崇拜的人是我爸爸。
48	惭愧	慚愧	cánkuì	to be ashamed; to feel abashed	你的無私讓我為自己的自私慚愧。/他因為忘了妻子的生日而感到很慚愧。
49	解释	解釋	jiěshì	to explain; to interpret	解釋語法/解釋問題/請用英語給我解釋一下？ /你別生氣，聽我給你解釋。/這件事很複雜，回頭我有時間再給你仔細解釋。/這件事怎麼向他解釋？
50	造成	造成	zàochéng	to cause; to create (sth. unpleasant)	造成麻煩/造成傷害/造成問題/造成他們之間的激烈競爭/這個問題是誰造成的？

51	重新	重新	chóngxīn	anew; afresh; re-	重新考慮/重新解釋/昨天的計劃沒有通過，我們得重新討論。
52	摆脱	擺脫	bǎituō	to get rid of, to cast off	擺脫困難的情況/擺脫麻煩/擺脫貧窮的生活/擺脫束縛
53	原谅	原諒	yuánliàng	to excuse; to forgive; forgiveness	我錯了，請你原諒我好嗎？/我希望得到你的原諒。
54	好强	好強	hàoqiáng	eager to put one's best foot forward; eager to proof one's capability	他是個好強的孩子，事事都要拿第一。/你別太好強，該請人幫忙的時候還是得請人幫忙。
	清华	清華	Qīnghuá	name of a Chinese university	
55	电子	電子	diànzǐ	electronic	電子學/電子詞典/電子郵件(email)/電子手表/電子圖書館
56	工程	工程	gōngchéng	engineering; project	工程學/化學工程/建筑工程/電子工程/工程結構/工程師
57	系	系	xì	school department	中文系/法律系/工程系/他考上了歷史系。/他是數學系畢業的。
58	合资	合資	hézī	joint-venture	中日合資/中美合資/合資企業
59	通讯	通訊	tōngxùn	communication (of using electronic technology)	電話通訊/網絡通訊
60	培训	培訓	péixùn	to train; training	參加職業培訓/培訓新老師/培訓新職員
61	网络	網絡	wǎngluò	internet	電腦網絡/網絡教育 (網路 is more often used in Taiwan)
62	技术	技術	jìshù	technique; skill; technology	電腦技術/管理技術/開車的技術/生產技術/技術改革
63	发达	發達	fādá	developed; advanced	發達國家/發達的市場/技術很發達
64	尽快	儘快	jìnkuài	as soon as possible	我會盡快做完這個工作。/請盡快給我回信。
65	人事处	人事處	rénshìchù	office of human resources	
66	办	辦	bàn	to proceed with a task	辦簽證/辦離婚手續/辦一場晚會
67	签证	簽證	qiānzhèng	visa	工作簽證/旅遊簽證/辦簽證/申請簽證

68	踏	踏	tà	to step on	我的書掉在地上，他不但不幫我拿起來，還在上面踏了一腳。/踏上中國的土地。/踏上留學這條道路。
69	土地	土地	tǔdi	land	
71	难得	難得	nándé	hard to come by; rare; rarely	這是一個難得的機會。/她難得到我家玩一次。/他這麼自私的人竟然願意捐錢，真難得！
	洛杉矶	洛杉磯	Luòshānjī	Los Angles	
	既然	既然	jìrán	since	見語法
72	提	提	tí	to mention; to bring up	她常常跟我提她的男朋友。/請你別再提墮胎那件事了。/提起共產黨，你就會想到毛澤東。/上課的時候，他提了一個問題。/他提出了他的看法。
73	想不通	想不通	xiǎng bùtōng	cannot think through, cannot know why	我想不通他為什麼不愛我。/我想不通他是怎麼考上北京大學的。/你想通了沒有？
74	擦肩而过 擦肩而過		cājiān érguò	to pass by shoulder to shoulder/ to bump into each other without knowing	和某某人擦肩而過。/每天上學都要和一個時髦的女孩擦肩而過。
75	偶尔	偶爾	ǒuěr	occasionally; once in a while	我一般做美國飯，一兩個月才偶爾做次中國飯。/我常常踢足球，偶爾也打籃球。
76	议论	議論	yìlùn	to comment; to discuss; to gossip	不要在背後議論別人。/ 你們在議論什麼？
77	可怜	可憐	kělián	to have a pity on; pitiful; pitiable	可憐的孩子/這個小孩真可憐。/我很可憐他，這麼小就得賺錢養家。
78	厨师	廚師	chúshī	cook, chief	
79	干	幹	gàn	to hold the post of; be engaged in; to do	他幹過廚師。/我這幾年一直在幹管理工作。/他什麼壞事都幹過。
80	自杀	自殺	zìshā	to commit suicide; suicide (n.)	

81	可惜	可惜	kěxī (Taiwan: also kěxí)	unfortunately; it's a pity; it is too bad	我想幫你，可惜我沒時間。/這女孩長得很漂亮，可惜就是笨了點。/這工作不錯，可惜離我家太遠。**(見口語用法)**
82	搞	搞	gǎo	to play; to be engaged	他和一個壞女人搞在一起。/你在搞什麼鬼？好好睡覺。/他是搞電腦的。

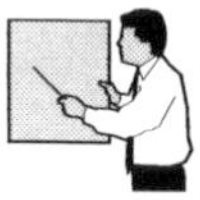

句型和語法

- **Verb +得住 or Verb+ 不住 (When "住" is used as a complement after a verb, it conveys a meaning of being stable or of holding up something. "記住" means to remember something and have it fixed in your memory; "忍住" means to hold up something and to bear it. If you say someone is "靠得住", it indicates that he is stable to rely on).**

課本裏的生詞這麼多，我怎麼可能全都記得住呢？
There are so many new words in the textbook. How can I remember all of them?

一想到當時的情景，他的眼淚就忍不住掉了下來。
Once he began to think about what had happened back then, he couldn't stop shedding a drop of tear. .

你不要相信這家中介公司的話，聽人說，他們一點兒都靠不住。
Don't believe what this agency tells you. People say they're not reliable at all.

你說的話真是太有意思了，我想不笑出來都不行。
(也可以說) =〉

你覺得日商比較值得相信還是美商比較值得相信？
(回答問題) =〉

- **將 ("將," going to or about to [do something]; used with a verb expressing future action, is usually used in written Chinese or formal speech. Note : "將" also means "把" as in "請將這本書放回去。")**

說一說"將"在下邊的句子的意思：

母親終於還是將這個殘酷的事實告訴了英英。
Her mother finally told Yingying the cruel truth.

通訊公司決定將英英派往日本受三個月的訓。
The communications company decided to send Yingying to Japan for three months of training.

為了拿到綠卡，他將和那個洋女人結婚。

In order to get a green card, …

如果你同意，我們將請人事處盡快替你辦好簽證手續。
If you agree, …

- 不管 (**"不管" is used in front of a interrogative sentence, meaning "regardless if", "no matter" or "not care").**

  不管你曾經有過什麼樣的遭遇，你都得勇敢面對下半生。
  No matter what kind of troubles you have had, you should face the rest of your life bravely.

  他根本不管我害怕不害怕，就是要我冒這個險。
  He doesn't care one bit whether I'm afraid or not. He still wants me to take this risk.

  他們有默契或沒有默契都沒關係。我已經決定讓他們在同一個機構工作了。(也可以說) =〉
  (……, 我都會…)

- 更加+**Adj./V ("更加" simply means "更". It occurs in written Chinese and needs to be followed by a two-syllable adjective or verb).**

  爸去世以後，媽的生活變得更加寂寞。
  After Dad died, Mom became even lonelier.

  當我知道她把一輩子都奉獻給貧窮的兒童之後，我對她更加崇拜了。
  Ever since I found out that she dedicated her whole life to help poor children, I idolized d her even more.

  自從在網上交了一個網友後，她對海外的留學生活更好奇了。
  (也可以說) =〉

- 再怎麼地，也**… (a very colloquial way to say "不管怎麼樣"，"不管發生什麼"。)**

  你就原諒他吧！再怎麼地，他也是你的父親啊！
  Just forgive him! No matter what happened, he's still your father!

  你快去跟人事室說說，讓他們再怎麼地，也要在一個星期內幫你把簽證手續給辦好。

Go quickly and talk to the personnel office. Tell them no matter what, you need the visa arrangements made within a week.

(完成句子) =〉 "別忘了，你現在是中國的逃犯，這是機票。記著！踏上了美國的土地後，____________________。"

- 為的是… **(same as"是為了"."為的是" occurs in the second clause to indicate the reason or the purpose).**

公司派你去受訓，為的是培養你當高級主管。
The company sent you to training for the purpose of grooming you for a high-level management job.

醫生讓你躺著別下床，為的是讓你的傷口早點兒好起來
The reason that the doctor made you lie down and not get out of bed is to have your wound heal faster.

(回答問題) =〉 他的父母為什麼逼他上補習班呢？

- 這些動詞可以怎麼用？

弄　搞　辦　幹

1. 這孩子每天回來，都把衣服_______得很髒。
2. 你每天跟那些吸毒的孩子_______在一起，我看你肯定上不了什麼好大學。
3. 電子工程和網絡通訊技術這兩個專業畢業以後哪個更容易賺錢，你一定要先_______清楚再做選擇。
4. 聽說廚師老王這幾天正在忙著_______退休的事，他怎麼這麼年輕就要退休？
5. 不管你長大以後_______什麼，都會面對各種各樣的競爭。
6. 小張，你明天下午有事嗎？如果有時間的話，能不能請你幫我_______件事？

Key: 1. 弄/搞 2. 搞 3. 弄/搞 4. 辦 5. 幹 6. 辦

課堂活動

(一) 用課文裏學到的生詞和句型回答問題:

- 何文看了信以後為什麼這麼興奮？張華呢？她也很興奮嗎？(錄取，放棄，拒絕，成績，夢想，考慮，)
- 何文離家以後，張華的生活有什麼改變？(挑，重擔，節省，眼淚)
- 何文在美國的生活怎麼樣？他為什麼不回中國了？(碩士，不景氣，解雇，綠卡)
- 張華和何文離婚了嗎？她一開始為什麼不把事實告訴英英呢？(協議書，簽字，天真，忍心，心靈，傷害)
- 當張華將她和何文離異的事實告訴英英時，英英有什麼反應(reaction)？(撲，懷裏，拋棄，狠心，崇拜，原諒，好強)
- 英英為什麼會到洛杉磯去？媽媽知道英英要去洛杉磯，跟她說了些什麼？(合資，派， 培訓，技術，手續，說不定)
- 英英到了洛杉磯以後真的碰到了爸爸嗎？(偶爾，擦肩而過，聚，可憐，自殺)

(二)從不同的角度(jiǎodù)來討論:

- 對一個外國學生來說，畢業後留在美國真的更好嗎？
  - 工作機會上
  - 生活條件上
  - 政治環境上
  - 婚姻關係上
  - 身份認同上(self-identity)

- 請從不同的角度談談你對美國移民(yímín: immigration) 政策的看法。
  - 關心社會福利的人
  - 加州某大農場(farm)的老板
  - MIT 校長
  - 高科技公司負責人
  - 從其他國家來的逃犯
  - 移民局官員

(三) 你的看法

- 你會為了事業(career)或學業而離開家人，到陌生的地方去嗎？為什麼？
- 如果你是英英，你在加州找到了爸爸，你希望他跟你回中國嗎？為什麼？

練習題

一 詞彙練習：

（一）*不景氣 被迫 節省 暫時 拒絕 回憶*

1. 沒辦法，那時候經濟_______，好多人都丟了工作，_______下崗的不只我一個人。
2. 他過得非常_______，能不花的錢就不花，總是在家裏做飯吃，很少上飯館。
3. 別擔心，這種現象只是_______的，不會一直繼續下去。
4. 他申請了五所學校，但是都被_______了。
5. 童年生活對他來說是一段非常美好的_______，她常常想起小時候快樂的情景。

（二）*撲　掉　提　踏*

1. 她_______向媽媽的懷裏，大哭了一場。
2. _______上教書這條路以後，她就知道自己這一輩子不可能賺大錢。
3. 我急匆匆跑到教室，卻發現我的中文書不見了，肯定是剛才_______在路上了。
4. 我父母最討厭談毛澤東了，尤其是上個世紀六十到八十年代的事，因此，你明天跟他們見面的時候，千萬別_______那段歷史。

二 口語表達練習：

1. A: 聽說你們公司跟一個大公司簽了一筆大生意？
   B: ____。
   (哪裏是..., (只)是...)
2. A: 這些孩子真可憐，一輩子都要待在這個落後的農村，難得有機會出去看看外面的世界。
   B: ____。
   (**...是..., 可是/但是...** such as in "好是好，可是那樣我壓力太大")
3. 媽媽，爸爸這次只邀請了三個人來家裏吃飯，而且他們晚上八點才來，
   ____。***(用不著)***

三 綜合練習：

小紅的先生小劉在一家中美合資公司當主管，由於經常到美國 __1__，有機會認識一些洋女人，他__2__太太，跟一個性感的洋女人發展出了情人的關係。兩人不見面時也天天__3__網絡聯系。小紅什麼都不知道，在他心目中小劉是個又能幹又老實的好先生，因此她每天都是笑盈盈的，一副很幸福的樣子。而小劉天真地以為 有情人這件事可以一直 __4__下去。然而，一年以後，一個不幸被小劉公司__5__了的員工卻把小劉有個美國情人這件事告訴了小紅。，小紅一下子根本沒法接受這個殘酷的 __6__，傷心得想要 __7__，朋友們勸了半天，小紅才想通了， 下決心跟小劉離了婚，過起了單身生活。漸漸地，小紅又 __8__ 快樂起來了，但前一段婚姻在心靈上__9__的傷害，卻永遠無法忘記。她對婚姻再也不像以前那樣 __10__幻想了。

1. a. 簽證 b. 出差 c. 土地
2. a. 通過 b. 瞞 c. 瞞著
3. a. 通過 b. 通知 c. 瞞著
4. a. 相信 b. 瞞 c. 瞞著
5. a. 擺脫 b. 避免 c. 解雇
6. a. 事實 b. 實際 c. 情景
7. a. 幻想 b. 自殺 c. 放棄
8. a. 恢復 b. 放棄 c. 重新
9. a. 造成 b. 接受 c. 曾經
10. a. 激烈 b.充滿 c. 避免

四 翻譯練習：

1. 想不通 根本 再怎麼地
I feel sorry for her. I can't figure out how you can have the heart to hurt her young soul? You don't know how much she worships you at all. No matter what, you should ask her to forgive you.

2. 為的是； 既然 更加 仍然
Colleague A: Don't feel ashamed. The boss said that for your own good. What everyone wants is to have Japan sign a joint-venture agreement with us. Since you know the company still supports you, you should work even harder. Don't ever give up.

3. 盡快 難道 不管怎麼樣
No matter what, you should not forgive him. He did cruel things to you and made you cry every day. How can you not remember? You should break up with him as soon as possible.

4. 難得 挑 可惜 or 可憐
Studying abroad for a master's degree in Management had been his dream. His wife carried the burden of taking care of the family for him. Don't you think what she has been doing is hard to come by? It is a pity that his grades are so low. No school is willing to accept him.

五. 作文：(從下邊幾個題目中, 選擇一個, 寫一篇不少於 500 字的作文。你至少要用六個所提供的句型或詞彙)

再也不/再也沒...	用不著	忍不住
每當...的時候	既然	可惜
不管...,...都/也	再怎麼地	為的是

- "單親家庭"
- 談移民政策
- 親愛的爸爸□
  --英英給爸爸的一封信。
- 親愛的英英：
  --爸爸給英英的一封信。

第八課 學成語

Let's warm-up with a review exercise!

Match the words in characters with Pinyin and English:

漢字	拼音	英文	哪兒學過
成語			二年級
文章			二年級
類			二年級
隨便			二年級
困難			二年級
生長			二年級
關注			第一課
按照			第三課
因此			第四課
使用			第四課
儘管			第五課
傻			第五課
存在			第六課
既然			第七課

拼音

1. ànzhào	2. chéngyǔ	3. cúnzài	4. guānzhù
5. jìrán	6. jǐnguǎn	7. kùnnan	8. lèi
9. shǎ	10. shēngzhǎng	11. shǐyòng	12. suíbiàn
13. wénzhāng	14. yīncǐ		

英文

a. even though	b. article; essay	c. casual; careless	d. difficulty
e. (four-word) idioms	f. to exist	g. to pay close attention	h. to grow
i. therefore	j. according to	k. category	l. since
m. stupid; silly	n. to use		

聽力&口語

聽錄音回答問題

對話一

1.	2.	3.	4.	5.

生詞：夜郎自大，坐井觀天，典故，謙虛，猜
複習：事實，(全部，解釋，了解，流利，觀察)

對話二

1.	2.	3.	4.	5.

生詞：猶豫不決，結構，下手，大體上
複習：煩，肯定，千萬，考慮，選擇，感受，耐心，這一陣子，(租)

對話三

1.	2.	3.	4.	5.

生詞：默不做聲，一成不變，裝聾作啞，生龍活虎，一敗涂地，班門弄斧
深藏不露，一見鐘情，三心二意，一帆風順，不聞不問，對牛彈琴
複習：感情，願意，球賽，冠軍，驕傲，不管怎麼樣，慚愧

根據對話一回答問題：
1. 大為昨天用中文和女朋友聊天時，女朋友說了什麼他不懂？為什麼？他的朋友小華是怎麼給他解釋的？
2. 小華又用了哪個成語說大為太驕傲了？請解釋一下這個成語的意思。

根據對話二回答問題：
1. 小張看的頭兩個房子，各有什麼好的地方和不好的地方？她的朋友老李給了她什麼建議？
2. 小張覺得找到一個百分之百滿意的房子重要嗎？這陣子找房子的經驗讓她很興奮嗎？她先生對看房子是什麼態度？她的朋友老李的先生當初在看房子的時候態度也是這樣嗎？

根據對話三回答問題：
1. 阿麗為什麼不願意說他愛阿文？她是怎麼跟阿文解釋的？
2. 阿麗為什麼喜歡看小陳打球？如果小陳和阿文比賽打籃球，阿麗覺得誰會贏？為什麼？
3. 當初阿文和阿麗一見面就互相喜歡嗎？他們的戀愛出現過問題嗎？現在阿麗為什麼不喜歡阿文了？

口語用法

1. 總是問她，多沒面子啊。(“面子” means “reputation, face, self-respect”. If something “讓你有面子”, that’s something makes you proud. If you feel “沒面子”, you feel that you lose your face. If you “給 Sb. 面子”, you take care not to offend one’s susceptibility).

丟了工作讓我挺沒面子的，你別到處跟人說去。
Losing the job made me lose my face. Don’t tell around people.

兒子呀！你好好學。你想想，要是拿個第一，老爸多有面子！
My son, you have to study hard. Think that, if you win first place, how proud I will be as the father of yours.

邀請你你怎麼不來呢？真是不給我面子！
I invited you, why didn’t you come? You disappointed and embarrassed me.

2.“夜郎”在這裏指的是古代一個叫“夜郎”的國家。(“指的是…” or “…是指” means “to refer to”).

A: “小秘” 是什麼意思？
B: 小秘是指大老板們在辦公室裏養的情人。
What does “小秘” refer to?
“小秘” refers to those office secretaries with whom the boss has affairs with.

我說的女強人指的是她，不是指你。
When I said “女強人”, I meant her, not you.

3. 沒錯！(“That’s right!” “That’s correct!”，“Exactly”)

A: 我想，這件事對她心靈的成長有很大的影響。
B: 沒錯，她這一輩子都忘不了這個傷痛的。
I think this incident has a big impact on the development of her mind.
You are right. She won’t forget this pain her whole life.

A: 在他們家，挑起生活重擔是他的母親
B: 沒錯。她父親一點責任感都沒有。
In his family, it is his mother who carries the burden of supporting the family.
That’s right. His father doesn’t have a sense of responsibility at all.

4. 我告訴你啊！學校不好的房子千萬不要考慮. ("我告訴你啊" means "Let me tell you…"; listen to me". It is used when you give a warning or a clarification).

我告訴你啊！你再不乖(guāi) 點兒，我可要教訓人了！
Let me tell you, if you don't behave, I'll teach you a lesson.

我告訴你啊！老張已經向我求婚了，從今以後你別再來煩我了！
Let me tell you, Old Zhang proposed to me already. From now on, don't bother me any more.

我告訴你啊！我是自己不想幹了，不是讓人逼走的！
Let me tell you, I myself didn't want to stay in the job. Nobody forced me to leave.

5. 差不多就行了, 不可能有百分之百讓你滿意的房子。(When you say "差不多就行了", you think something less perfect should also do, or you ask someone not to be too picky, too greedy, or too ambitious, etc).

差不多就行了，別那麼講究！
The difference is not that great. Don't be so picky.

念吧！這所大學雖不算是個名校，但差不多也就行了。
Why don't you go to that university? Thought it's not a famous school, it's not that bad either.

你那麼用功幹什麼？成績差不多就行了，難道你要考一百分呀？
Why do you study so hard? a mediocre score is enough. Do you think you can get a hundred on your test?

6. 這買房子的事都快把我煩死了. ("死了" can also be used after a verb to exaggerate the degree. The pattern is "(把) + Sb. + V+ 死了". See also Adj.+ 死了 in Lesson 3 口語用法)

找房子這事快把我煩死了。
I'm almost agonized to death looking for a house.

你不知道他那個傻樣子，簡直把我笑死了。
You don't know how silly he was. I almost laughed to death.

我的小寶貝，你終於回來了，真是把奶奶想死了。
My baby, you finally came back. You really made Grandma miss you to death.

7. 慢慢來，小張，一定能買到你滿意的。(“慢慢來” means “take it easy; slow down, don’t rush”. It is often used to comfort or remind the others).

找男朋友這種事得慢慢來，不能急。
Things like finding a boyfriend have their own pace. You can’t rush.

你小心點，慢慢來，別把湯給灑(sǎ)了。
Be careful, go slowly, and don’t spill the soup.

先別急著做決定，咱們慢慢來，先聽聽那老頭怎麼說。
Don’t rush to make the decision. Let’s slow down. Listen to what the old man says first.

8. 有時候真想隨便買一座房子算了。(“算了” can be used alone meaning “forget it; or “let it go at that”. When you use “算了” after a verb phrase, you suggest an undesired but the best solution to the given situation).

這麼貴？算了，別買了吧！
Is it this expensive? Forget it. Don’t buy it.

算了！別人要說我們的閑話就讓他們說吧！你生氣有什麼用呢？
Let it be. If other people want to gossip about us, you can just let them do so. Being angry is not helpful.

你要是真不喜歡我，咱們分手算了。
If you really do not like me, it might be better for us to break up.

他不支持算了，反正我要參加這個組織。
Just drop the matter if he doesn’t support it. I will join this organization anyway.

沒想到辦個簽證這麼麻煩，算了，我們還是別去辦了。
I didn’t expect this much trouble for getting a visa. Maybe it’s better for us not to go.

9. 他這樣做就不對了，回頭我跟他談談。(“回頭” literally means: “to turn one’s head. However, in spoken Chinese, it can also be used as a time phrase, meaning “later”).

我得走了，回頭再跟你聊。
I have to go. Talk to you later.

怎麼能吸毒呢？你回頭見了他得好好跟他說說。

How can he use drugs? You have to have a good talk with him when you see him later.

你考慮考慮，要是同意了，我回頭讓人事處給你辦手續。
You may consider it. If you agree, I'll ask the human resource department to help you with the process.

10. 怎麼著？我去看他打球不行嗎？(“怎麼著” is used to response to negative comment or doubting, meaning “So what?”).

怎麼著？我就是這麼殘酷，不行嗎？
So what? I'm really this cruel. Isn't that all right?

沒錯，我是為了綠卡才娶那個洋女人的，怎麼著？
You are right, I married that white woman to get a green card, so what?

11. 哼！好男人不怕找不到女朋友。(“哼” is spelled as “hèng” , but pronounced with a stronger nasal sound. It is used to give a snort of contempt when you belittle someone).

哼！在外商通訊公司工作有什麼了不起的？
Heng! What is great about working in a foreign communication company?

哼！不派我去受培訓有什麼？我一點也不在乎！
Heng! What makes it a big deal that they don't send me for the training? I don't care about it at all.

12. 誰知道你是不是在說大話。(“誰知道” means “who knows”. It can be followed by a phrase or a question to indicate one's doubt, surprise or indifference. “說大話” means to boast).

他說他很慚愧，誰知道是不是真的。
He said he was ashamed. Who knows if it's true?

我本來以為他放棄了。誰知道他好強得很，又跑來找我挑戰。
I thought he gave up at an early stage. Who knows that he is so eager to win, and he would come to challenge me again.

你餓了就先吃吧，別等你爸爸了，誰知道他什麼時候回來。
If you are hungry, you can go ahead and eat. Don't wait for your Dad. Who knows when he will come back?

13. 你死了這條心吧！(When you say “死了這條心吧！”, you tell someone to stop hoping. In our dialogue, the woman said “你對我死了這條心吧” to tell the man it is impossible for her to return to him).

你死了留學這條心吧！
Stop hoping to study abroad.

你死了這條心吧！她是不可能原諒你的。
Stop hoping. It is impossible for her to forgive you.

口語練習：請用聽力對話裏學到的生詞和口語用法討論下面的問題：

有面子/沒面子 / 指的是…/是指… / 沒錯，…/ 我告訴你啊，…
差不多就行了/ 把我 Verb 死了/ 說實在的/ 慢慢來/ (…)算了
回頭…/ 怎麼著，…/ 哼！/ 你少說大話/ 誰知道…/ 死了這條心吧

1. A- 你是中國人，喜歡用成語。你覺得美國人太驕傲了，以為自己是世界警察。B- 你是美國人，討厭用成語。你覺得中國人太驕傲了，總以為中國文化最好。

2. A- 你想趕快買個房子，但看了幾所還是做不了決定。
B- 你當初買房子沒考慮清楚，現在後悔了，你想給 A 一點建議。

3. A- 你喜歡上另一個男孩子，但你還沒有準備好怎麼跟你現在的男朋友說。
B- 你發現你女朋友特別喜歡去看某個男人打球，你想告訴她你比那個男人好。

課文

第一部分

老黃：嘿，老張，咱們剛才談小雲對你怎麼怎麼一見鐘情，你還一副生龍活虎的樣子，怎麼話題一轉到股票，你就默不做聲啦？

老張：什麼默不做聲？股票你老黃懂多少？我跟你談啊，就象是對牛彈琴！

老黃：éi, 你這話是什麼意思？股票的事，我知道的可不比你少！

老張：哦(ó)？可我看你這兩年對股票的事情不聞不問的，怎麼可能知道多少呢？

老黃：我這叫裝聾作啞，深藏不露！

老張：哦(ó)，那我可得向您好好請教請教嘍！

老黃：別別別！既然你不想對牛彈琴，那我也不敢班門弄斧。

老張：哎呀，你別這麼謙虛嘛。我剛開始玩股票的時候雖然是一帆風順，後來卻是一敗涂地！您哪，懂股票的話，就多指教指教吧！

老黃：這個股市的行情嘛，不是一成不變的。您真要我給您些建議，我只能說，第一，要多關注新聞，多收集信息，可千萬不要坐井觀天，夜郎自大。

老張：那，第二呢？

老黃；第二嘛，就是看準了，就趕快下手。不能老三心二意，猶豫不決。

中國人喜歡用成語，寫文章的時候用，說話的時候也用。上面的對話並不難懂，但你得知道一點成語才能了解他們在說些什麼。到底什麼是成語呢？一般來說，成語由四個字構成。這短短的四個字，卻準確生動地表達了好幾句話才能表達的意思。漢語裏的成語成千上萬，大體上，可分為結構性和典故性兩大類。

和典故性的成語相比，結構性成語對外國學生來說比較容易。前面我們用到的"成千上萬"就屬於結構性成語。從"千"和"萬"兩個字，我們可以猜出"成千上萬"指的是"大量的、非常多的"。"成千上萬"說得更口語、更白話一點，就是："有幾千幾萬個那麼多"。值得注意的是，在每個成語裏，四個字的組合一般是固定的，不能隨便用別的字來代替。因此，"據我所知"雖然也是四個字，但我們一般不把它看作成語，因為你也可以說"據他所知"，"據你所知"。

生詞用法

1	一见钟情 一見鍾情	yījiàn zhōngqíng	fall in love at first sight	小王對小張一見鍾情。/你相信一見鍾情嗎？/你覺得一見鍾情的戀愛靠得住嗎？
2	生龙活虎 生龍活虎	shēnglóng huóhǔ	doughty as a dragon and lively as a tiger -- full of vim and vigor	上課時她沒什麼精神，一下課她就生龍活虎起來了。/年輕人嘛，就應該生龍活虎一點兒。
3	股票	gǔpiào	stock; shares	玩股票/炒股票/買股票/股票市場
4	默不做声 默不做聲	mòbú zuòshēng	to be silent	你說話啊！你默不做聲，我怎麼知道你心理想什麼？/他好像對我們的話題不感興趣，一直坐在那兒默不做聲。/跟一個整天默不做聲的人在一起，實在太悶了！

5	对牛弹琴 對牛彈琴	duìniútánqín	to play lute for the cow (to speak to the wrong audience)	我完全不懂電腦，你跟我談電腦就像是對牛彈琴。/你別對牛彈琴了，他根本聽不懂。
6	不闻不问 不聞不問	bùwénbúwèn	be indifferent to sth; neither care to inquire nor to hear	他是你的父親，怎麼能對你的生活完全不聞不問呢？/某些領導對一些事實完全不聞不問。
7	装聋作哑 裝聾作啞	zhuānglóng zuòyǎ	to pretend to be ignorant of sth.; pretend ignorance (聾: deaf; 啞: dumb)	你不要跟我裝聾作啞，我今天一定得讓你把話跟我說清楚。/父母讓她做什麼事情她都裝聾作啞。
8	深藏不露 深藏不露	shēncáng bú lòu	to hide one's great ability; to be modest about one's skill	他這個人深藏不露，你不要以為他什麼都不懂。/跟那種深藏不露的人打交道，我總是緊張。
9	请教 請教	qǐngjiào	to consult; to ask for advice	向老師請教一個問題/你常常向你的同屋請教哪方面的問題？/我想請教你一下，中國人見面怎麼打招呼？
10	班门弄斧 班門弄斧	Bānmén nòngfǔ	to display one's light skill (insignificant experience) before an expert;	你別在這些專家面前班門弄斧了，你會鬧笑話的。/雖然我會彈鋼琴，可我真不敢在你們面前班門弄斧。
11	谦虚 謙虛	qiānxū	modest; modesty	他是一個謙虛的領導。/你應該謙虛一點，別太驕傲！/謙虛使人進步。
12	一帆风顺 一帆風順	yìfān fēngshùn	as smooth and pleasant as a perfect sailing	他在工作上雖然一帆風順，但在婚姻生活上，卻有一大堆的問題。/祝願你生活一帆風順！ (Taiwan: yìfánfēngshùn)
13	一败涂地 一敗塗地	yíbàitúdì	to suffer a crushing defeat; to suffer a complete loss	那次戰爭(zhànzhēng-war)，中國真是一敗涂地。/那次比賽我們球隊把另一個球隊打得一敗涂地。
14	指教	zhǐjiào	to give advice or comments to; advice or comments	你比我有經驗，請你多指教我。/很感謝您的指教。
15	股市	gǔshì	stock market	
16	行情	hángqíng	market quotations; market trend	股票行情/市場行情/這個商品的行情
17	一成不变 一成不變	yìchéng búbiàn	invariable; immutable and never-changing	這種一成不變的日子我真過夠了，我想換換環境。/世界上沒有一成不變的愛情。

18	建议 建議	jiànyì	to propose; to suggest; suggestion	我建議你多聽錄音，把發音再好好練習練習。/希望你能接受我的建議。/對這件事，你有什麼好建議？
19	收集	shōují	to collect; to gather	收集資料/收集郵票
20	信息	xìnxī	information	收集信息/市場信息/信息技術 訊息 (xùnxí) or 資訊 (zīxùn) are more commonly used in Taiwan
21	坐井观天 坐井觀天	zuòjǐng guāntiān	to look into the sky from sitting in a well -limited outlook; to take a narrow view of things	如果我們公司坐井觀天，一定會在競爭中一敗涂地。/ 你不要坐井觀天，應該知道外邊的世界更大。
22	夜郎自大 Yèlángzìdà [Yelang people think their country is bigger than China]		to be too proud of oneself out of ignorance; ignorant boastfulness;	你雖然有了一點進步，但可不能夜郎自大，還得繼續努力。/他太夜郎自大了，總是把自己當成世界的中心。
23	准	zhǔn	accurate; precise	他的球都很準，只要出手，一定得分。/你的聲調還是說得不太準(or 準確)。/你說得真準，她果然又遲到了。
	赶快 趕快	gǎnkuài	immediately; in a fast pace; ; to hurry up	就快考試了，你還不趕快準備？/你趕快把功課做完，就可以出去玩了。見語法
24	下手	xiàshǒu	to put one's hand to; to start; to set about	我想申請到美國留學，但不知道從哪兒下手。/她幾次都想殺了那個色鬼，但總下不了手。
25	三心二意	sānxīnèryì	cannot make up one's mind; to be of two minds	你再三心二意，機會就沒了。趕快做決定吧！/我看你就好好在這個公司工作吧，不要再三心二意了。/她對你那麼好，你要是對人家三心二意，就太對不起人家了。
26	犹豫不决 猶豫不决	yóuyù bùjué	to remain undecided to poise; (猶豫=to hesitate)	我在猶豫要不要跟他們一起旅遊。/你不要猶豫不決了，來跟我們一起玩吧。/這個人幹什麼事都很猶豫，不適合黨領導。
27	构成 構成	gòuchéng	to constitute; to form	由兩部分構成/他那些不三不四的話已經構成了犯罪事實。

28	准确 準確	zhǔnquè	precise; accurate	發音準確/準確地解釋
29	生动 生動	shēngdòng	lively; vivid	生動的語言/生動的小說/生動地講故事/他講故事講得很生動。
30	表达 表達	biǎodá	to express; to deliver	你喜歡她，為什麼不向她表達？/我的中文還不夠好，很多時候我不知道怎麼表達自己的看法。/他的表達能力很差。/這個成語表達了一個人不怕困難的決心。
31	成千上万 成千上萬	chéngqiān shàngwàn	tens of thousands of	誰說成千上萬中國人練法輪功練得走火入魔？/被美國家庭收養的孤兒成千上萬。
32	大体上 大體上	dàtǐshàng	on the whole; roughly; by and large	從大體上說，這輛車還不錯。/經理大體上同意了我們的要求。
33	结构 結構	jiégòu	structure; construction	成語的結構/這個句子的結構/房子的結構/這張桌子的結構很奇特。
34	典故	diǎngù	literary quotation	歷史典故/名人典故/成語典故/文學典故
35	猜	cāi	to guess	你猜我今天給你買什麼了？/我猜不出來。/你可以猜三次。/你猜錯了。/我猜出來了。/你猜猜看？
36	大量	dàliàng	a large number; a great quantity	大量的財富/大量的時間/大量事實/大量地收集這方面的信息。
37	白话	báihuà	colloquial, clear and easy to understand	
38	组合 組合	zǔhé	to compose; to assemble; composition; combination	這張床由三部分組合在一起。/我們三個人是很好的組合。/球隊的組合很重要。
39	固定	gùdìng	to fasten; to fix (and not change); fixed	把這個桌子固定在這裏。/請你固定一個時間找我作輔導。/他固定三點鐘來。/我剛來兩天，住的地方還不固定。/她還沒有固定的男朋友。/固定收入/固定財產
40	代替	dàitì	to substitute for; to replace	今天你們的老師生病了，我代替他上課。/媽媽在孩子心中的地位是沒有人能代替的。

課文

第二部分

至於典故性成語，之所以對外國學生比較難，是因為理解這一類成語需要對中國的一些歷史人物和文化背景有一些了解。舉例來說，中國人都知道"愚公移山"這個成語。按照字面的意思，這四個字是說："一個很愚笨的老人要把一座山搬走"。但了解了這個歷史典故之後，你會知道，這個成語強調的是不怕困難的決心。愚公家前有一座大山，出入很不方便，但愚公不想搬家，因為在古代中國人看來，你生長的地方，就是你的根，隨便搬家是件令人忌諱的事，因此愚公帶領全家人移山。儘管人們都笑他傻，但愚公固執地認為，只要他的子子孫孫堅持下去，最終會把山移走。

之前在對話裏出現的"班門弄斧"，也屬於典故性成語。"班"是指歷史上一位叫魯班的人物；"班門"就是說在魯班的家門前；"斧"對工匠來說是必不可少的工具。"班門弄斧"意思是在魯班的家門前玩弄你的斧頭。這是什麼意思呢？原來，魯班是古代最有名的一位建筑師傅。如果你在他家門前賣弄你那一點手藝，可是會鬧笑話的。現在我們用這個成語來形容一個人自不量力，在專家面前炫耀。

無論是結構性成語還是典故性成語，在使用上，都有它的特別之處。一般來說，成語後不能直接加賓語，比方說"我一見鐘情他"是錯誤的，正確的應該是："我對他一見鐘情。" 另外，成語前常常不能加"很"，"非常"等副詞，但可以加上 "是"、"真是"、"實在是"來發表個人主觀意見或者表示感嘆。因此，你不可以說"我們很一敗涂地"，但你可以說"我們真是一敗涂地"；你不可以說"他非常坐井觀天"，但你可以說"他實在是坐井觀天"。

成語的大量存在和使用，是漢語的一個特色。對外國人來說，雖然不那麼容易，但只要了解了其中的基本規則，多聽多用，還是可以學好的。

生詞用法

	至于 至於	zhìyú	as for; as to	見語法
41	理解	lǐjiě	to comprehend; to understand	理解能力/很難理解/我不理解這本書想表達的意思。
42	背景	bèijǐng	background; setting	家庭背景/生活背景/歷史背景/背景知識/文化背景/不同文化背景的人看問題的角度(jiǎodù)自然不同。/我很喜歡這個電影的背景音樂
43	举例 舉例	jǔlì	to give an example; to cite an instance	我還是不懂，你給我舉例說一下。/她舉了很多例子來解釋這個道理。/理解典故性的成語需要背景知識，舉例來說，…
44	愚公移山	Yúgōng yíshān	to be as determined as the old man's attempt to move the mountain	要完成計劃，我們必須要有愚公移山的精神。/要是你有愚公移山的精神，世界上沒有你做不好的事。
45	强调 強調	qiángdiào	to emphasize; to stress	老師總是向我們強調要完成功課。/我把今天的重要語法再強調一次。
46	字面	zìmiàn	literal; literal meaning	按照字面上理解。/這個成語的意思跟字面上的意思不一樣。
47	愚笨	yúbèn	foolish; stupid	
48	出入	chūrù	to come in and go out; to go out and come in	這座建筑出入不方便。/出入平安。
49	根	gēn	root	樹根/草根
	令/令人	lìng/lìngrén	to make happen; to let	見語法

50	忌讳 忌諱	jìhuì	to avoid as a taboo; to abstain from; taboo (n.)	她忌諱別人叫她的小名(nickname)。/中國人忌諱數字四，美國人忌諱數字十三。/結婚那天，中國人有什麼忌諱？
51	带领 帶領	dàilǐng	to lead; to guide	上回你跟著做過一次，這次你帶領其他人做吧！/在他的帶領下我們把對方的球隊打得一敗涂地。
52	固执 固執	gùzhí	stubborn; wilful	固執的老頭/ 固執的想法/ 他這個人太固執了。/ 他固執地相信他的女朋友不會變心。
53	坚持 堅持	jiānchí	to insist on; to persist in; to hold on	他堅持他的看法。/他堅持每天跑步。/我們都堅持用原來的計劃。/我知道你很累，請再堅持一會兒，很快就到家了。/我堅持不下去了。
54	最终 最終	zuìzhōng	at last; finally; at the end	最終的結果/最終的成績/最終，我們把他說服了。
55	指	zhǐ	to point to, to refer to	你說的是哪個人？你給我指一下。/“夜郎自大”中“夜郎”指的是古代一個國家。/歐盟是指歐洲聯盟。
56	工匠	gōngjiàng	craftsman	
57	必不可少	bìbùkěshǎo	absolutely necessary	學好外語，一本好字典是必不可少的。
58	工具	gōngjù	tool	交通工具/建筑工具/語言是人們交流的工具。
	鲁班 魯班	Lǔ Bān	name of a master carpenter	
59	玩弄	wánnòng	to play with; to dally with men/women	她對你是全心全意的，你不要玩弄人家的感情。/玩弄外交手段/你就那一點知識，沒什麼好賣弄的。
60	斧头 斧頭	fǔtou	axe	一把斧頭
61	建筑 建築	jiànzhù	to build; to erect; building; architecture	建筑一座高樓/建筑一條公路/一座建筑/古代建筑/現代建筑/建筑師

62	师傅 師傅	shīfu	master worker; a polite form to address blue-collar workers	她小時候跟幾個師傅學過做飯。/你問問路邊的那位師傅，到火車站怎麼走？
63	卖弄 賣弄	màinong	to show off	賣弄小聰明(show one's smartness)/向別人賣弄他剛學到的技術
64	手艺 手藝	shǒuyì	workmanship; skill	做飯的手藝/畫畫的手藝/他做菜的手藝很高。
65	闹笑话 鬧笑話	nàoxiàohua	to make a fool of oneself	要是你不懂裝懂，一定會鬧笑話。/大為把"問"說成了"吻"(wěn-to kiss)，鬧了一個大笑話。/你鬧過什麼笑話？
66	形容	xíngróng	to describe (形容詞: adjective)	我沒法形容我的感受，太複雜了。/他的房子什麼樣？你形容一下。/有些東西用語言是 形容不出來的。
67	自不量力	zìbúliànglì	to do sth. beyond one's ability; be unaware of one's own limitation	你那點知識還想當他的老師，你太自不量力了。
68	专家 專家	zhuānjiā	an expert	電腦專家/環境專家/向專家請教
69	炫耀	xuànyào	to show off; to flaunt	炫耀他的財富/在陌生人面前炫耀/向同學炫耀他的女朋友
70	直接	zhíjiē	direct; directly; (間接: inderct; indirectly)	直接原因/直接關係/別再瞞她 了，直接告訴她吧！/下課以後，我直接去吃飯，不回宿舍了。
71	宾语 賓語	bīnyǔ	object (in linguistics)	直接賓語/"我看書"這個句子的賓語是"書"。
72	错误 錯誤	cuòwù	wrong; incorrect	錯誤的想法/錯誤的句子/犯了一個嚴重的錯誤
73	正确 正確	zhèngquè	correct (adj.); right	正確的政策/正確的句子/你說得很正確。/正確估計
74	副词 副詞	fùcí	adverb	
75	发表 發表	fābiǎo	to manifiet, to publish (an article); to present (a paper); to express (an opinion)	在報紙上發表文章/ 發表論文/ 發表你的看法

76	主观 主觀	zhǔguān	subjective; subjectivity; (客觀 = objective; objectivity)	主觀感受/主觀認識/你的看法太主觀了。/看問題不要太主觀。
77	意见 意見	yìjiàn	opinions; view; objection and complain	你對這個問題有什麼意見？ / 請提出你的意見。 / 我同意你的意見。/你對我的安排有什麼意見，請你直接告訴我。/他總是對別人有意見，沒有人能讓她滿意。
78	表示	biǎoshì	to show, to express	向父母表示關心/向朋友表示感謝/在信中他表示他很喜歡他的學校。/對這件事，他沒做什麼表示。
79	感叹 感歎	gǎntàn	to exclaim out of surprise; to sigh over sth.	他常感嘆時間過得太快。/看到朋友妻子做的菜，他感嘆："你太幸福了"。
80	特色	tèsè	characteristic, distinguishing feature	上海菜的特色/中國建筑的特色/這個飯館的特色菜
	其中	qízhōng	among (which, them, etc)	見語法
81	基本	jīběn	basic; fundamental 基本上=basically; by and large	基本觀點/基本問題/基本條件/基本知識/這個工作基本上已經做完了。
82	规则 規則	guīzé	rules; regulation	交通規則/成語構成的規則/一成不變的規則

句型和語法

- 怎麼怎麼+Adj./Stative verb (**"怎麼怎麼" is used to replace the detailed description when retelling something to bring a sense of vividness and emphasis of the degree).**

    他總是跟別人埋怨他妻子對他怎麼怎麼不好。
    He always complains to people about how his wife treated him badly.

    你總是說他生活怎麼怎麼節省。他這次怎麼會捨得買這麼貴的東西呢？
    You always tell me how thriftly he lives his life. How could he decide to buy such an expensive thing this time?

    她常告訴我她有多崇拜念電子工程的人。
    (也可以說) =>

- **person+ 這/那 ("我", "你", "他", "我們", "你們", "他們"or names can occur in front of "這"and "那". A combination like "我這" or "你那" serves as subject in the sentence, meaning 'my/your doing this/that' or 'my/your going through this/that').**

    我這叫深藏不露。
    My action can be explained as 'not revealing the deeply hidden ability.'

    老陳那是班門弄斧。
    Old Chen' is showing off in front of experts.

    你這是幹嗎呢？人來就好，帶什麼禮物(lǐwù)嘛！
    Why are you doing this? (You shouldn't have done this). Your visiting is really enough. There is no need for you to bring a gift.

- **趕快("趕快" is often used in an imperative sentence to urge someone to hurry up. It can also be used in a narration to indicate that someone speeds up his action. "趕快" cannot be modified by adverb such as "很", "非常", and "特別").**

    同事老王的孩子又上補習班，又請家教，我們也得趕快把孩子送去學鋼琴。

My colleague Mr. Wang's child not only goes to cram school but also has a tutor. We should also send our child to piano lessons as soon as possible.

這本很暢銷，你要買就趕快去，去晚了就買不到了。
This book is really popular. If you want to buy it you need to hurry. It might get sold out if you are too late.

聽了他的建議以後，小李趕快去買股票。
After listening to his suggestions, little Li took an immediate action and bought the stocks.

(完成句子) => 你不是九點有課嗎？現在都已經八點一刻了，
________________________________。

- **把…分為/分成…(to divide Sth into； to categorize as)**

我們一般把成語分為結構性和典故性兩種。
Generally, we divide Chengyu into two categories: structural Chengyu and story-based Chengyu.

老師把學生分成三組來做口語討論。
The teacher divided the students into three groups to practice oral discussions.

這些組織，有的是非法的，有的是合法的。
(也可以說) =>

- **(A) 和 B 相比/比起來, (A)…… (To compare with B, A …)**

和過去相比，現在重男輕女的觀念越來越淡了。
Compared with the past, male-centered values are less and less emphasized.

你總是不滿足，和那些殘疾人比起來，你已經夠幸運了。
You are always unsatisfied; however, compared to those who are handicapped, you are really lucky.

A: 美國人常常換工作嗎？
(回答問題) => B:____________________。

A: 你籃球打得那麼好，差不多算是職業水平了。
(完成句子) => B: 哪裏，哪裏，__________________。

- **VP 的是，…. (“的是” is used after a verb phrase in the first part of the sentence to emphasize the information stated after.)**

  值得注意的是，那些最好的建筑師傅絕對不會隨便在人面前炫耀他們的手藝。
  What is worthy to notice is that the best architectural masters would never show off their skills in front of other people.

  讓人感到安慰的是，他並沒有坐井觀天。
  What is comforting is that he did not have a narrow view like sitting in the well to watch the sky.

  他永遠不會了解的是，為什麼小雲從此對他不聞不問。
  What he will never understand is that why Little Yun lacks interest in him since that time.

  跟他說話就像是對牛彈琴，真是讓我生氣！
  (也可以說) =>

- 至於 **(“as to”; is used to introduce another topic and is immediately followed by the comment on this topic).**

  我只知道他決定提前退休了，至於為什麼，我不清楚。
  I only know that he decided to have an early retirement, as for the reason I'm not sure.

  這種藥對艾滋病很有效，至於怎麼用，你得聽醫生的。
  (I only know that) this medicine is effective in treating AIDS, as for how you will use it, you have to consult a doctor.

  我的中文發音很好，至於______，我覺得我還得更努力。

  和你談談道教、佛教還可以，至於______，我可不敢班門弄斧。

- 令人 **XX (“令人” is often followed by a multiple-syllable word, meaning “make people XX”. For example, “興奮” means “excited”, “令人興奮”means “exciting”. “令” is same as “讓”, meaning to make or to cause. “讓” is more colloquial than “令”).**

  搬家是件令人忌諱的事。
  Moving is a taboo to people.

他為那些孤兒所作的一切令人十分感動。
All the things he dedicated to help those orphans make people feel very touched.

聽了這個故事以後，所有的人都很難過。
(也可以說) =>

- **無論/不論+ question +....都 ... "no matter what/how; regardless of"; used to indicate that the result or the conclusion won't change under the condition stated).**

不論我說什麼，他都不聽。
No matter what I said, he wouldn't listen.

無論你是中國人還是外國人，都得按照基本規則去做。
Whether you are a Chinese or a foreigner, you have to follow the basic rules.

無論她跟你說得多好聽，你都得裝聾作啞，別三心二意。
No matter how pleasant her words are, you have to play deaf and dumb. Do not change your mind.

A: 如果情況繼續壞下去，我們有可能一敗涂地嗎？
(完成句子) => B: 你別胡思亂想，____________________________________。

- **...，其中，("其中"means "among (which, them, etc) "其" is used like a pronoun, refers to something or some people mentioned earlier).**

今天考試我出了很多錯，這是其中的一個。
I made a lot of mistakes today on the test. This is one of the mistakes.

這些東西對我們來說都很重要，其中，斧頭更是一個必不可少的工具。
Those tools are all important to us, among them, axe is a necessary tool.

(回答問題) => 成語有哪兩種？哪一種對外國學生來說比較難？

課堂活動

(一)舉些例子說一說這些成語的意思：

愚公移山	成千上萬	生龍活虎	班門弄斧	一帆風順
深藏不露	三心二意	對牛彈琴	裝聾作啞	一見鐘情

(二)下邊幾個成語的用法是錯的。請你說說錯在那裏，要怎麼用才對。

1. 他畢業以後很一帆風順。
2. 中國的成語是成千上萬。
3. 小張一見鐘情他的女朋友。
4. 我不聞不問股票。

(三)角色扮演：

- 用你學過的成語寫一段戀人的對話：
  A: “我喜歡上了別的男孩子”
  B: “你怎麼可以…….”
- 小董，小郭，老米這三個人，應該為他們的退休計劃買什麼樣的股票呢？請給他們一些建議。說你的建議的時候，成語用得越多越好哦！

	小董	小郭	老米
年齡	30 歲	45 歲	55 歲
月收入	\$3,000	\$9,000	\$1,200
存款	\$18,000	\$2,897,000	\$78,000

	最近三個月	最近五年	最近十年	股價變化
中國股票	☹ ☹	☺ ☺	☺ ☺ ☺ ☺ ☺	+- \$\$
俄羅斯股票(Éluósī)	☺	☺ ☺ ☺	☹	+-\$\$\$
歐洲股票(Ōuzhōu)	☺ ☺ ☺	☺	☹	+-\$\$\$\$
美國股票	☹	☹☹☹☹☹	☺☺	+-\$\$\$\$\$

一成不變	一帆風順	一敗涂地	三心二意
班門弄斧	默不作聲	對牛彈琴	不聞不問
裝聾作啞	深藏不露	坐井觀天	夜郎自大

(四) 你的看法

- 說一說愚公移山的故事。你認為愚公傻嗎？為什麼？
- 為了三峽大壩 (Sānxiá dàbà: Three Gorge Dam)，部分住在長江附近的人得搬家。如果你是中國政府，你會怎麼做讓老百姓高高興興地搬走呢？

練習題

一. 詞彙練習:

(一) *(請教 指教 建議 帶領)*

1. 我是新來的，對這些規則完全不懂，還請您多多________。
2. 不管我向他_____什麼問題，他都能給我很好的_____。
3. 我這孩子從小就被嬌慣，現在他跟著您這個大師傅，不但要請你教他手藝，還請你多_____他一些怎麼跟人打交道的知識。
4. 我們對這個城市的結構不熟悉，好在他也去了，在他的_____下，我們的訪問基本上還算順利。
5. 這個孩子喜歡玩股票，對股市行情非常清楚，他想_____他媽媽買某家公司的股票，可是媽媽很固執，不聽他的。

(二) *(賣弄 玩弄 炫耀)*

1. 一有機會他就向別人_____ 他的大房子，實在是令人討厭。
2. 我研究生的時候學的是中國歷史，你不要給我__________你那一點中國歷史知識。
3. 別的同學都很注意聽老師說什麼，他卻低著頭_______他的新手表，什麼也沒聽進去。
4. 我以為咱們倆是認真的，沒想到你只是在_______我的感情。

(三) *(發表 出版 表達 表示 形容)*

1. 他在信中 _____， 他剛剛 _____了一篇關於中國古代建筑學的文章。
2. 他新 ____的書是關於一位母親。通過這個故事他向讀者 ____了他對偉大母愛的尊敬。看完以後，我的感受真的無法用語言來__(multiple answers possible__。

二. 口語表達和語法練習:

(一) *慢慢來 指的是 死了這條心吧 怎麼著 回頭*

1. 想當醫生？你父母就這麼一點工資怎麼能付得起那麼貴的學費，_____________。

2. 典故性成語________那些跟歷史人物或歷史故事有關的成語。______我有時間，可以給你找幾本關於成語典故的書看看。你才剛開始學中文，先別急，________。一兩年以後你就會知道一些常用的成語了。

3. A: 我警告你，以後你最好別來找麗麗了。
   B: 我喜歡她， 我就要來找她，______？

(二) *怎麼怎麼 說大話 沒錯 說實在的*

A: 他總是告訴我他在股票方面______厲害，誰知道他是不是在______。
B: ______,我也覺得他並沒有那麼厲害。______我真不喜歡這個人，太喜歡賣弄了。

三. 綜合練習：

不聞不問 一帆風順 一見鐘情 對牛彈琴

默不做聲 一成不變 三心二意 裝聾作啞

王紅和李明第一次見面時就互相喜歡，朋友們都說，他們倆是____1___。從戀愛到結婚，他們也可說是____2___，從來沒有遇到過什麼問題。然而，結婚沒幾個月後，李明就變得不怎麼愛說話了。王紅問他的工作情況，他也不回答，有時候竟然還說“你對我的工作完全不懂，我幹嗎____3___呢？”以前，李明挺關心王紅的工作，現在，他對王紅的工作____4___， 完全不在乎似的。在家事方面，王紅和李明兩個人應該輪流做的，但每次輪到李明該做家事的時候，他就____5___，裝出一副什麼都不知道的樣子，好像這些家事跟他完全無關。

王紅的母親知道了這個的情況以後，氣得不得了，她打電話問李明這到底是怎麼回事。李明聽了先是____6___，什麼話都沒說。過了一會，他嘆了口氣， 說：“人不是____7___的嘛! 誰有可能一直跟從前一樣呢？再說，以前是以前，現在是現在。結婚了哪能總像談戀愛的時候，累不累呀！”王紅的母親說：“我老實告訴你吧！王紅雖然結了婚，但還是有人追。原本，她還告訴自己，只可以愛你一個人，不應該____8___，但你現在對她這麼不好，我看她不會再有這樣的想法了。你們的婚姻很危險，如果到時候出了問題，你應該負最大的責任。”

四. 翻譯練習：從下面的句型中，選出合適的，把英文翻成中文

把...分為..../ 和…相比/ …的是/ 至於/ 令人 XX/
無論\不論…都 / 其中/ …指的是/ 到底/ 大體上

1. The stock specialist divided us into two groups. Compared to the other team, our group collects more information, whether it is on the internet or from the newspaper, therefore; we can always make a better decision.

2. She can comprehend most of the structure-oriented Chengyu. As for Chengyus based on ancient stories, their forms don't have a rule . It is really hard to say how much she really understands.

3. What is worthy to notice is that most of those who wrote the basic rules are very subjective. Some of them are even naively arrogant and as narrow-sighted as frogs sitting in a well.

4. What makes people sigh is that young people nowadays are naively arrogant and narrow-sighted. Comparing with the old generation, they are not modest enough. They disregard old taboos and see things very subjectively.

五. 作文：(從下邊幾個題目中, 選擇一個, 寫一篇不少於 500 字的作文。你至少要用五個所提供的句型或詞彙)

無論...，...都...	至於	指的是
和 B 相比，A...	令人...	其中
VP 的是...(as in 值得注意的是...)	大體上	

1. 你是一個反對美國政府的外國人，你認為美國政府太自大了，請舉例談談為什麼。
2. "別三心二意了！"----寫一段男女朋友之間的對話。
   --- 小麗：小王的女朋友，卻開始喜歡小張了，很猶豫，不知道該怎麼辦
   --- 小王：小麗的男朋友，想說服小麗跟自己在一起才會永遠幸福
3.因為建三峽大壩(sānxiádàbà-Three Gorge Dam), 許多住在長江(Yangzi River) 附近的人得搬家，你估計中國政府得面對什麼樣的問題，你對此有什麼看法？

第九課　俗語和順口溜

Let's warm-up with a review exercise!

Match the words in characters with Pinyin and English:

漢字	拼音	英文	哪兒學過
私生活			二年級
打招呼			二年級
麻煩			二年級
熟悉			二年級
大概			第一課
領導			第二課
方式			第三課
退休			第五課
複雜			第六課
遭遇			第六課
放棄			第七課
拒絕			第七課
充滿			第七課
代替			第八課
典故			第八課

拼音

1. chōngmǎn	2. dǎzhāohu	3. dàgài	4. dàitì
5. diǎngù	6. fàngqì	7. fāngshì	8. fùzá
9. jùjué	10. lǐngdǎo	11. máfan	12. sīshēnghuó
13. tuìxiū	14. zāoyù	15. shúxi	

英文

a. be full of	b. complicated	c. to encounter misfortune	d. to give up
e. to greet	f. leader	g. literary quotation	h. private life
i. probably	j. to refuse	k. to retire	l. to replace
m. trouble	n. style, way	o. familiar	

聽力&口語

聽錄音回答問題

對話一

1.	2.	3.	4.	5.

生詞：放屁，屁股，背黑鍋，場合，禮貌，炒冷飯

複習：正式，沒面子，嫌，控制(不住)，過分，享受，演講，(道歉 dàoqiàn)

對話二

1.	2.	3.	4.	5.

生詞：開夜車，拼命，拍馬屁，抱怨，老婆

複習：領導，普通，主管，商業，資料，受得了 / 受不了
煩，固執，允許，答應，爭取，為你好，算了

對話三

1.	2.	3.	4.	5.

生詞：丑聞，表現，犧牲，半瓶醋，通俗，幽默，文雅
諷刺，押韻，打退堂鼓，暗示，坐冷板凳，浪漫

複習：情人，默不作聲，感受，拒絕，表現，自大，狠心
原諒，感動，一見鐘情，求婚

根據對話一回答問題：

1. 對話開始時，屋子為什麼有一股臭味(yìgǔ chòuwei)？肚子不舒服的小李擔心什麼？為什麼？
2. 小張和小李喜歡校長演講的題目嗎？為什麼？
3. 校長演講到一半，小李為什麼生氣走了？

根據對話二回答問題：

1. 為什麼太太叫阿強起床他起不來呢？
2. 阿強工作認真嗎？為什麼阿強的太太要他學他的同事小王？
3. 對於老婆的話，阿強都聽了嗎？他同意做什麼？不同意做什麼？

根據對話三回答問題：

1. 一開始，記者問了希拉裏什麼問題？對這個問題希拉裏是什麼態度？
2. 希拉裏和克林頓在法學院讀書的時候表現得怎麼樣？她覺得自己為克林頓做了很多嗎？為什麼？
3. 她認為老百姓為什麼喜歡克林頓？她愛克林頓什麼？她想過離婚嗎？為什麼？
4. 希拉裏和克林頓是怎麼戀愛、結婚的？克林頓不當總統以後，希拉裏的生活有什麼改變？

口語用法

1. 不好意思，　…(“不好意思” can mean “embarrassed.” It is also often used to apologize for an incontinence one brings to people. “不好意思” is softer than “對不起” and it lessens the distance between the listener and speaker by implying the speaker’s thankfulness for the listener’s understanding or toleration. It is also often used to show humility or politeness).

不好意思，讓你久等了。
I’m sorry I made you wait so long.

阿華，不好意思，我今天晚上可能要晚點回家吃飯，你別等我了。
A’hua, I am sorry but I probably will be home a little late for dinner tonight. Please don’t wait for me.

不好意思，能不能向您請教一下…
Excuse me, may I ask you…

那我就在大家面前班門弄斧了。不好意思。
Well, then I’ll show off my inadequate skills in front of all you experts. Sorry about that.

2．怎麼這麼說話，不夠朋友。 (“夠” can mean “to be up to a certain standard.” “夠朋友” or “不夠朋友” is an idiomatic way of saying a friend is a true friend or a friend does not value the friendship enough).

怎麼一要你幫忙你就皺眉頭呢?真不夠朋友。
How come right when I start asking you for help you frown? You really don’t value our friendship.

你再對小王的事不聞不問，可別怪我不夠朋友。
If you remain indifferent to Little Wang’s business, don’t blame me for not valuing our friendship.

你知道我忌諱“四”還讓我住四樓，這樣做太不夠朋友了。
You know that the number ‘four’ is unlucky for me (and staying on fourth floor is a taboo to me), but you still let me stay on the fourth floor. I can see that you really don’t value our friendship

3. 明明就是你放的屁，幹嗎讓我替你背黑鍋！("明明" is an adverb meaning "obviously," "undoubtedly," or "by all appearances." It is always used before a verb phrase in one clause to emphasize the truth even while the other clause relates some contradictory comment).

他怎麼會不知道？明明就是在裝聾作啞！
How can he not know it? He is obviously playing dumb and deaf.

你明明知道我沒有錢，幹嗎還一直逼著我還錢？
You obviously know that I don't have any money. Why do you keep forcing me to pay you back?

剛才我還明明看見我的字典就在這裏，怎麼一下子就不見了？
Undoubtedly I just saw my dictionary; how come it disappeared all of a sudden?

("明明" can also be used in a rhetorical question or in a complaint to enhance affirmation).

你怎麼會不知道今天有考試？我昨天不是明明告訴你了嗎？
How can you not know that we have a test today? Didn't I tell you yesterday?

你這不是明明在躲著我嗎？
Aren't you blatantly hiding from me?

4. 等等，怎麼說走就走啊。(If someone"說 V 就 V", he "acts as soon as he says he will act." In other words, he forcefully takes the action without being distracted by the concerns of others).

這孩子說做功課就做功課，馬上就關了電視開始了。
This child started working on his homework without any distraction, since he immediately turned off the TV.

你怎麼能說走就走，回來，把話說清楚啊！
How can you leave like that? Come back, you have to clarify what you meant.

我說教訓他就教訓他，別以為我在開玩笑！
I'll teach him a lesson as I said I would. Don't think I'm just joking.

你說不打就不打？不行！我就不能讓你這樣嬌慣孩子。
Just because you said not to beat him you think I won't? No way. I won't let you spoil the child like this.

5. 你昨晚又開夜車了吧？我問你呢！ (Besides being used at the end of an interrogative sentence， “呢” can be used to soften the tone at the end of a declarative sentence to emphasize doubt, disgust, conceit, or admiration).

我問你呢！你怎麼不說話呢？
I'm asking you. Why aren't you talking?

我正忙著呢，你找媽媽幫你吧。
I am busy now. Go to Mom for help.

你沒看我正吃飯呢！有事等會兒再來。
Don't you see I'm eating now? Come back later.

他這是笑你夜郎自大呢！難道你聽不出來嗎？
He was laughing at you for being foolish and arrogant. Can't you tell?

6. …， 再說了，你這樣拼命有什麼用？ (“再說了” is used as a conjunction to introduce the second clause which discloses a further concern or reason. It can be translated as “…, besides,…” , “moreover .” You can also say “再說,” but “再說了” is stronger in tone than “再說”).

要蓋(gài)房子你也得先有地，再說(了)，要找個好的建築師父也沒那麼容易。
To build a house you should first own land. Besides, finding a good architect isn't that easy.

這些成語的規則本來就很複雜，再說(了)，有些還帶有典故，外國學生更是難懂。
The rules for 成語 usage are already complicated as they are, but moreover some of them are based on ancient stories, making them even harder for foreign students to understand.

7. 老婆，你有完沒完呀，大早上就開始抱怨。(“有完沒完” is used to indicate a complaint and means “aren't you going to stop?” or “can't you just stop it?” It is used when you are really fed up with something and want it to be stopped).

同樣一件事你都說了三天了，你有完沒完？
You have been talking about the same thing for three days. Aren't you going to stop?

你到底有完沒完？不是告訴你別再給我打電話了嗎？

Are you going to stop or not? Haven't I told you not to call me again?

(When a speaker uses "大早上" or "一大早", he implies that things the listener does or suggests shouldn't be happening so early in the morning).

大早上的，小點聲，別把大家都吵醒了。
It is still early morning. Keep your voice down. Don't awaken everybody.

一大早起來就喝酒？
Why are you drinking this early in the morning?

口語練習：請用聽力對話裏學到的生詞和口語用法討論下面的問題：

不好意思/ (不)夠朋友/　明明/　說 Verb 就 Verb
… 我問你呢？/ 再說了，…/　你有完沒完啊!/

1. 小明拉肚子，但是等一會兒得去聽一個關於改革開放的演講。
   A，B-你們替小明想個辦法，決定他到底該不該去聽演講。

2. A – 你是個認真的職員，但這次別人的工資都增加了，你的工資沒增加，你很生氣，要跟老板談。
   B- 你是老板，你只喜歡拍你馬屁的人。

3. A- 你是克林頓。
   B-你是希拉裏。
   希拉裏對記者說了很多克林頓的壞話。克林頓很生氣，和希拉裏吵，希拉裏也跟他吵。

課文

第一部分

成語以外，漢語裏還有另一種慣用詞語，一般我們把它叫做“俗語”。這裏的“俗”，也就是“通俗”，和“文雅”的“雅”是相對的。俗語通常是在比較隨便的場合中使用，同時也得注意使用的對象，否則就會引起麻煩。舉個例子，你可以用“脫褲子放屁”來說一個人所做的事情是多余的，沒有必要的。這雖然是極不文雅的比喻，但既簡單又生動，在日常生活中常常聽到，但用在正式場合或者關係不夠親近的人身上，就顯得非常不禮貌，好像在罵人。

俗語的來源比較複雜，一些俗語和歷史典故有關。比方說，過去蒙古人打招呼，習慣拍拍對方的馬屁股，要是碰上了高官，更得邊拍馬屁股邊稱贊他的馬兒好。現在，這種習慣已消失，但“拍馬屁”卻成為慣用的俗語，比“奉承”多了份通俗生動的味道。再比方說，從前審判完罪犯，打鼓表示退堂，現在沒有所謂的打鼓退堂了，但“打退堂鼓”卻仍是個普遍的用法，表示因害怕而放棄了原本的打算。

很多俗語的來源我們並不清楚，但有不少說的都是老百姓日常生活中很熟悉的東西，例如: “背黑鍋”指的是代替別人承受指責和處罰；“碰釘子”說的是遭遇到冷冷的拒絕；“炒冷飯”是指在老題目上一說再說卻提不出新的看法；“半瓶醋”是用來諷刺那些沒有能力卻愛賣弄的人；“把某人的話當耳邊風”指的是你對某人的話毫不在乎、也不會認真對待；“開夜車”意思是為了完成一個任務晚上睡得很晚；“坐冷板凳”比喻一個人在工作上不受重視，沒有表現的機會；“騎驢找馬”是說一邊利用已經擁有的，一邊尋找更好的。從以上的例子我們可以看出，這些俗語充滿了活潑生動的感覺，並且都很適合在日常生活裏用，因此，即使不靠文字記錄，也能以口語的方式流傳下來。

生詞用法

1	俗语	俗語	súyǔ	common saying	
2	顺口溜	順口溜	shùnkǒuliū	short, rhymed, slang verse	
3	惯用	慣用	guànyòng	idiomatic	慣用語
4	通俗	通俗	tōngsú	popular; common	通俗文學/通俗的語言/通俗文化/用通俗的話來解釋複雜的問題。
5	文雅	文雅	wényǎ	refined; educated; elegant	文雅的語言/說話很文雅/這個女孩子很文雅。
	相对	相對	xiāngduì	to be opposite, relative (opposite of “absolute”)	見語法
6	场合	場合	chǎnghé	occasion	外交場合/正式場合/教室不是談戀愛的場合。
7	对象	對象	duìxiàng	object; boyfriend or girlfriend	批評的對象/開玩笑的對象/他是我的對象。/你幫我找個對象。
8	脱裤子放屁	脫褲子放屁	tuōkùzi fàngpì	to take off one’s pants to fart (to do something that is unnecessary and superfluous)	你都已經做好決定了幹嗎還來問我。脫褲子放屁！/ 你別脫褲子放屁了！都打電話說好了，幹嗎再發 e-mail 問他一次。
9	多余	多餘	duōyú	extra; surplus	你這些話都太多余了。/這些都是多余的解釋，前面你已經解釋得很清楚了。/我有多余的一枝筆。/我們把多余的錢寄給了父母。
10	必要	必要	bìyào	necessary; essential	必要的幫助/必要的培訓/必要的條件/做決定之前的集體討論是很必要的。/你這樣做，實在沒必要。

11	比喻	比喻	bǐyù	metaphor or simile; to compare one thing to another	這是一個比喻。/人們常常把男人比喻為太陽(sun)，把女人比喻為月亮(moon)。/人們喜歡拿火比喻熱情。
12	亲近	親近	qīnjìn	to approach; close (adj.); intimate	他這個人很孤僻，不太容易親近。/這個老師很友好，學生們都願意親近她。/她和媽媽非常親近，什麼事都會跟媽媽說。
13	显得	顯得	xiǎnde	to appear (to be); to seem	她說話做事都顯得很文雅。/你穿上這件衣服顯得特別年輕。/他跟你說話的時候顯得有點兒緊張。
14	礼貌	禮貌	lǐmào	polite; courtesy; politeness	聚會的時候遲到不太禮貌。/這個孩子很有禮貌。/你這樣跟老人說話顯得非常沒有禮貌。
15	骂	罵	mà	to curse; to scold; to criticize; to reprimand	他不是打孩子就是罵孩子。/你不要罵他，這不是他的錯。/他罵我是個笨蛋。
16	來源	來源	láiyuán	source; origin	成語的來源/典故的來源/經濟來源/明天的幸福生活來源於今天的努力學習和工作。
17	蒙古	蒙古	Ménggǔ	Mongolia	
18	拍	拍	pāi	to pat; to slap	拍桌子/拍手/她拍了我肩膀一下。
19	屁股	屁股	pìgu	buttocks; hip	
20	称赞	稱讚	chēngzàn	to praise; praise (n.)	稱贊他的努力/稱贊學生的進步/得到家長的稱贊/受到負責人的稱贊
21	消失	消失	xiāoshī	to disappear; to vanish	她消失在人群中。/這樣的現象已經消失了。
22	拍马屁	拍馬屁	pāimǎpì	to pat the horse's butt (to flatter excessively; to be a sycophant; to lick sb.'s shoes)	他常對老板拍馬屁。/他常拍老板的馬屁。
23	奉承	奉承	fèngcheng	to flatter	奉承別人/說奉承話
24	味道	味道	wèidào	scent; flavor; taste	這個菜的味道不錯。/屋子裏有股怪味道。/你的話有點諷刺我的味道。/這幅畫有點日本畫的味道。

25	从前	從前	cóngqián	in the past; before	從前有一個國家叫夜郎。/那是從前，現在不一樣了。
26	审判	審判	shěnpàn	to bring to trial; to try; trial (n.)	審判罪犯/ /受審判/審判長/審判的規則
27	罪犯	罪犯	zuìfàn	criminal (n.)	
28	打鼓	打鼓	dăgŭ	to beat the drum (to feel uncertain; to feel nervous)	他又會彈琴，又會打鼓。/能不能得到領導的批準，我心裏一直在打鼓。
29	退堂	退堂	tuìtáng	to leave the court	
30	打退堂鼓		dă tuìtánggŭ	to beat the step-down-the-stage drum (to give up a pursuit without attaining one's goal)	你要堅持下去，不要動不動就打退堂鼓。
31	普遍	普遍	pŭbiàn	universal; common; ubiquitous	普遍的要求/普遍的現象/普遍地存在
32	背黑锅	背黑鍋	bēihēiguō	to carry the black wok (to take the blame for others; to be made a scapegoat)	我不要替別人背黑鍋。/他讓老張替他背了兩次黑鍋。
33	承受	承受	chéngshòu	to bear; to endure	承受壓力/承受批評/承受生活的重擔/承受不了這麼大的壓力。
34	指责	指責	zhĭzé	to blame; to accuse	指責某人/他指責我說他的閑話。/我受不了他的指責。
35	碰钉子	碰釘子	pèng dīngzi	to bump into the nail (to be rebuffed)	畢業以後他找工作處處碰釘子。/我請他幫忙，她卻讓我碰了一個大釘子。
36	炒冷饭	炒冷飯	chăo lěngfàn	to heat leftover rice (to say or do the same old thing; to repeat without any new content)	你的文章又在炒冷飯。
37	半瓶醋	半瓶醋	bànpíngcù	a half-bottle of vinegar (one who has only a superficial knowledge of something; a charlatan)	他是個半瓶醋。/你要認真學習，不要當半瓶醋。

38	讽刺	諷刺	fěngcì	to mock; to lampoon; satire	他諷刺我寫文章總是炒冷飯。/我諷刺他缺乏創造性。/這是一個諷刺的說法。/我受不了她對我的諷刺。
39	把…当耳边风	把…當耳邊風	ěrbiānfēng	to let something go in one ear and out the other; to turn a deaf ear to something	他總是把妻子的話當耳邊風。
40	毫不在乎		háobúzàihu	to not care about	父母的感受他毫不在乎。/我對他的諷刺毫不在乎。/ 他毫不在乎地在教室裏大聲說笑。
41	对待	對待	duìdài	to treat	對待客人要有禮貌。/你不能讓他殘酷對待罪犯。
42	开夜车	開夜車	kāiyèchē	"to burn the midnight oil"	她考試前總開夜車。/你昨天晚上開夜車開到幾點?
43	任务	任務	rènwù	mission; task	接受任務/拒絕任務/完成任務/很重要的任務/他給我派了一個新任務。
44	坐冷板凳		zuò lěng-bǎndèng	to sit on the cold bench (to be idled from important tasks)	老板一直讓他坐冷板凳。/坐了三年的冷板凳以後，他終於接到了一個重要任務。
45	表现	表現	biǎoxiàn	to show; to manifest; performance	表現你的能力/表現做飯的手藝/他在學校的表現好不好？/老板對他最近的表現很滿意。
46	骑驴找马 騎驢找馬		qílǘ zhǎomǎ	to ride the donkey while looking for a horse (to retain while looking for something better (usually said of a job or a boyfriend or girlfriend)	你要集中精力在這兒好好工作，不要騎驢找馬，總是想換工作。
47	利用	利用	lìyòng	to use or take advantage of; to exploit	利用關係/好好利用時間/利用這個機會了解中國社會。/他被朋友利用了。
48	寻找	尋找	xúnzhǎo	to seek; to search for	尋找方向/尋找機會
49	适合	適合	shìhé	to suit; to fit; to be appropriate for	這個工作很適合你。/這個電影不適合孩子看。

	即使...也		jíshǐ...yě	even if	見語法
50	记录	記錄	jìlù	to write down; to record; record (n.)	記錄歷史/記錄下她說的話/會議記錄/破世界記錄
51	流传	流傳	liúchuán	to pass on; to hand down	流傳下去/這個故事一直在老百姓中流傳。/民間流傳著這樣的說法，…。

課文

第二部分

順口溜和俗語一樣，和古書、文學沒什麼關係。 它流傳在平民老百姓中，常常是幾個短句組合在一起，有點像詩，通常還押韻，並帶有幽默，諷刺的味道。以下我們來看幾個例子。

(一) 領導四怕：

一怕老婆拼命, 二怕小姐有病
三怕情人懷孕, 四怕群眾反映

不管是在美國還是在中國，性丑聞都是讓官員們最頭疼的。這首順口溜描寫了某些領導官員，諷刺他們最怕的不是工作做不好，而是婚外關係和私生活出問題。

(二)

青春獻給黨, 老了沒人養
本想靠兒女, 兒女下了崗

改革必然要犧牲一些人的利益，也會引起一些抱怨。一些老年人為黨、為國貢獻了幾十年，到了該退休的年紀，制度卻變了，該享受的福利享受不到，甚至連兒女也靠不上。這首順口溜暗示了這些老一輩人的無奈和不滿。

(三)

到了北京才知道自己官小，
到了上海才知道自己錢少，
到了重慶才知道自己結婚太早。

北京、上海和重慶是中國三個很重要的大城市。這首短短的順口溜生動地反映了這三個城市的特色: 北京是政治文化中心, 上海是中國的經濟文化中心，重慶則是美女滿大街的浪漫地方。

通過上面這幾個例子，我們可以看出，一個順口溜常常反映某個群體的生活感受，反映一些有趣的社會文化現象。它的流行范圍是有限的，隨著時代的發展，一些順口溜將會消失，而新的順口溜也會不斷出現。

生詞用法

52	平民	平民	píngmín	common people	平民百姓/平民教育
53	诗	詩	shī	poem	一首(shǒu)詩/現代詩/詩人
54	押韵	押韻	yāyùn	to rhyme; to have a correspondence of terminal sounds of words or of lines of verse	這兩個句子押韻。/這首詩押韻押得不太好。
55	幽默	幽默	yōumò	humorous (幽默感 = sense of humor)	缺乏幽默感的人/幽默小說/他很幽默。
56	老婆	老婆	lǎopo	wife	娶了大老婆之後他又接著娶了兩個小老婆。

57	拼命	拼命	pīnmìng	to risk one's life to do something; to exert the utmost strength; to put up a desperate fight	逃犯拼命地往前跑，警察在後頭拼命地追。/他只知道拼命工作，從來不管孩子。/你不還我錢，我就跟你拼命。/這種工作不值得你那麼拼命。
58	群众	群眾	qúnzhòng	the masses; the general public	
59	反映	反映	fǎnyìng	to reflect; to report	向領導反映問題/一個人的行為反映一個人的觀念。
60	丑闻	醜聞	chǒuwén	scandal 丑：ugly	政治丑聞/性丑聞
61	描写	描寫	miáoxiě	to describe; to portray	他的人物描寫很生動。/他在小說中仔細描寫了女人的穿著。
62	婚外关系 婚外關係		hūnwài guānxi	extra-marital affair	
63	青春	青春	qīngchūn	youth (n.)	把青春獻給了國家。/ 他充滿了青春活力(vigor)
64	贡献	貢獻	gòngxiàn	to contribute; contribution	貢獻自己的時間和精力/他對我們的公司作了很大的貢獻。
65	必然	必然	bìrán	inevitable; certain; necessarily	必然的結果/必然會贏/這是必然的。
66	牺牲	犧牲	xīshēng	to sacrifice; to do something at the expense of another	犧牲財產/為國家犧牲生命/ 犧牲個人休息時間為公司工作。
67	利益	利益	lìyì	interest (n.)	群眾利益/公共利益/個人利益
68	抱怨	抱怨	bàoyuàn	to complain; complaint	他是一個愛抱怨的人。/ 他總抱怨先生不努力工作賺大錢。/他對職員的抱怨毫不在乎。
69	制度	制度	zhìdù	system	考試制度/工廠的制度/管理制度/教育制度
70	福利	福利	fúlì	benefits；welfare (see also Lesson 6 福利院)	公共福利/社會福利/公司的福利/兒童福利院
71	暗示	暗示	ànshì	to hint; to imply; hint(n.)	他暗示了他這次訪問的原因。/他給我了好幾次暗示，可是我沒懂他的意思。
72	无奈	無奈	wúnài	can't help but; to have no choice (usually used as an adjective)	我很無奈，只好按照他說的做。/我很喜歡他，無奈沒有機會向他表達。

73	不满	不滿	bùmǎn	resentful; unsatisfied; discontented	對同屋不滿/他有很多不滿。
	重庆	重慶	Chóngqìng	name of a city in China	
74	浪漫	浪漫	làngmàn	romantic	浪漫的生活/浪漫的氣氛/浪漫的詩人/浪漫的顏色/一個浪漫的夜晚。
75	群体	群體	qúntǐ	collective unit; group	老師這個群體/醫生這個群體
76	有趣	有趣	yǒuqù	interesting; amusing	有趣的電影/有趣的話題/這種現象很有趣。/ 這本書很有趣。
77	现象	現象	xiànxiàng	phenomenon	自然現象/社會想象/暫時的現象
78	范围	範圍	fànwéi	scope; range	活動范圍/研究范圍/適用范圍/大范圍/小范圍
	随着	隨著	suízhe	along with	見語法
79	不断	不斷	búduàn	constant; constantly; (斷: to discontinue; to break apart)	這種現象將不斷出現。/他不斷地給我打電話。/你不聽話，小心我打斷你的腿。/哎呀！我的鉛筆斷了！

句型和語法

- **A 和 B 是相對的 (This phrase means "A and B are relative" , "A and B are connected" , or "A is the opposite of B").**

"俗"和"雅"是相對的。
Vulgarity and grace are relative terms.
Vulgarity is the opposite of grace.

鄧小平的某些觀點和毛澤東的是相對的。
Some of Deng Xiaoping's points of view are the opposite of Mao Zedong's.

你所得到的和你所付出的是相對的。想得到多少，就得付出多少。
How much you gain is relative to how much you pay. You have to give as much as you want to get.

*相對 (於 XX) 來說，A … **("Comparatively speaking, A …;" "as compared to XX, A …")**

相對來說，私立學校的教育水平比公立學校的高些。
Comparatively speaking, education in private schools is a little better than education in public schools.

中國的生活水平雖然提高了許多，但相對於美國的來說，還差一大段距離(jùlí-distance)。
Though the living standard in China has improved a lot, compared to the living standard in the US, it's still far behind.

A:　和中國相比，印度的人口問題怎麼樣？
(回答問題) => B:
____.

A：一個月賺三千塊錢算得上是有錢人嗎？
(回答問題) => B：
____.

- **即使…也　(the equivalent of "就算…也" (See L4); "即使...也…" is less colloquial than "就算…也").**

別怕！即使說錯了也沒關係。
Don't be afraid. Even if you say the wrong thing, it will be ok.

即使我們知道最後有可能一敗涂地，也不願意打退堂鼓。
Even if we know that we might ultimately have a big failure, we're still unwilling to give up.

沒有我的幫助，你即使再聰明也沒有用。
You won't succeed without my help no matter how smart you are.

A：是不是只要考試考得好，期末就能得到 A？
Do you only need to do well in exams to get a final A?
(完成句子) => B：誰說的？要是你不來上課，
____

- **以…的方式/+VP ("以" in this context is like the colloquial "用" .We use "以…的方式" in front of a Verb Phrase meaning "to do something by means of ….". "以口語的方式流傳下來" means "to hand down in the form of a colloquial expression" . See also L6 "以").**

過去，她是個好強的人，大大小小的事都想管，現在，她學會了以裝聾作啞的方式來避免麻煩。
In the past, she liked to show her ability and to take charge of everything. Now she has learned to avoid trouble by pretending that she hears nothing and making no comments.

醫生教他以聽音樂的方式讓孩子開朗起來。
The doctor taught him to cheer up his child by playing music.

你覺得吸毒可以幫助人減輕(jiǎnqīng)壓力嗎？
(回答問題) =>

- **A…, B 則… ("A…, whereas B…" "則" is used in written Chinese to emphasize the difference between A and B. "則" needs to go after the subject).**

中國的歷史有五千年，美國的歷史則只有兩百多年。
China has a history of five thousand years, whereas the United States has a history of only about two hundred years.

按照他的方式做，會有人抱怨，按照你的方式做，則會犧牲我們的利益。
Doing it his way, some people will complain; however, by doing it your way, we will sacrifice our own interests.

A: 在你看來，男女在選擇對象的時候，條件上有什麼不同？
(回答問題) => B:

____

- **毫+Neg. + multiple-syllable words ("毫"originally meant "a small, fine hair" . When it is used with "不" or "沒", it means "not at all" [literally "not a small hair at all"])**

把某人的話當成耳邊風指的是你對某人的話毫不在乎。
"把某人的話當成耳邊風" means that you don't care about somebody's words at all.

股票價格的高低跟我毫無關係。
The rise and fall of stock prices have nothing to do with me.

他一點也不受影響
(也可以說) =>

- 隨著 **("隨著" means "along with … " and indicates that a certain thing changes in tandem with something else. It must be followed by a noun phrase. When the subject is placed in front of "隨著", "而" can be used in front of the verb to indicate a transformation).**

  隨著夏天的到來，到海邊游玩的人漸漸多了起來。
  到海邊游玩的人隨著夏天的到來而漸漸多了起來。
  With the arrival of summer there are more and more people come play at the beach.

  隨著經濟的發展，家長們對孩子的教育也越來越重視。
  Along with the development of the economy, parents treat the education of their children more and more seriously.

  某些順口溜會隨著時代的發展而漸漸消失。
  Along with the passing of time, some 順口溜 will disappear.

<u>說一說，這些現象會帶來什麼問題？</u>
(Remember that "隨著" needs to be followed by a noun phrase).

• 人口越來越多
• 男女朋友見面時間減少
• 油價上升

課堂活動

(一)

1. 說一說俗語和成語有什麼不同?	相對來說…, 文雅, 通俗, 場合, 對象, 親近, 禮貌, 生動, 比喻, (指的是/是指)
2. 什麼是順口溜?	流傳, 結構, 詩, 押韻, 幽默, 諷刺, 反映, 描寫, 現象, 范圍
3. 舉例子說說這些俗語的意思。	炒冷飯, 背黑鍋, 拍馬屁, 耳邊風, 打退堂鼓, 坐冷板凳, 半瓶醋, 開夜車, 騎著驢找馬

(二)角色扮演: role play

記者覺得"領導幹部四怕"這首順口溜非常有意思, 於是想進行一些采訪, 聽聽不同人的意見。如果你是 XXX 你會對記者說些什麼呢?試試看, 在你和記者的對話裏, 用上這些俗語:

炒冷飯/ 背黑鍋/拍馬屁/ 坐冷板凳/ 開夜車/ 耳邊風/ 打退堂鼓/ 騎著驢找馬

受采訪者:

領導幹部	幹部的老婆	幹部的情人	小姐	群眾

- 記者: 聽說……….,是真的嗎? 您能不能說一下您的看法?
- 受采訪者:

- 記者: 為什麼…….呢?
- 受采訪者:

(三)你的看法:

- 有首校園裏的順口溜是這麼說的: "大一嬌, 大二俏(qiào: pretty), 大三拉警報(set off the alarm), 大四沒人要。"意思是說, 女同學大學一二年級的時候可愛漂亮, 不怕沒有人追, 如果大學三年級還沒有男朋友, 就開始緊張, 大四大概就沒有希望了。你覺得這首順口溜反映了你的大學生活嗎? 說說你對大學生談戀愛的看法。

練習題

一. 詞彙練習:

(一) ***(表現 表示 表達 顯得 反映 描寫)See Lesson 8 for 表達 and 表示.***

1. 新雇來的廚師工作_____很好，我們應該給他增加工資。
2. 打掃乾淨以後，你的房間______比原來大了一倍。
3. 只要是跟中國有關的東西，這個老外都______出極大的興趣。
4. 要是你對領導有什麼看法或建議，你應該向他們______。
5. 他在小說中把人物的心理的活動______得很生動。
6. 一個學生的成績並不能全部______他的水平和能力。

(二) ***(半瓶醋 / 拍馬屁 / 碰釘子/ 炒冷飯 / 耳邊風/ 背黑鍋/打退堂鼓 / 騎驢找馬 / 坐冷板凳)***

1. 他的論文並沒有提出新的觀點，完全是在__________________。
2. 電話推銷員常常_______，打一百個電話，能做成兩個生意就不錯了。
3. 他這個人，喜歡人家給他______________。你要是說他帥，說他有能力，他就高興得不得了。
4. 老師上課強調的東西，都很重要,你千萬別當成__________________。
5. 她的能力不差，但老板總是不給她機會做重要的事情，總讓她_______________。
6. 她本來想學中文課，但一聽說功課很重，加上每天有小考，她就________________。
7. 打破杯子的是他，我卻替他______________，讓媽媽教訓了一頓。
8. 雖然她對目前的男朋友不太滿意，但也不想和他分手，只是________________，總希望碰上條件更好的男人。
9. A: 老張總跟我們說，他在公司裹表現怎麼怎麼好，他一定非常有能力吧？
   B: 他只是個 ____________________。真正有能力的人，是不會到處跟人說自己有多了不起的。

二. 語法和口語表達練習:

(一) 請用提供的句型改寫句子或完成對話

1. 你付出多少努力，你就有多大的進步。***(A 和 B 是相對的)***
2. 這個任務太重了，三天時間根本完成不了，開夜車也不行。**(即使…，也…)**
3. 他的父母怎麼教育他，他就怎麼教育自己的孩子。***(以…的方式)***
4. A: 你常常去中國，能不能談談中國年輕人跟美國年輕人有什麼不同？
   B: ______________________________。***(…，則…)***
5. A: 在中國能不能找到美式的快餐店？
   B: ______________________________。
   (滿+location +都是+NP)
6. A: 你跟我借的書，什麼時候還給我呀？
   B: ______________________________。***(明明…)***

(二)從下面的口語表達中選擇一個完成句子：

(不夠朋友　說 v 就 v　不好意思　再說了)

1. 你這個人真__________，說好今天一起去打球，你卻要陪女朋友看電影。
2. 等等，你別__________，聽我把話說完啊！
3. _______，我老婆做的飯味道可能不適合你們的口味，還請大家原諒。
4. 你這個題目是炒冷飯，不會有人感興趣的。_________，像你這樣一個半瓶醋，哪寫得出什麼好文章來？
5. (電話中)：對不起，路上塞車(sāichē)，我會晚點到。真_________，天氣這麼熱，還讓你等。

三．綜合練習；

老王在我們單位做部門負責人已經十幾年了，開始那幾年，大家都 1_____他有領導能力，而且能平等 2______每一個人。最近幾年，我們單位在福利 3______方面進行了一些改革，從此以後，我不斷聽到員工對老王的 4_____。大家普遍反映老王缺乏專業知識，不 5_____當領導。有人還指責老王 6______領導地位，給那些喜歡 7______他的人特別的照顧。最近有人甚至向我 8______老王私生活有問題。在我看來，即使一個人能把單位管理得很好，但有婚外關係或性丑聞 9______對單位的影響不好。10______是我所了解到的情況，請大家討論一下，我們要不要解雇老王。

1．a. 拍馬屁　b. 稱贊　c. 奉承
2．a. 對待　b. 利益　c. 承受
3．a. 群體　b. 制度　c. 中心
4．a. 奉承　b. 抱怨　c. 對待
5．a. 適合　b.合適　c. 拼命

6. a. 使用　b.利用　c. 親近
7. a. 拍馬屁　b. 議論　c. 奉承
8. a. 暗示　b. 諷刺　c. 表現
9. a. 儘管　b. 畢竟　c. 既然
10. a.其中　b.以上　c. 以下

四. 翻譯練習;

1. (review : 進行 Lesson 1, 資料 Lesson 6， 挑戰性 Lesson 4, 處罰 Lesson 2)

This is not a good time to try this criminal because we haven't collected enough data. We need to continue looking for it. The record shows that he was caught three times but was never punished. I know our task is very challenging. Though we might encounter difficulty, I hope we won't give up.

2. 隨著…，…　　相對來說

Along with the change in the system, the phenomenon of new employees needing to sacrifice weekends will gradually disappear. The senior employees express their frustration and discontent for this. They think that they made greater contributions to the company, but comparatively speaking, the company does't care about their benefit as much.

五. 作文: (從下邊幾個題目中, 選擇一個, 寫一篇不少於 500 字的作文。你至少要用四個所提供的句型或詞彙)

明明	A 和 B 是相對的	相對（…）來說	即時…也…
以…的方式…	A…， B 則…	豪不/無…	隨著…

1. 本課學了很多"審判"、"對待"、"碰釘子"等等這樣的詞，請你用這些詞寫一篇文章：

"請聽我解釋…"
--------------一個罪犯的心裏話

2. 談談在你的社會和文化中，在老百姓的眼中，政府領導都有什麼樣的形象 (xíngxiàng-image)。

第十課 談"吃"

Match the words in characters with Pinyin and English:

漢字	拼音	英文	哪兒學過
熟人			二年級
勺子			二年級
學問			二年級
瀉/拉肚子			二年級
特點			二年級
講究			第二課
吃苦			第三課
解決			第四課
幸福			第六課
雇			第七課
情景			第七課
工具			第八課
構成			第八課
感嘆			第八課
味道			第九課
反映			第九課

拼音

1. chīkǔ	2. fǎnyìng	3. gǎntàn	4. gōngjù
5. gòuchéng	6. gù	7. jiǎngjiū	8. qíngjǐng
9. sháozi	10.shóurén	11.tèdiǎn	12.wèidào
13.jiějué	14.xièdùzi	15.xìngfú	16.xuéwèn

英文

a. characteristic	b. flavor	c. happiness	d. spoon
e. knowledge	f. scene	g. to constitute	h. tool
i. to hire	j. to reflect; to report	k. to solve	l. to have a diarrhea
m. to sigh over sth.	n. acquaintance; friend	o. to be particular about	p. to suffer hardships

聽力&口語

聽錄音回答問題

對話一

1.	2.	3.	4.	5.

生詞：不外乎，食欲，生菜，牛排，吃驚，優秀
複習：老婆，反正，可憐，手藝，出差，炫耀，說 vp 就 vp，真是的

對話二

1.	2.	3.	4.	5.

生詞：蘿蔔　土豆，蒸，燒，蔬菜，營養
複習：討厭，原本，無所謂，限制，(刀叉，西紅柿，黄瓜，魚，肉，豐富，新鮮)

對話三

1.	2.	3.	4.	5.

生詞：左宗棠雞，色香味，無處不在，北京烤鴨，地區
向往，先進，禁不住，相聚，精通，氣候，(特色菜)
複習：手藝，可惜，懷念，真正，味道，何況，技術，發達
寂寞，貢獻，追求，個人，享受，感動，事業，一帆風順

根據對話一回答問題：

1. 朋友請阿強吃飯，阿強為什麼回家還那麼餓 (è) 呢？
2. 阿強為什麼建議老婆周六做二十個菜？
3. 為什麼阿強的老婆不希望外國男人娶中國女人？這改變了他們周六的計劃嗎？阿強怎麼認為？

根據對話二回答問題：

1. 小強的媽媽今天給他做了哪些顏色的漂亮好菜？她做了土豆嗎？
2. 媽媽做的魚小強喜歡嗎？為什麼？
3. 小強不喜歡吃肉嗎？媽媽怎麼說呢？小強聽媽媽的話嗎？為什麼？

根據對話三回答問題：

1. 安妮來找阿健，想讓阿健教她什麼？阿健教她了嗎？為什麼？
2. 安妮覺得在美國吃中國飯容易嗎？為什麼？阿健對美國的中國飯館有什麼看法？安妮同意嗎？安妮喜歡中國菜嗎？你怎麼知道？
3. 阿健在美國學什麼？安妮為什麼覺得阿建畢業以後應該在哪兒工作？為什麼？阿健覺得呢？他如果回了中國，會懷念什麼？

口語用法

1. 你一會兒這樣，一會兒那樣，像個孩子似的。(“一會兒這樣，一會兒那樣” is used when you complain about someone changing his mind from time to time. You can also replace “這樣” and “那樣” with a verb phrase if you want to be more specific, such as “一會兒想去，一會兒又不想去”).

你一會兒這樣，一會兒那樣, 真煩人。
It is such an annoyance when you change your mind from time to time.

你一會兒想去，一會兒不想去。我不管你了！
You want to go one moment, but don't want to go the next moment. I'll leave you alone.

他一會兒說她很文雅，一會兒又說她沒有禮貌？你怎麼這樣變來變去？
Why did he say that she is graceful at one moment and then say that she has bad manners at the next moment? How can you flip-flop like a silly frog?

2. 來了來了！ (“來了來了” is used to tell people that you are coming now, or that someone / something is coming now after a long wait).

A: 該上車了！我們馬上就要離開了！
B: 來了來了！
A: It is time to get on the bus! We will depart soon.
B: I am coming.

來了來了，不好意思，讓你們久等了。
Here I am. Sorry about making you wait.

(服務員)：來了來了。這是您要的炒飯，和您的牛肉麵。
(Waiter): Here you are. This is your stir-fried rice and your beef noodles.

A: 等了這麼久，小張怎麼還不來啊！
B: 來了來了，你看連女朋友也一起帶來了。
A: We have been waiting for so long. Why hasn't Little Zhang shown up yet?
B: Here he is. Look, he brought his girlfriend too.

3. 你喜歡也得吃，不喜歡也得吃。("…也+VP, …也+VP" means there is only one possible outcome regardless of which of the opposite situations mentioned in the two clauses actually happens).

你喜歡也得吃，不喜歡也得吃。
Whether you like it or not, you have to eat it.

你要繼續住也好，要搬走也好，明天以前得讓我知道。
Whether you want to stay or move out, you have to give me an answer by tomorrow.

我瞞著他他也抱怨，告訴他他也抱怨。
Whether I tell him or not, he complains.

4. 那倒也是。(When you use "那倒也是", you indicate that, upon further consideration, you agree with the speaker).

A: 我們找小林幫忙吧！
B: 他是個挺固執的人，找他幫忙很可能會碰釘子，說不定他會反對我們做這件事。
A: 那倒也是。咱們還是先瞞著他好了。
A: Let's ask Little Lin for help
B: He is a stubborn person. We are likely to be snubbed if we ask him for help. Perhaps he will even give us opposition.
A: Yeah, I guess you are right. Let's not let him know about it for now.

A: 小李對公司的利益怎麼一副毫不在乎的樣子？我真想把他給解雇了！
B: 他雖然有一點不在乎，但對公司還是有很大貢獻的。再說，把他解雇了，要重新找人也不容易啊！
A: 那倒也是。
A: How come Little Li appears not to care about the interests of the company at all? I really want to fire him.
B: He is a little indifferent to the company's interests, but he still makes a big contribution to the company. Besides, if you fire him, it also wouldn't be easy to recruit a new person.
A: Yeah, I guess you are right.

5. 這裏中國飯的味道的確很差.("的確" means "indeed, really" .It can also be said as "的確是", "的確"and "的確是"are used to strengthen one's positive response to another's comments or questions).

你說的沒錯，他這個人的確很喜歡炫耀。
You were right. He indeed likes to show off.

官僚作風的確是很難避免的。
Bureaucracy is indeed hard to avoid.

他的確不太了解當時的情況。
It's true that he didn't really understand the situation at the time.

6. 別提了！(I don't want to talk about it; I don't want to mention it)

A: 人家說重慶美女滿大街。怎麼樣？你碰到美女沒有？
B: 別提了，不但沒碰到美女，還被丑女罵了。
A: They say that there are beauties everywhere on the streets of Chongqing. How was your experience? Did you encounter beauties?
B: I don't want to talk about it. I didn't encounter any beauty; instead, I was reprimanded by some ugly women.

A: 你進的是大公司，福利制度應該不錯吧！
B: 別提了，什麼福利都沒有，還得小心，做不好會被解雇呢。
A: You joined a big company. I suppose that they have good benefits.
B: Don't talk about that. I don't have any benefits at all; besides, I have to be careful not to make mistakes or they will fire me.

7. 別這麼說，我都不好意思了。("別這麼說" means "please don't say that." It can be used to respond to praise or to give others a comfort or suggestion).

A: 你真是了不起，懂得那麼多，卻從來都不自大。
B: 別這麼說，我都不好意思了。
A: You are really something. You are so knowledgeable but you never show off in front of others.
B: Don't say so. I'm embarrassed.

A: 真是不好意思，我在這兒就像是多余的，什麼也幫不上。
B: 你別這麼說。有你在我們就高興得很，什麼忙也不需要你幫。
A: I'm really sorry. I feel like I'm unneeded. There is nothing I can do to help.
B: Don't say that. We are so happy that you are here. You don't need to help with anything.

你別這麼說，他會生氣的。Don't say that. He will be angry.

8. 怪不得 (When“怪不得” means “no wonder” , it is equal to “難怪”; When there is an object after “怪不得”, it means “can’t blame”).

A: 這道菜是從餐廳買的，不是我自己做的。
B: 怪不得 **(/難怪)** 這麼好吃，我還以為你有這麼好的手藝呢！
This was bought from a restaurant, not made by me.
No wonder it’s so delicious. I almost thought you had great cooking skills.

他給你打了那麼多次電話你都不回，怪不得 **(/難怪)**人家現在不理你了。
He called you so many times and you never answered. No wonder he does not want to talk to you now. (You can’t blame that he doesn’t talk to you now).

這工作是你自己要做的，現在弄得這麼累，只能怪你自己，怪不得別人。
You are the one who wanted this job. Now you get so tired. There is no one but yourself to blame.

口語練習：請用聽力對話裏學到的生詞和口語用法討論下面的問題：

(S) + 一會兒…，一會兒… (as in 你一會兒這樣，一會兒那樣)
(S)…也得，不…也得… (as in 你喜歡也得吃，不喜歡也得吃)
那倒也是 /　　的確 /　　別提了 /　　別這麼說 /
難怪/怪不得/　來了來了

1. A B- 你們是中國人，打算請美國朋友到家裏用飯。
   A 覺得應該做美國菜
   B 覺得應該做中國菜。

2. A- 你是媽媽，你的孩子不喜歡吃蔬菜，你想逼他吃。
   B- 你是孩子，喜歡吃肉，你覺得自己想吃什麼就吃什麼，媽媽不應該管。

3. A B – 你們現在在美國。A 是美國人，在中國留學過一年。B 是中國人，現在在美國留學。你們討論 B 畢業後應不應該回中國。

課文

第一部分

中國有句古話叫“民以食為天”。對中國人來說，“吃”向來都是頭等大事。現代漢語中，“吃”這個字可以說是無處不在。不但能吃肉、吃菜，還能“吃苦、吃驚、吃虧”；“受不了”可以說“吃不消”；“一個人很受歡迎”可以說他“吃得開”；熟人見面會問“你吃過了嗎”；老朋友相聚則要一起吃頓飯，好像只有在飯桌上才能找回曾經無話不說的感覺。

中國人重視吃，也很會吃。中國菜，從材料到做法，五花八門，豐富多樣。有人開玩笑說“天上飛的，地上跑的，水裏游的，沒有中國人不吃的”；做法上，煎、煮、炒、炸，燒、烤、燜、蒸等等，可以說是千變萬化。另外，不同地區，菜的做法和味道也不盡相同，但都講究“色、香、味”，也就是說，一道菜要看著好看、聞著好聞、吃著好吃才算是好菜。

中國菜的材料和做法很複雜，但中國人用餐的工具卻很簡單，一個勺子一雙筷子就解決了所有吃的問題。相比之下，西方人吃的不外乎生菜、沙拉和牛排，但刀叉盤子，桌布餐巾，每一樣都不能少。用餐時，中國人喜歡用蔥、薑、蒜、醋、辣椒等佐料，這不但能增進食欲、幫助消化，而且也能起殺菌的作用。飯桌上，中國人喜歡熱鬧。生意好的飯館，遠遠地就能聽到人們說笑或者勸酒勸菜；為了增加熱鬧氣氛，過去飯館的老板還專門雇人來唱歌唱戲。

生詞用法

1	民以食为天	民以食為天	mínyǐshí wéitiān	Food is the most important thing in the eyes of the people.	
2	向来	向來	xiànglái	always; all along	我爸爸向來都不吸煙。/ 他向來喜歡遲到一會兒。
3	头等	頭等	tóuděng	first-class	
4	无处不在	無處不在	wúchù búzài	to exist everywhere	在美國，中國飯館無處不在。/ 這種迷信觀念無處不在。
5	吃惊	吃驚	chījīng	to be surprised; to be shocked; to be amazed	他說他離婚了，我們都很吃驚。/聽他這麼說，我吃了一驚。/ 他小小年紀就挑起養家的重擔，讓我們大吃一驚。
6	吃亏	吃虧	chīkuī	to suffer loss; to be taken advantage of	我吃了她的虧。/他這筆生意吃大虧了。/ 他很老實，跟別人打交道的時候總是吃虧。/你小心一點，他一點虧都不會吃的。
7	吃不消	吃不消	chībùxiāo	can't take it; can't endure it	一天工作十個小時，你吃得消嗎？/這件事讓我累得吃不消。
8	吃得开	吃得開	chīdekāi	to be popular; to get along well	他很帥(shuài)，在那群女孩子中很吃得開。/ 真正有能力的人在哪兒都能吃得開。
9	相聚	相聚	xiāngjù	to get together	跟朋友相聚/跟親戚相聚/老同學們偶爾相聚一次。
10	无话不说	無話不說	wúhuà bùshuō	to talk about everything; to hide nothing	他和媽媽無話不說。 /他們倆是無話不說的好朋友。
11	材料	材料	cáiliào	ingredient; material	建筑材料/學習材料/做菜的材料
12	五花八门	五花八門	wǔhuā bāmén	a wide variety of; a motley variety of	五花八門的商品/五花八門的服務/那條街很熱鬧，五花八門的商店一直開到晚上十二點。
13	丰富多样	豐富多樣	fēngfù duōyàng	to allow to choose from many kinds and many categories	豐富多樣的選擇/商店裏的水果豐富多樣。(used as an adjecive)
14	煎	煎	jiān	to pan fry; to fry in a shallow oil	煎餃子/煎魚/煎豆腐/煎肉/這牛排還沒煎熟呢！
15	烧	燒	shāo	to stew after frying or to fry after stewing; to cook	燒雞/燒豆腐/燒牛肉/燒茄子(qiézi-eggplant)/你休息吧，我來燒飯。

16	烤	烤	kǎo	to bake; to roast; to toast; to BBQ	烤蛋糕(dàngāo)/ 烤麵包(bread)/ 烤鴨/烤雞/烤羊肉串(chuàn: skewer)
17	焖	燜	mèn (also as mēn in Taiwan)	to allow to simmer in a covered pot	燜飯/燜羊肉/燜牛肉/紅燜羊肉/把肉放在鍋裏再燜一會兒。
18	蒸	蒸	zhēng	to steam	蒸饅頭(mántou-bun)/蒸包子/清蒸魚
19	千变万化	千變萬化	qiānbiàn wànhuà	to vary in thousands of ways; kaleidoscopic change	家常菜(home-style cooking)也可以千變萬化。/毛衣有千變萬化種織法。
20	地区	地區	dìqū	region; area; district	多山的地區/發達地區/貧窮地區/你住的那個地區環境怎麼樣?
21	不尽相同	不盡相同	bújìn xiāngtóng	not completely the same	美國英語和英國英語的詞彙和語法不盡相同。見語法
22	色香味	色香味	sè xiāng wèi	color, smell, and flavor	中國人做菜講究色香味俱全(jùquán)。
23	道	道	dào	a measure word designating a course of a meal	一道川菜/你想點幾道菜? /這個飯館上一道菜需要這麼長時間，我等得都沒有耐心了。
24	用餐	用餐	yòngcān	to dine	用餐習慣/用餐時間/ 用餐工具/先生，請用餐。
25	不外乎	不外乎	búwàihū	nothing else but	他的歌不外乎愛呀、情呀。/他每天哭喊不外乎兩個原因，一是被逼練鋼琴，一是被迫吃蔬菜。見語法
26	生菜	生菜	shēngcài	an uncooked vegetable; lettuce	
27	沙拉	沙拉	shāla	salad	
28	牛排	牛排	niúpái	beef steak	羊排/ 豬排/ 魚排
29	刀叉	刀叉	dāochā	fork and knife	一副刀叉
30	桌布	桌布	zhuōbù	table cloth	一塊桌布
31	餐巾	餐巾	cānjīn	napkin (餐巾紙 = paper napkin)	麻煩你給我一張餐巾紙。
32	葱	蔥	cōng	green onion; scallion (洋蔥 = onion)	一根蔥/一把蔥
33	姜	薑	jiāng	ginger	一塊薑/幾片薑

34	蒜	蒜	suàn	garlic (usually appears as 大蒜)	一頭大蒜/一瓣(bàn : a glove of)蒜
35	辣椒	辣椒	làjiāo	hot pepper; chili	紅辣椒/辣椒粉(fěn: powder)/辣椒醬(jiàng: sauce)
36	佐料	佐料	zuǒliào	sauce	吃餃子得要醋、醬油(jiàngyoú-soysauce)、香油(sesame oil)等佐料。
37	增进	增進	zēngjìn	to enhance	增進食欲/增進健康/增進友誼(yǒuyì-friendship)/增進文化交流/增進了解/增進父母和孩子之間的關係
38	食欲	食欲	shíyù	appetite	運動可以增進食欲。/我的問題不是沒食欲，而是食欲太強。/跟這樣的人一起吃飯，讓我一點食欲都沒有。
39	消化	消化	xiāohuà	to digest; digestion	這個東西很難消化/ 我這幾天消化不好，總是沒食欲。/每天下課以後要複習一下，這樣才能消化學過的東西。/今天學了這麼多生詞，我一天消化不了。
40	杀菌	殺菌	shājūn	to sterilize; to kill germs	(Taiwan: shājùn)
41	作用	作用	zuòyòng	effect; function	這個藥沒什麼作用。("起…作用"見語法)
42	劝酒劝菜 勸酒勸菜		quànjiǔ quàncài	to urge sb. to drink and eat more	在西方，過分勸酒是不禮貌的。/中國人認為勸酒勸菜是很有必要的。
43	增加	增加	zēngjiā	to increase; to add	增加工作量/學中文的學生人數每年都在增加。
44	气氛	氣氛	qìfen	atmosphere; air	學習氣氛/工作氣氛/友好的氣氛/緊張的氣氛/競爭的氣氛/ 西方人講究用餐時的氣氛。
45	专门	專門	zhuānmén	special; specialized; specially	專門的技術/專門為兒童寫的故事/專門為你做的飯/為了你，他專門從紐約開車來到這裏。
46	唱戏	唱戲	chàngxì	to act in a Chinese opera or play	

課文

第二部分

討論中國菜，不能不提菜名，中國菜名裏藏著很多學問。一般來說，菜名中常常會看到烹調方法和材料，例如“涼拌黃瓜”、“紅燒牛肉”、“炒土豆絲”、“西紅柿炒雞蛋”、“青椒肉絲”；有時候菜名由菜的味道和材料構成，例如“甜酸雞”、“麻辣羊肉”、“香辣肉片”；有的菜名中出現一個地方的名字，表示這個菜是該地方的特色菜，例如“北京烤鴨”，“四川泡菜”；有的菜名跟歷史典故有關係，例如“左宗棠雞”；有的菜名則完全看不出來是什麼材料做的，比方說你聽到東北菜“大豐收”，一定不知道是什麼東西，但當你看到黃瓜、西紅柿、蘿蔔等五顏六色的蔬菜放在一起，你一定會聯想到秋天收獲的季節、大豐收的情景，也禁不住會感嘆“大豐收”這個菜名的美好創意。

講究的中國人還非常重視食物的涼性和熱性。魚呀、蝦呀等海鮮屬於涼性，羊肉則屬於熱性。涼性的菜吃多了會瀉肚子，熱性的菜吃多了則會上火。因此，優秀的廚師不但注意菜的營養，也會根據食物的涼熱性，配合氣候的特點、季節的變化來決定該做什麼菜。記得一位精通中西文化的大學者曾說過，世界上最令人向往的幸福生活，就是在英國的鄉下，住一個帶有最先進水電系統的美國式大房子，娶一個日本老婆，擁有一個法國情人，再加上一個中國廚師。聽起來很可笑，但也幽默地反映了中國菜在這位大學者心中的地位。

生詞用法

47	藏	藏	cáng	to hide	你把錢藏在哪兒了？/ 他藏在床下面。/快把這本書藏起來了，別讓他看見。
48	学问	學問	xuéwen	learning; knowledge (有學問 = knowledgeable)	他的學問很高。/中國人的名字裏藏著很多學問。/ 他是一個很有學問的教授。
49	烹调	烹調	pēngtiáo	to cook (dishes); cooking	烹調中國菜/烹調方法/我喜歡中國式的烹調。
50	凉拌	涼拌	liángbàn	(said of food) cold and dressed with sauce	涼拌菜/涼拌面/涼拌生菜
51	黄瓜	黃瓜	huánggua	cucumber	一根黃瓜/兩條黃瓜/ 涼拌黃瓜
52	红烧	紅燒	hóngshāo	to braise or stew in soy sauce	紅燒肉/紅燒魚
53	土豆丝	土豆絲	tǔdòusī	shredded potato (土豆 is also called 馬鈴薯 [mǎlíngshǔ]) (絲 = thread or thread like thing)	炒土豆絲/土豆炒肉絲
54	西红柿	西紅柿	xīhóngshì	tomato (also called 番茄[fānqié])	西紅柿湯/西紅柿炒雞蛋
55	青椒	青椒	qīngjiāo	green pepper	
56	甜酸鸡	甜酸雞	tiánsuānjī	sweet and sour chicken	
57	麻辣 麻辣		málà	numbing-hot	四川麻辣鍋(guō: pot)
	该	該	gāi	this; that; the aforementioned (used in written Chinese or formal speech)　見語法	
58	北京烤鸭 北京烤鴨		Běijīng kǎoyā	Peking duck	一只北京烤鴨
59	四川泡菜 四川泡菜		Sìchuān pàocài	Sichuan pickled vegetables	(泡菜 = pickles)
60	左宗棠鸡 左宗棠雞		Zuǒ Zōng-táng jī	General Tso's Chicken	also known as 左公雞、宮保雞丁 (Gōngbǎo jīdīng)
61	丰收	豐收	fēngshōu	bumper crop; a good harvest	蘋果豐收的季節/ 今年玉米(yùmǐ: corn)能獲得豐收。

62	萝卜	蘿卜	luóbo	radish	白蘿蔔/胡蘿蔔(or 紅蘿蔔)：carrot
63	五颜六色	五顏六色	wǔyán liùsè	colorful	你看那些五顏六色的魚在水裏自由地游來游去。/這裏的花五顏六色，漂亮極了。
64	蔬菜	蔬菜	shūcài	vegetables; greens	蔬菜豐收了。/這片土地上種了很多蔬菜。
65	联想	聯想	liánxiǎng	to associate with; to connect in the mind	提起美國，人們就會聯想到自由女神(statue of liberty)。/聽到那個音樂，我就會聯想到我的那次夏威夷(Xiàwēiyí-Hawaii)旅行。/你那麼說容易讓人引起不好的聯想。
66	收获	收獲	shōuhuò	to harvest; to gather in the crops; to gain; the harvest; gain (n.)	農人忙著收獲桔子(júzi) / 我的努力很有收獲。/你觀察了那麼長時間，有什麼收獲？
67	季节	季節	jìjié	season	收獲季節/開花的季節/季節變化/一年有四個季節。/這是一種季節性的現象。
68	禁不住	禁不住	jīnbuzhù	can't help doing sth; can't refrain from; = 不禁	看見她的頭發，我們都禁不住(/不禁)大笑起來。/這麼好吃的菜，我禁不住(/不禁)吃了一盤又一盤。
69	美好	美好	měihǎo	fine; happy and beautiful	美好的回憶/美好的風景/美好的日子
70	创意	創意	chuàngyì	originality	廣告(guǎnggào)創意/美好的創意/你的畫非常有創意。
71	虾	蝦	xiā	shrimp	一盤紅燒大蝦/一只大龍蝦(lobster)
72	海鲜	海鮮	hǎixiān	seafood	
73	上火	上火	shànghuǒ	to suffer from excessive internal heat (according to traditional Chinese medicine)	我昨天吃了太多辣椒，上火了。
74	优秀	優秀	yōuxiù	outstanding; excellent	優秀運動員/優秀的老師/這個學生向來表現優秀。/他的成績很優秀。

75	营养	營養	yíngyǎng	nutrition (有營養 = nourishing; nutritious)	雞肉的營養很高。/ 這個菜很有營養。/你只吃這些東西營養不夠。
76	配合	配合	pèihé	to coordinate; in step with	我們一塊兒工作，不能總是讓我配合你，你也得配合我。/他們非常有默契，兩人總是配合得很好。
77	气候	氣候	qìhòu	climate	溫和的氣候/熱帶氣候/ 寒帶(hándài)氣候
78	精通	精通	jīngtōng	to get a thorough knowledge of; to have a good command of	他精通英語。/他精通中國歷史。/你至少要精通一門手藝。
79	学者	學者	xuézhě	scholar	訪問學者 = a visiting scholar
80	向往	向往	xiàng wǎng	to yearn for; to look forward to	向往自由/ 令人向往的幸福生活/
81	乡下	鄉下	xiāngxià	countryside	他一向住在鄉下，剛搬到城裏，很不適應。
82	先进	先進	xiānjìn	advanced	先進的網絡技術/先進的教育制度/ 先進和落後是相對的。
83	系统	系統	xìtǒng	system; systematically	消化系統/組織系統/經濟系統/先進的網絡系統/ 要系統地學習中國歷史。/他系統地研究了一下中國各個地區的建筑特點。

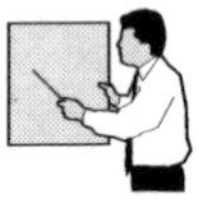

句型和語法

- 從 … 到 …　　**(“From …to …”).**

中國菜從材料到做法，五花八門，豐富多樣。
From ingredients to methods of preparation, Chinese cuisine is complex and full of variety.

這個旅遊網站從旅遊景點到酒店價錢都有很好的介紹。
This travel website offers very good explanations of everything from tourist attractions to hotel rates.

他的興趣很廣，從歷史小說到電子工程方面的書他都看。

His interests are varied; his reading matter ranges from historical fiction to texts on electrical engineering.

- 不盡(相同) **(不盡 means "not completely". It is usually followed by a two-syllable verb, and used as a prefix such as in 不盡滿意，or 不盡相信. A 和 B 不盡相同 means "A and B are not completely the same".)**

雖然他們都來自中國，他們普通話的口音卻不盡相同。
Although they all come from China, their accents are not completely the same.

對於為什麼分手，他們兩人的說法不盡相同.
The reasons they gave for the break-up were not completely the same.

他說的和做的不太一樣。
(也可以說) =>

- …，相比之下，… **("comparatively speaking"; This pattern is used to emphasize a comparison. The main point always comes in the second clause after the pattern. See also "和…相比" in Lesson 8)**

中國菜的做法很複雜，相比之下，美國菜的做法就簡單得多。
The methods of preparation of Chinese food are very complex; comparatively speaking, American cuisine is much simpler.

美國教育重視孩子的獨立性和和創造力；相比之下，中國父母比較重視孩子的學習成績。
Encouraging independence and creativity in children is viewed as important in American education; comparatively speaking, Chinese parents are more focused on their children's grades.

日文，法文的語法都很複雜；相比之下，中文的語法就簡單得多。
Japanese and French are complicated in terms of grammar; comparatively speaking, Chinese grammar is much easier.

私立大學的學費非常貴，公立大學呢？
(回答問題) =>

- 不外乎 **(to be) no more than; (to be) just**

中國人認為西方人吃的不外乎生菜，沙拉和牛排。

Chinese people think Westerners eat nothing but raw vegetables, salad and steaks.

語言課考試的方式不外乎筆試和口試兩種。
Tests in language classes involve nothing but writing and oral examinations.

一個人的成功不外乎努力加上運氣。
Individual success depends only on determination and luck.

要怎麼學好中文？
(回答問題) =>

- 起(…的)作用　　**(to take effect ; to cause an effect; to take action)**

佐料中的蔥、薑、蒜都能起殺菌的作用。
Among spices, onion, ginger, and garlic all have the effect of killing germs.

古代的萬裏長城對當時的中國起了很重要的保護作用。
In ancient China, the Great Wall was instrumental in the protection of China.

1972 年中國乒乓球隊訪問美國，這對兩國交流起了很重要的促進作用。
The 1972 visit of the Chinese national Ping-Pong team to the US had a very important impact on the communication between the two countries.

為什麼要養成一個好的運動習慣？
(回答問題) =>

- 該 + **Noun ("該" in front of a noun in written Chinese or formal speech means "this; that; the aforementioned ")**

我去過北京大學，並和該校的大學生進行過多次交流。
I have been to Beijing University and have exchanged ideas with the college students there many times.

他最後選擇了臺北醫院，原因是該(醫)院大多數醫生擁有五年以上的經驗。
In the end he chose Taipei hospital. The reason was because most of the doctors there have more than five years of experience.

學校將派劉小麗到重慶接受培訓。該(學)生曾經多次贏得全省數學比賽冠軍，在四川是個有名的人物。

The school will send Liu Xiaoli to Chongqing for training. This student was the champion of the Province Math Competition, and is a well-known person in Sichuan.

- 禁不住 **(Same as"不禁"; "can't help (doing something)"; This phrase is followed by a verb or a verb phrase).**

看到五顏六色的蔬菜放在一起，令人禁不住/不禁感嘆"大豐收"這個菜名的美好。
On seeing the many colors of the different vegetables next to each other, people can't help but exclaim that "The Great Harvest" is a well-named dish.

看到朋友穿的新外套又時髦又好看，她禁不住/不禁也去買了一件。
Seeing her friend wearing the new, fashionable jacket, she couldn't resist going out to buy one herself.

聽到父親病重的消息，他禁不住/不禁哭了起來
Receiving the news of his father's illness, he couldn't help but cry out loud.

(完成句子) => 看到朋友領養的中國小孩這麼可愛，______________

- **...a 呀, b 呀 (The particle "呀" can be used after each of the similar things in the list when you give examples).**

中國菜的做法千變萬化，煎呀、蒸呀、炸呀什麼的比較容易，燒呀、烤呀什麼的，就複雜一點。
There are thousands of ways to make a Chinese dish. Pan-frying, steaming, and deep-frying are examples of easy ways; as for stewing and roasting, they are a little more complicated.

他吃飯時喜歡加佐料，蔥呀、蒜呀、薑呀什麼的，一樣不能少。
He likes to add sauce and seasonings when he eats. Things like scallions, garlic, and ginger can't be absent.

課堂活動

(一) 用課文裏學到的生詞和句型回答問題：

- 我們可以從哪些方面看出“吃”對中國人的重要？(民以食為天，頭等大事，無處不在，無話不談)
- 請談談中國菜的材料和做法。(五花八門，豐富多樣，千變萬化，不盡相同，色香味)
- 和西方人吃西餐相比，中國人的用餐習慣有什麼特點？(不外乎，相比之下，佐料，食慾，消化，起…作用， 勸酒勸菜)
- 中國菜的菜名藏著什麼樣的學問？(烹調，材料，由…構成，聯想)
- 什麼是食物的涼性、熱性？這對中國人做菜有什麼影響？(營養，配合，氣候，優秀，精通)

(二)從不同的角度(**jiǎodù**)來討論:

- 在北京一個外國人集中的地區，開什麼飯館生意最好？
  - 中國廚師
  - 法國廚師
  - 喜歡麥當勞的中國政府官員
  - 精通中西文化的學者

- 這條魚該怎麼做最好？
  - 美國人
  - 中國人
  - 印度人
  - 日本人

(三) 你的看法

- 佛教認為，人應該吃素。近年來，素食(sùshí: vegetarian dinning)的觀念在世界各地也越來越流行。 你同意佛教的看法嗎？你覺得為什麼素食越來越受歡迎？你會吃素嗎？
- 你相信食物的涼性熱性嗎？有人把這看成迷信，你的看法是什麼？

練習題

一. 詞彙練習：(請選用最合適的詞來完成句子)

(一) 吃驚／吃虧／吃得開／吃不消

1. 李老板做生意很厲害；賺錢第一，向來不__________。
2. 聽說老張這個老實人也搞婚外關係，真令人__________。
3. 他性格開朗，又常幫助人，非常受歡迎，到哪兒都__________。
4. 我這學期選了六門課，幾乎天天都得開夜車，真有點兒__________。

(二) 無處不在／無話不說／五花八門／五顏六色／千變萬化／不盡相同

1. 這個商場裏的商品______________，什麼都有。
2. 他是我最好的朋友，我跟他 __________。
3. 大湖邊的風景 __________,隨著季節與氣候的變化天天都不同。
4. 春天到了，花園裏開滿了______________的花，美麗極了。
5. 在紐約(New York)，中國飯館 ______________，可見中國菜有多麼受紐約人歡迎了。
6. 這兩家四川飯館菜單差不多都一樣，但菜的味道 ______________。

二. 句型和口語表達練習：(請用提示的句型完成下面的句子)

1. 一般人心目中的英國名校，______________________________。*(不外乎)*
2. 交中國朋友對我學習中文____________________________。*(起了…的作用)*
3. 老一輩的中國人很忌諱搬家，___________________________。*(相比之下)*
4. 那部關於領養孤兒的電影太讓人感動了，__________________。*(禁不住)*
5. A: 這些沙拉看起來一點都不好吃。
   B：我們沒有別的選擇，______________________________ 。*(X 也得…，不X 也得…)*

三．閱讀練習：

喝酒為什麼要碰杯？

不管在哪個國家，親朋好友相聚的時候，都免不了要喝酒。雖然各國的酒，味道不盡相同，但各地的人喝酒時似乎都有碰杯的習慣。喝酒為什麼要碰杯呢？

目前有兩種說法。一種說法是古希臘人(Xīlà-Greek)創造的。據說古希臘人注意到這樣一個事實：在舉杯飲酒之時，人的五官都可以分享到喝酒的樂趣，鼻子能聞到酒的香味，眼睛能看到酒的顏色，嘴巴和舌頭都能夠嘗到酒的香味，而只有耳朵最可憐，什麼也享受不到。怎麼辦呢?希臘人想出一個辦法：在喝酒之前，互相碰一下酒杯，杯子發出的清脆的響聲傳到耳朵中，這樣，耳朵就和其他部位一樣，也能享受到喝酒的樂趣了，同時也給喝酒增加了一種熱鬧的氣氛。

另一種說法是，喝酒碰杯源於古羅馬(Luómǎ -Rome)。古代的羅馬人喜歡功夫，常常進行比較危險的比賽。開始比賽以前，比賽者習慣飲酒，以此表示互相鼓勵。由於酒是事先準備的，為了防止有的人在給對方喝的酒中放毒，人們想出一個辦法，就是在比賽前，比賽者將自己的酒向對方的酒杯中倒一些，然後再喝。漸漸地，這個規定發展成一個習慣，人們喝酒的時候都禁不住碰一下杯子。也許只有在“叮當”一聲中，這酒喝起來才更有味道。

毒 dú: poison

<u>根據上文判斷對錯：（True or False）</u>

1. 作者認為，喝酒碰杯這種習慣，在世界各國都很普遍。
2. 根據上文，“五官”指的是人身上的五個部位。
3. 從上文中我們可以知道，羅馬人常常進行喝酒比賽。
4. 當初古羅馬人喝酒碰杯為的是安全(ānquán)，古希臘人喝酒碰杯為的是樂趣。
5. 從上文中我們可以知道，關於碰杯，作者認為第二種說法更值得相信。

四．　翻譯練習

1. I like to go to the country in harvest season; although houses in the countryside lack advanced plumbing and electrical systems, you can eat all kinds of fresh vegetables and fruits everyday. We barbecue under the trees, we eat on the grass, and the atmosphere is extremely relaxed.

2. 向來　　從…到…

Professor Shi is not just a scholar with deep understanding of Eastern and Western cultures; he is also an outstanding cook. He has always enjoyed cooking. From ingredients, to cooking methods, he is particular about everything. He thinks spicy food is best for increasing appetite, so when he has a get-together with friends, he always wants to eat Szechuan food.

3. 的確　　別這麼說

A: Your cooking skills are really good! These dishes look great, smell great and taste great.

B: Don't say so. I am embarrassed. Actually, when I cook, I only care about the nutrition and whether it is easy to digest.

4. 配合　　向往　　一會兒…，一會兒…

I am his secretary, so of course I should coordinate with him. However, he changes his mind every other minute. One minute he wants this, the next minute he wants something else. I don't know how much longer I can stand it. I really look forward to the day of my retirement.

五．作文：(從下邊幾個題目中，選擇一個，寫一篇不少於500字的作文。你至少要用六個所提供的句型或詞彙)

A…, 相比之下, B…	不外乎	的確
起…的作用	…不盡相同	該(as a pronoun)
a 呀，b 呀，...	從...到...	禁不住

1. 根據你所熟悉的文化，也談談"吃"。

2. 談談你對中國菜的了解，你相信食物有涼熱性嗎？

3. 一個地方的飲食(diet)習慣和當地人們的性格有沒有關係？請舉例說明。

4. 最近，吃素(vegetarian dinning)的觀念越來越流行，這些人吃素有哪些原因？你的看法？

5. 你是一位美食雜誌(Gourmet Magazine)的記者，請你介紹一家有特色的飯館。請包括：地點(location)，飯館的特點，廚師的介紹，有什麼特色菜(材料，作法)，飯館的氣氛，服務態度，價錢，適合什麼樣的客人，你為什麼推薦(tuījiàn: to recommend) 等等。

第十一課 中國的搖滾歌手崔健

Match the words in characters with Pinyin and English:

漢字	拼音	英文	哪兒學過
警察			二年級
深			二年級
廣			二年級
方向			二年級
與			二年級
末			二年級
聲音			二年級
初			二年級
追求			第一課
出版			第三課
挑戰			第四課
感受			第六課
表達			第八課
大量			第八課
隨著			第九課
浪漫			第九課

拼音

1. biǎodá	2. chū	3. chūbǎn	4. dàliàng
5. gǎnshòu	6. guǎng	7. jǐngchá	8. mò
9. shēn	10. làngmàn	11. fāngxiàng	12. suízhe
13. tiǎozhàn	14. zhuīqiú	15. yǔ	16. shēngyīn

英文

a. to publish	b. a great quantity	c. along with	d. to challenge
e. the beginning of	f. to experience; feelings	g. direction	h. and
i. deep	j. the end of	k. to express	l. to pursue
m. voice	n. broad; wide	o. police	p. romantic

聽力&口語

聽錄音回答問題

對話一

1.	2.	3.	4.	5.

生詞：**體育館，抗議，謠言，氣溫，吶喊**

複習：鍛煉，食堂，抱怨，福利，退休，計劃，帶領
領導，爭取，一成不變，起作用，動不動就

對話二

1.	2.	3.	4.	5.

生詞：**取消，演唱會，歌手，幾乎，懷疑**

複習：聚會，反正，值得，瞞，果然，夠朋友
(交通，堵車 dǔchē，開玩笑，目的)

對話三

1.	2.	3.	4.	5.

生詞：**天才，樂隊，專輯，歌迷，歌頌，搖滾樂**
震撼，邪惡，偷偷，墮落，風格，叛逆

複習：收集，保守，老一輩，發現，追求，吶喊，不滿
無奈，表達，感受，了解，羨慕，(軍人)

根據對話一回答問題：

1. 丹尼想去哪兒鍛煉身體？那天的天氣怎麼樣？他為什麼鍛煉不成？
2. 什麼樣的人在進行著那個活動？丹尼聽以前說過這件事嗎？
3. 那些人為什麼要進行這個活動？ 他們怎樣進行這個活動？
4. 學校領導對這個活動持什麼樣的態度？丹尼和朋友呢？

根據對話二回答問題：

1. 先生為什麼回家晚了？他本來準備回家後和太太一起做什麼？後來呢？
2. 太太讓先生吃完晚飯一起做什麼？先生知道後態度怎麼樣？
3. 太太為這個活動花錢了嗎？她告訴先生真話了嗎？先生相信不相信她？為什麼？

根據對話三回答問題：

1. “披頭四”是什麼？丹尼和阿華都知道“披頭四”嗎？阿華的爸爸喜歡“披頭四”嗎？你怎麼知道呢？
2. 五十年代，中國人聽的音樂和“披頭四”的音樂有什麼不同？早些時候中國老一輩的人限制孩子聽搖滾樂？為什麼？
3. 六十年代到七十年代，美國的流行音樂對臺灣有什麼影響？為什麼？
4. 丹尼為什麼羨慕阿華和她爸爸的關係？

口語用法

1. 上哪兒？(“上哪兒” means “where are you going” . Saying “上哪兒”or “上 XX 啊！ ” is a common way for the Chinese to greet people. When you don’t think they need to know where you are going, you can response with “不上哪兒”).

A: 上哪兒？
B: 上店裏買點東西去。
A: Where are you going?
B: I’m going to buy something at the store.

A: 上學校接孩子啊？
B: 是啊。
Are you going to the school to pick up the kids?
That’s right.

A: 你上哪兒？
B: 不上哪兒， 隨便出去走走。
A: Where are you going?
B: I’m not going anywhere. I am just having a walk.

2. 完了, 看來這幾天體育館都不開。(You say“完了!” , when you find something bad has happened or you know something bad is about to happen. It is like “un-oh”, “oops” or “I’m toast” in English You can also say someone or something is “完了” when bad things are happening to another person or an object).

完了，看來這幾天體育館都不開，鍛煉不成了。
Oh no! It looks like the gym won’t be open for a few days. I won’t be able to exercise.

完了！等會兒林叔叔一定又要勸酒，爸爸想不喝醉都不行了！
Oh no! Uncle Lin will be here later to urge father to drink again. I feel father will definitely get drunk.

A: 他在公司的性丑聞好像上報了。
A: His sex scandal in his company seems to be in the newspaper.
B: 他完了。不但老婆會跟他拼命，工作大概也得丟了。
B: He’s done for. His wife will want to kill him; plus, he will probably also lose his job.

哎呀！我一下子放了太多辣椒，這盤菜完了！
Aiya! I put too much hot pepper by accident. This dish is ruined.

3. 取消就取消了，有什麼好氣的。("就" in "XX 就 XX" indicates one's passive acceptance, resignation, or indifference. Please also see Lesson 3: 口語用法 "二十分就二十分". "有什麼好+VP" means, "What's the big deal," or, "It is nothing worth X").

晚會取消就取消了，有什麼好氣的。
Canceling the party it is no big deal; it is nothing worth getting angry about.

去就去，有什麼好怕的！
Just go, it is nothing to be afraid of.

吃虧了就吃虧了，有什麼好難過的！
Being taking advantage of is not a big deal. There is nothing to be upset about.

吃不開就吃不開吧！你有什麼好抱怨的。
If people don't buy it they don't buy it. No big deal. There is nothing worth complaining about.

這事有那麼難決定嗎？有什麼好猶豫的呢？
Is this thing that difficult to resolve? What is making you hesitate?

4. 你想哪兒去了？我可沒別的目的。(You use "你想哪兒去了？" when you think people might have misunderstood).

你想哪兒去了？我可沒有別的目的。
What made you think that? I don't have any other purpose.

你想哪兒去了？我讓你多運動是為你的身體好，不是嫌你胖啊！
What brought you a thought like that? I asked you to have more exercise for the good of your health. I wasn't saying you are too fat.

我沒有指責你的意思，你想哪兒去了？
I never meant to blame you. What made you think that?

5. 原來是這樣，我說呢！ (You use "我說呢！" when you are fooled or confused momentarily, but then realize the truth. It is often used in conjunction with "原來" or "以為").

原來是這樣，**我說呢!**
Now I see. It's really like this.

他的中文好原來是因為他的中國女朋友在幫他，**我說呢！**
His Chinese is good because of his Chinese girlfriend's help. Now I see.

A: 這孩子今天回來沒有看電視就開始學習，是因為他明天要考試。
A: This child started studying as soon as he came home, without watching TV, because he has a test tomorrow.
B: 哦，**我說呢**。
B: Oh, I see.

6. 看把你 **Adj** 得！(“看把你 Adj 得” means, “Look at you,” or, “Look how XX you are”).

不就是請你吃個北京烤鴨嗎？**看把你高興得!**
Wasn't what he did as simple as treating you to the Peking duck? Look how happy it made you.

沒事沒事，別哭了。**看把你難過得**。
It's ok, stop crying. Look how sad you are.

其他的員工也該輪流一塊做啊！**看把你**一個人**累得**。
Other staff members should also take turns doing it. Look how tired it makes you.

7. 在老年人看來，放著好好的歌你不唱，在那兒喊什麼？ (The pattern “…放著…不…” indicates one's disagreement. The speaker values the thing stated after “放著”, and belittles the thing mentioned in the second clause).

放著好好的歌你不唱，在那兒喊什麼？
Why do you put aside those great songs only to shout out there?

他放著好好的書不念，跑去玩什麼搖滾樂！氣死我了！
He put aside studying and ran off to listen to rock and roll music. It made me so angry I could die.

唉，我不該放著好好的律師不嫁，嫁給了一個沒讀過書的！
Sigh! I shouldn't have denied the lawyer to marry an illiterate person.

8. 有時候年輕人心裏的感受，老人說什麼也不會理解的。(“說什麼也…” means, “There is no way…,” or, “No matter how/what…”).

有時候年輕人心裏的感受, 老人說什麼也不會理解的
Sometimes there is no way for the elderly to understand the deep feelings of the young generation.

我媽說什麼也做不出味道這麼好的菜來。
There is no way my mom could cook a dish as delicious as this.

口語練習：請用聽力對話裏學到的生詞和口語用法討論下面的問題：

上哪兒?/上…/　　完了，/　　XX 就 XX 了 /　　有什麼好+Verb Phrase +(的)
你想哪兒去了？/　　我說呢! /　　看把你 XX 得 /　　說什麼也…
…放著…不…，… (as in 放著好好的歌你不唱，在那兒喊什麼？)

1. A- 你是職工抗議活動的代表，你要向學校領導表達不滿，並提出要求。
   B- 你是學校領導，你覺得這些職工的抗議很煩，你也不想改善他們的情況。

2. AB- 你們是夫妻。先生想讓太太今晚跟她去聽演唱會，太太想讓先生今晚跟她去參加朋友聚會。你們得一起做個決定。

3. A- 你是爺爺或奶奶，是個老一輩的傳統中國人，你反對年輕人聽搖滾樂。
   B- 你是孫子或孫女，你最喜歡搖滾樂，最討厭革命歌曲。
   B 希望 A 給他錢買演唱會的票。

課文

第一部分

一九九零年一月。六四後的第一個冬天。二十八號晚上的北京，大雪紛飛，氣溫只有零下十五度,而此時此刻的工人體育館裏，擠滿了激動萬分的群眾，吶喊聲一浪高過一浪。這不是什麼政治抗議，這是崔健的演唱會，也是他在天安門廣場的學生群中大唱《新長征路上的搖滾》後第一次公開露面。

看著崔健和他的樂隊走上舞臺，緊張的觀眾們才終於相信，演唱會並不會被取消，崔健被警察帶走了只是個謠言。他們興奮地跟著崔健大聲唱：

怎樣說，怎樣做，才真正是自己,
怎樣歌，怎樣唱，這心中才得意
一邊走，一邊想，雪山和草地
一邊走，一邊唱，領袖毛主席
噢！一、二、三、四、五、六、七

一九八四年崔健出版了第一張專輯，專輯中的《不是我不明白》是崔健的第一首搖滾歌曲。兩年後，崔健的第二首歌《一無所有》紅遍各地，並給中國的流行樂壇帶來了無比的震撼。一直到二零零三年，音樂評論家談起崔健時仍說:

"崔健是搖滾樂的天才。"
"崔健的音樂宣布了中國搖滾樂的誕生。"

"崔健的歌，表現了八十年代年輕人潛意識裏想要表達的東西。"

"談到本土的音樂創作者，影響最深、最廣的，只有崔健。"

生詞用法

1	摇滚	搖滾	yáogǔn	rock and roll	搖滾樂/搖滾歌手
2	歌手	歌手	gēshǒu	singer	流行歌手/鼓手/吉他手
	崔健	崔健	Cuī Jiàn	name of a Chinese singer	
	六四	六四	Liùsì	June 4th, 1989, Tiananmen Square Incident	
3	纷飞	紛飛	fēnfēi	to blow and to fly	大雪紛飛/落葉(falling leaves)紛飛
4	气温	氣溫	qìwēn	air temperature	
5	度	度	dù	degree	氣溫十五度/一個圓有三百六十度。/婚後，他有了一百八十度的轉變, 和過去完全不一樣了。
6	此时此刻	此時此刻	cǐshícǐkè	at this very moment	此時此刻你在做什麼？
7	体育馆	體育館	tǐyùguǎn	gymnasium; stadium	體育課: PE class
8	挤满	擠滿	jǐmǎn	to be at full capacity	(verb+滿) 見語法
9	激动万分	激動萬分	jīdòng wànfēn	very agitated; excited	你別那麼激動，有話慢慢說。/知道婚姻出現了第三者後，他激動得哭了起來。/ 演唱會場擠滿了激動萬分的觀眾。/這實在是一件令人激動萬分的事。
10	呐喊	吶喊	nàhǎn	to shout loudly; loud shouts in support (of something)	他們在吶喊。/他們的吶喊聲很大。/為自由吶喊。
11	浪	浪	làng	wave	聲浪/海浪/一浪高一浪
12	抗议	抗議	kàngyì	to protest; to object; remonstrate; protest (n.)	向政府抗議/跟老師抗議/提出抗議/學生們抗議功課太多。/老百姓向政府提出抗議。
13	演唱会	演唱會	yǎnchàng huì	music concert with vocals	開一場演唱會/辦一場演唱會/鋼琴演奏會(yǎnzòuhuì)/小提琴演奏會
	天安门广场	天安門廣場	Tiānānmén guǎngchǎng	Tiananmen Square	

14	长征	長征	chángzhēng	a long march; The Long March (Aug.1934 -Oct.1936)	
15	公开	公開	gōngkāi	to make public; public; publicly	公開一個秘密/公開他們的婚外關係/公開的場合/公開的活動/公開表示/公開露面/公開反對/他們倆雖是男女朋友，但一直沒有公開他們的關係。
16	露面	露面	lòumiàn	to show up; to make public appearances	露了一次面/總統有一周沒有露面了，是不是病了？
17	乐队	樂隊	yuèduì	orchestra; band	in Taiwan, "搖滾樂團" is more often used than "搖滾樂隊".
18	舞台	舞臺	wǔtái	stage for performances	
29	观众	觀眾	guānzhòng	audience; viewer	
20	取消	取消	qǔxiāo	to cancel	我們取消了那個聚會/考試(被)取消了
21	谣言	謠言	yáoyán	rumor	
22	得意	得意	déyì	to be proud of oneself; to be pleased with oneself	又賺了一大筆錢，真得意。/你看她那一副得意的樣子，好像沒人比他強似的。/你還不知道最後會怎麼樣呢，別得意得太早！
23	草地	草地	cǎodì	lawn; meadow; field	一片草地
24	领袖	領袖	lǐngxiù	leader	領袖毛澤東/天才領袖/偉大的領袖/領袖的作用
25	噢	噢	ō	an exclamation; a particle	
26	专辑	專輯	zhuānjí	music album	一盤專輯/一張專輯
27	明白	明白	míngbai	to understand; clear; coherent; clearly; coherently	你講的我都明白了。/她說得很明白。/你聽明白了沒有？
28	歌曲	歌曲	gēqǔ	songs	一首流行歌曲/愛國歌曲/鄉村歌曲(country music)
29	一无所有	一無所有	yìwú suǒyǒu	to have nothing at all in the world	除了我身上穿的這身衣服，我一無所有。

30	红	紅	hóng	to be hot; to be popular	Andy Lau (劉德華) 在華人世界紅了二十多年了。/ 這部電影紅遍美國。/這個歌手一直沒有紅起來。
31	乐坛	樂壇	yuètán	musical circles (of people); music world	流行樂壇/海外樂壇/華人樂壇
32	无比	無比	wúbǐ	incomparable; unparalleled	他是一個優秀無比的運動員/這個消息讓人無比激動。/聽到兒子被名校錄取了，他感到驕傲無比。
33	震撼	震撼	zhènhàn	to shake, to shock; shock (n.) , shaking,	九一一事件震撼了全世界。/父親的死，對他來說是個很大的震撼。/令人震撼的電影/震撼人心的故事
34	评论	評論	pínglùn	to comment on; critique (of movie, article, current events)	我不想評論這件事。/很多人都在評論那個政府官員的丑聞。/文學評論/新聞評論/電影評論
35	天才	天才	tiāncái	talented; talent; genius	天才兒童/天才音樂家/他有數學方面的天才/他是一個天才。
36	宣布	宣布	xuānbù	to announce; to declare	宣布了他們要結婚的消息/宣布與中國開始外交關係/宣布會議開始/我要給大家宣布一件事。
37	诞生	誕生	dànshēng	To be born, birth; to come into the world	毛澤東誕生於 1893 年。/1949 年毛澤東向世界宣布新中國誕生了。
38	潜意识	潛意識	qiǎnyìshi	sub-consciousness (意識 = consciousness, 潛= potential; to go under water)	有人說做夢夢見的東西是你潛意識裏的東西。/你說你不討厭這種風格的音樂，可是潛意識裏你並不喜歡它。
39	本土	本土	běntǔ	local; indigenous; native; (with in the) mainland territory	本土音樂/本土作家/本土文化/美國本土
40	创作	創作	chuàngzuò	to create (artwork); creation	文學創作/藝術創作/電影創作/他創作了一首很好聽的歌。

課文

第二部分

為什麼崔健的音樂能夠給中國人帶來這麼強的震撼？為什麼他能夠擁有這麼多的歌迷？也許有兩個原因，一是在於他音樂的搖滾風格，二是在於他的歌詞所反映的時代聲音。

五十到七十年代，凡是中國人公開聽的、唱的，都是歌頌社會主義、歌頌毛主席的革命歌曲。現今二十歲以上的中國人，都能唱上幾句這一類的革命歌曲，比方說，“東方紅，太陽升，中國出了一個毛澤東”，或者“工農兵，聯合起來，向前進，消滅敵人”，“社會主義好，社會主義好，社會主義國家，人民地位高”。那時，資本主義和邪惡腐敗幾乎是同義詞。如果唱一些來自資本主義社會的流行歌曲，會被認為是思想墮落的表現。這些歌，人們只能偷偷聽，偷偷唱。

七十年代末到八十年代初，港臺的流行音樂悄悄進入中國大陸。年輕人聽到那些軟綿綿的愛情歌曲，以及浪漫的校園歌曲，才發現音樂原來可以這樣表達自己的生活和內心感受。隨著改革開放的深入發展，大量的港臺文化與西方文化進入中國，許多傳統的觀念受到了挑戰。剛剛經歷了文化大革命的中國人開始思考，開始懷疑。從小到大接受社會主義教育的年輕人在這樣的中西文化碰撞中失去了方向，而崔健的搖滾歌曲正唱出了這些年輕人的掙扎、叛逆，喊出了他們的茫然和不滿。

我曾經問個不休
你何時跟我走
可是你卻總是笑我
一無所有
我要給你我的追求
還有我的自由
可你卻總是笑我
一無所有

噢---你何時跟我走

腳下這地在走
身邊那水在流
可你卻總是笑我，一無所有
為何你總笑個沒夠
為何我總要追求
難道在你面前
我永遠是一無所有

聽一聽上面這首《一無所有》，你是否聽到了那個時代的聲音？是否也感受到了同樣的震撼？

生詞用法

41	歌迷	歌迷	gēmí	music fans (迷 = fans)	書迷/球迷/影迷/我是麥克杰克遜(Michael Jackson)的歌迷。
42	在于	在於	zàiyú	to lie in; to reside in; to be found in	見語法
43	风格	風格	fēnggé	style	做事的風格/寫作風格/音樂風格/建筑風格/這幅畫的風格跟他從前的創作不盡相同。
44	歌词	歌詞	gēcí	lyrics	這首歌的歌詞非常感動人。
45	声音	聲音	shēngyīn	voice; sound	他說話的聲音很好聽。/在電話上我能聽出是她的聲音。/溫柔(wēnroú)的聲音

46	凡是	凡是	fánshì	every; any; all	見語法
47	歌颂	歌頌	gēsòng	to sing and praise	歌頌雷鋒的偉大精神/歌頌共產黨/歌頌社會主義
48	社会主义 社會主義		shèhuì zhǔyì	socialism	社會主義制度/社會主義道路
49	革命	革命	gémìng	revolution	法國大革命/文化大革命/革命精神/革命歌曲/革命性的做法
50	太阳	太陽	tàiyáng	sun	太陽出來了/太陽下山了
51	升	升	shēng	to rise; to promote	太陽升了起來。/他今年升上二年級了。/他從一個普通職員升為主管了。
52	工农兵	工農兵	gōng nóng bīng	worker, farmer, and solder	八十年代以前，人們常常會聽到"工農兵"這個說法。
53	联合	聯合	liánhé	to unite; to ally; united	把所有的人都聯合起來。/這些大國家聯合起來壓迫這個小國家。/這兩個公司聯合起來了。//他們聯合爭取更高的福利待遇。/聯合國(UN)
54	消灭	消滅	xiāomiè	to exterminate; to wipe out	消滅敵人/消滅反對的聲音/消滅薩達姆(Sàdámǔ)政府/消滅病菌
55	敌人	敵人	dírén	enemy	
56	资本主义 資本主義		zīběnzhǔyì	Capitalism	資本主義制度/資本主義市場
57	邪恶	邪惡	xié'è	evil; malicious	邪惡的思想/邪惡的心靈/邪惡的做法
58	腐败	腐敗	fǔbài	corrupt (adj.); rotten (morally, ethically)	官僚腐敗/人性的腐敗/腐敗的制度/腐敗的行為/腐敗的生活
59	几乎	幾乎	jīhū	almost	她幾乎要哭了。/你變化太大，我幾乎認不出你來。
60	同义词	同義詞	tóngyìcí	synonym(s); 反義詞：antonym(s)	這兩個詞是同義詞。/"太太"是"妻子"的同義詞。
61	思想	思想	sīxiǎng	frame of mind, outlook, principles; thoughts	革命思想/健康的思想/思想落後/思想墮落/用語言表達你的思想。

62	堕落	墮落	duòluò	to decline (morally); corruption; decay (of morals); indulgence	思想墮落/精神墮落/墮落的生活/你怎麼墮落成這個樣子？
63	偷偷	偷偷	tōutōu	secretly; sneakily (偷: to steal)	我偷偷告訴你，你別告訴別人喔！/爸媽不注意的時候，他偷偷地跑了出去。/考試的時候他偷偷看別人的答案。
64	港台	港臺	Gǎng Tái	Hong Kong and Taiwan	港臺歌曲/港臺文化/港臺電影
65	悄悄	悄悄	qiāoqiāo	quietly	她看到別人都在睡覺，就悄悄地把門關上了。/他們悄悄地搬了家，沒人知道為什麼。/他們倆說的是悄悄話，才不會讓你聽到呢！
66	进入	進入	jìnrù	to enter	進入那座很高的建筑/進入大學
67	软绵绵	軟綿綿	ruǎn miánmián	as soft as cotton	軟綿綿的草地/軟綿綿的聲音/軟綿綿的歌聲/我覺得身體軟綿綿的，一點力氣都沒有。
68	爱情	愛情	àiqíng	love (between a romantic couple)	真正的愛情/愛情生活/浪漫的愛情/愛情歌曲/永遠的愛情/愛情故事
69	内心	內心	nèixīn	of the heart; innermost	內心活動/內心世界/內心激動萬分
70	深入	深入	shēnrù	to go deep into; to penetrate; intensively	深入了解/深入改革/深入觀察/深入研究
71	经历	經歷	jīnglì	to experience; to live through; experience	經歷過各種不幸的遭遇/經歷了文化大革命/生活的經歷/共同的經歷/他想把他的經歷寫成一本書。
	文化大革命	文化大革命	Wénhuà dàgémìng	Chinese Cultural Revolution	(1966-1976)
72	思考	思考	sīkǎo	to reflect upon; to ponder over; to think deeply about	思考一個問題/獨立思考/我思考了一個晚上，終於決定放棄念這所學校。
73	怀疑	懷疑	huáiyí	to suspect ; to have doubts; suspicions	我懷疑你偷了我的書。/我對這個統計結果有懷疑。/他的懷疑是有道理的。

74	碰撞	碰撞	pèngzhuàng	to collide; collision	這兩輛車碰撞在一起了。/這兩輛車發生碰撞了。/文化的碰撞/思想的碰撞
75	失去	失去	shīqù	to lose (something important and/or significant)	失去父母/失去生活能力/失去信心/失去朋友/失去支持/失去了父母的愛/我對學中文失去了興趣。
76	挣扎	掙扎	zhēngzhá	to struggle; a struggle	你不要掙扎了，這次你一定跑不了。/她病得很嚴重，可還掙扎著起床給孩子做飯。/接受這樣的工作條件，他的內心存在很大的掙扎。
77	叛逆	叛逆	pànnì	to be disobedient (towards parents, traditions); treacherous	叛逆的想法/叛逆的行為/他是個叛逆的孩子。/你這樣做太叛逆，也太不尊重大人了。
78	茫然	茫然	mángrán	to feel lost; at a loss	大學畢業了，前面的路怎麼走？我感到很茫然。/我問他，可是他一臉茫然，顯然他對這件事一無所知。/我茫然地坐在這裏，不知道他會不會來見我。
79	不休	不休	bùxiū	endlessly; ceaselessly (V 個不休)	問個不休/吵個不休
	何时	何時	héshí	when (written expression)	何, a written form for "what" 何人-who; 何地-where; 為何-for what. 見語法
	是否	是否	shìfǒu	是不是；whether	是否相信/是否同意 見語法

句型和語法

- **V 滿 (We say "他打破了一個杯子", but we can't say "他破了一個杯子". Similar to "破", "滿" itself can't be used as a verb. "滿" is a resultative complement after a verb and means "to maximum capacity").**

    體育館裏擠滿了人。
    The gym is full of people. (There is a big crowd squeezed into the gym). (擠 jǐ= to squeeze)

A: 歡迎光臨新光加油站，請問加多少？
A: Welcome to Xinguang gas station. How much (gasoline do you want)?
B: 加滿。
B: Fill it up.

桌上都是東西=〉桌上放滿了東西。
The table is full of things. =〉 There are things all over the table.

Rewrite the sentences with the following words:
寫滿， 排滿，裝滿
(排, as in 安排= to schedule; 裝 zhuāng= to put in)

黑板上都是語法重點。
=〉

書包已經裝不下更多的書了。
=〉

我這個下午有很多的事要做，沒辦法和你見面。
=〉

- **V+ 遍 (“遍” can be used after a verb, meaning “all over”. “崔健的歌紅遍各地” means “Cui Jian’s music is popular all over the place”.)**

我整個城都找遍了，也找不到手藝像他這麼好的建筑師傅。
I searched all over the city, but I can’t find an architect as skilled as him.

他拍遍了公司上上下下主管們的馬屁。
He flattered all the managers in the company.

在北京住了三個月，他們吃遍了北京大大小小的餐館。
After living in Beijing for three months, they had eaten at every single restaurant there.

在找工作這件事上，她碰的釘子再多不過。
(也可以說) =〉

- **在於 (to be found in, to rest with； “於” is from classical Chinese. It can also mean “在”. “在於” is often used in written Chinese to explain a fundamental reason or to characterize a condition).**

他的錯誤不在於沒表現好菜的色、香、味，而在於沒搭配好菜的涼性和熱性。
His mistake does not lie in the expression of color, smell, and taste in the dish. It lies in his failure to match the 'cool nature' and 'hot nature' of the dish.

年輕人墮落的原因就在於整天聽那些搖滾歌曲。
The reason for moral decline among youth is to be found in the fact that they daily listen to rock and roll music.

這位廚師做飯的特點在於總能配合季節做出有創意的新菜。
The extraordinary quality of this chef's cooking is a matter of his ability to adjust to the seasons in creating new dishes.

你覺得農村的生活和城市的有什麼不同?
(回答問題) =〉

- **凡是+ noun+ 都…("凡是 N 都" means "all those N that fit the specification" . "凡是" is usually followed by 都/一定/沒有不/從來不/必 to emphasize that there are no exceptions to the situation).**

凡是要領養中國小孩的外國人，都得經過複雜的申請手續。
Any foreigner who plans to adopt a Chinese child must go through a complicated application process.

凡是女朋友所說的話，他從來不敢當耳邊風。
He never dares to ignore what his girlfriend says.

凡是那些邪惡腐敗的想法，我們都得消滅。
We have to extinguish all of those evil and corrupted thoughts.

A: 拍馬屁對那些想升官發財的人來說很重要吧！
(完成句子) =〉 B: 當然！ ____________________

- **是否 ("是否" means "whether" . It is usually placed before a verb phrase. The basic usage of "否" is as negation. In classical Chinese, it means "non-" or "is not". In modern Chinese, "否" is mainly used as a word component in a compound to mean "not").**

你是否對那女孩一見鐘情？
Did or did you not fall in love with that girl at the first sight?

那些人是否因承受了太多的指責而打退堂鼓了？
Did those people change their mind because there was too much blame falling on them?

一般群眾是否注意到環境保護的問題是值得考慮的。
Whether ordinary people pay attention to issues of environmental protection or not is a question deserving of consideration.

對是否應該冒險接受人工受孕，她一直猶豫不決。
She kept hesitating and wondering about whether or not to undergo artificial insemination.

法輪功是否是個迷信的組織？
Is Falun Gong a superstitious cult or not?

上次的審判太主觀嗎？
(也可以說) =〉

- **"何" ("何" means "什麼" as a written expression in modern Chinese compounds).**

如何= 怎麼，怎麼樣
何時/何人= 什麼時候/什麼人
為何= 為什麼

Use "何" to rephrase the following questions:

作者是怎麼描寫(miáoxiě)他們倆人的關係的=〉

這樣的潛意識是怎麼表現出來的？=〉

你會在什麼時候宣布這個消息(xiāoxi)? =〉

你為什麼這麼傻？=〉

課堂活動

(一) 用課文裏學到的生詞和句型回答問題：

- 請談談一九九零年一月二十八號的北京和北京工人體育館裏的情景。
  (大雪紛飛 氣溫 Verb+滿 激動 吶喊)
- 音樂會的聽眾一開始為什麼有點緊張？後來呢？
  (謠言 取消 樂團 舞臺 露面)
- 崔健是怎麼紅起來的？他的音樂為什麼特別？音樂家怎麼評論他？
  (專輯 紅遍各地 樂壇 震撼 天才 宣布 潛意識 本土 創作)
- 改革開放以前，中國人聽的是什麼樣的音樂？唱的是什麼樣的歌？為什麼？
  (凡是 歌頌 資本主義 邪惡 腐敗 墮落)
- 改革開放初期，港臺音樂和文化對大陸有什麼影響？崔健的《一無所有》和當時中國的社會變化有什麼關係？
  (悄悄 軟綿綿 懷疑 碰撞 掙扎 叛逆 茫然)

(二)角色扮演：**role play**

- 如果你是音樂公司經紀人(jīngjìrén: agent)，你會安排下面那一位歌手到中國大陸辦演唱會？為什麼？

歌手	背景	才藝
周杰倫 Zhōu Jiélún Jay Chou	兩千年左右在臺灣紅起來。沒念過大學。常換女朋友。非常討厭記者。拍過廣告。	鋼琴、說唱歌曲、寫歌、籃球。
空中補給 Kōngzhōngbǔjǐ Air Supply	來自澳洲的合唱團體。唱過許多流行的浪漫歌曲。七十年代到九十年代紅遍各地。	
小甜甜布萊尼 xiǎotiántián Bùláiní Britney Spears	美國流行歌手，出版過多張暢銷專輯，得過 Grammy Award。拍過廣告，並擁有香水(perfume)和服裝(apparel)公司。兩千零五年懷孕生子。	
克莉絲汀-阿奎萊拉 Akuíláilā Christina Aguilera	來自紐約的性感搖滾女歌手。得過 Grammy Award。出版過多張暢銷專輯。繼布萊尼之後成為美國的流行女王。	
你建議的某位歌手	(介紹該歌手的背景)	

(三) 你的看法

- 為了培養愛國精神，中國的有些學校要求小學生每天唱一次國歌。在你的國家呢？你對這有什麼看法？
- 你會花十五塊美金買一張上面只有一首歌你喜歡的 CD 還是會到網絡上非法下載？為什麼？

練習題

一.　詞彙練習：(請選用最合適的詞來完成句子)

(一) *(風格 / 向往 / 氣溫 / 謠言)*

1. 這位曾經紅遍各地的歌手已經很久沒有公開露面了，有______說他得了艾滋病。
2. 北京的夏天白天________高達一百度，出去玩要記得多喝水。
3. 在美國拉斯維加斯 (Las Vegas) 有許多人模仿貓王 Elvis 的演唱________，非常受歡迎。
4. 哪個年輕女孩不________浪漫的愛情呢？

(二) *(懷疑 / 歌頌 / 碰撞 / 創作 / 消滅 / 評論 / 掙扎)*

1. 許多文化大革命時期的歌曲都是________社會主義的歌曲，現在聽來有點可笑。
2. 音樂評論家們認為披頭四 (Beatles) ________的歌曲反映了六十年代年輕人的想法。
3. 他太太________他跟女同事有婚外關係，吵著要跟他離婚。
4. 這是一個很難做的決定，他________了好久才狠下心來辭(cí)掉那份工作。
5. 他沒有什麼固定工作，每天就是在報紙或網絡上發表文章，_______那些名人的行為、作風、私生活等等。
6. 這些迷信觀念已經存在了幾百年甚至上千年了，怎麼可能一下子就被完全________呢。
7. 他找女朋友不在乎她漂亮不漂亮，只在乎兩個人之間有沒有默契，能不能發生心靈的___________。

(三) *(進入／深入／悄悄地／偷偷地／默默地(Lesson 5)／充滿／擠滿)*

1. 經過激烈的競爭，他終於______了這所人人向往的名校。
2. 這位精通中文的美國學者對中國農村人口問題有非常______的研究。
3. 他昨天睡覺前_____給以前的女朋友打了個電話，沒想到被他太太發現了。
4. 為了不吵醒(chǎoxǐng)母親，他________走出去打電話。
5. 他問母親為什麼難過？但母親________流著淚，什麼都沒說。
6. 演唱會場裏______了激動萬分的觀眾，這些________了熱情的歌迷要求歌手在他們買的專輯上簽名。

(四) 1. *震撼　聯合　宣布　抗議　掙扎　吶喊*

全市退休老人_____部分仍然工作的中老年人向政府______新的退休制度改革。他們______，如果政府減少他們的退休金，他們就要集體絕食(juéshí-to fast)一個星期。這些老人一邊搖著手裏的小旗子(qízi-flag),一邊大聲______，那種精神和決心，實在是令人______。

2. *墮落　茫然　邪惡　得意　幾乎*

這幾個孩子，每天不是逃課就是喝酒，甚至吸毒，還偷別人的東西，打破人家的車窗什麼的，______是無惡不做。孩子都應該擁有一顆美好的、天真的心靈，可是他們的腦子裏卻充滿了______的想法。為何這些曾經天真可愛的孩子_____成這個樣子？我問他們的家長，他們卻一臉____地搖搖頭。

二.　口語表達練習：(選擇下面的口語表達完成或改寫句子)

放著…不…, …　　看把你…的　　你想哪兒去了

1. 阿文，__________，趕快坐下來休息休息。
2. A: 這個樂隊的歌手，鼓手，吉他(jíta)手，都這麼大了，也不結婚，他們是不是對女人不感興趣啊？
   B: ________________，你不知道人家都有女朋友嗎?
3. 你父母的大房子你不住，怎麼出去租(zū)別人的小房子住？

（也可以說）=>

三. 翻譯練習

1. Success lies in luck as well as effort. (…在於)
2. All teenagers are, more or less, a little rebellious; this is part of growing up.(凡是…都…)
3. When, where, and who are all written clearly on the invitation notice; how could you not understand? (何…)
4. These music critics believe that Cui Jian, as an artist, is the deepest influence on local Chinese rock n' roll; do you agree or disagree with them? (是否…)

四. 作文：(從下邊幾個題目中, 選擇一個, 寫一篇不少於 500 字的作文。你至少要用三個所提供的句型或詞彙)

location + verb 滿	verb 遍	是否	在於	凡是…都

1. 介紹一位音樂家，一位歌手或者一個樂團/樂隊。
2. 一個時代有一個時代的流行音樂。 請談談美國不同時代的流行音樂。你喜歡哪種風格的音樂？
3. 有句話說"學音樂的孩子不會變壞"。請談談你對這句話的看法。

口語用法索引 **Oral Expression Index**

第一冊語法索引 Volume 1 Grammar Index

第一冊詞彙　拼音索引(Volume 1 Pinyin Vocabulary Index)

A

愛情	àiqíng	love (between a romantic couple)	L11
艾滋病	àizībìng	AIDS	L4
安靜	ānjìng	quiet	(review) L1
暗示	ànshì	to hint; to imply; hint(n.)	L9, L16
安慰	ānwèi	to comfort; to console; comfort	L5, L7
按照	ànzhào	in accordance with; to follow (an instruction, a regulation)	L3, L8, L16

B

霸道	bàdào	bossy ; overbearing; high-handed	L3
白話	báihuà	colloquial, clear and easy to understand	L8, L17
擺脫	bǎituō	to get rid of, to cast off	L7, L12, L17
辦	bàn	to proceed with a task	L7, L12
傍晚	bàngwǎn	early evening; at dusk	L5, L8
班門弄斧	Bānmén nòngfǔ	to display one's light skill (insignificant experience) before an expert;	L8
半瓶醋	bànpíngcù	a half-bottle of vinegar (one who has only a superficial knowledge of something; a charlatan)	L9
伴兒	bànr	company; companion; partner	L6
半天	bàntiān	half of the day; a long time; quite a while	(review) L5
報	bào	to register for/in	L3
抱	bào	to carry; to hold with both arms; to embrace	L6
保持	bǎochí	to keep; to preserve	L6
保護	bǎohù	to protect ; to defend; protection	L4, L19
報社	bàoshè	newspaper office	L6
保守	bǎoshǒu	conservative	L4
抱怨	bàoyuàn	to complain; complaint	L9
背黑鍋	bēihēiguō	to carry the black wok (to take the blame for others; to be made a scapegoat)	L9
背景	bèijǐng	background; setting	L8
北京烤鴨	Běijīng kǎoyā	Peking duck	L10
被迫	bèipò	to be forced to; to be compelled to	L7, L13
被窩	bèiwō	comfort of the blanket or quilt	L5
笨	bèn	stupid; foolish; clumsy	L3
本年度	běnniándù	this year；the current year	L3
本土	běntǔ	local; indigenous; native; (with in the) territory	L11, L13, L19
逼	bī	to compel; to force	L3
表達	biǎodá	to express; to deliver	L8, L11, L17, L21
表面	biǎomiàn	surface (see grammar for "表面上")	L2
表示	biǎoshì	to show, to express	L8, L20, L21
表現	biǎoxiàn	to show; to manifest; performance	L9, L15, L19
必不可少	bìbùkěshǎo	absolutely necessary	L8
別無選擇	biéwúxuǎnzé	to have no choice	L4
比方說	bǐfangshuō	for example	(review) L8
比例	bǐlì	proportion; ratio	L2, L13
避免	bìmiǎn	to avoid; to prevent (something from happening)	L4, L6, L22
賓語	bīnyǔ	object (in linguistics)	L8, L21
必然	bìrán	inevitable; certain; necessarily	L9, L12
必要	bìyào	necessary; essential	L9, L22

比喻	bǐyù	to compare one thing to another; metaphor or simile	L9
不打不成器	bùdǎ-bùchéngqì	"spare the rod, spoil the child"	L3
不斷	búduàn	constant; constantly	L9, L14
不顧	búgù	to disregard; in spite of	L6
不盡相同	bújìn xiāngtóng	not completely the same	L10, L21
不景氣	bùjǐngqì	recession of (economy; market); financial depression;	L7, L22
不滿	bùmǎn	resentful; unsatisfied; discontented	L9
不三不四	bùsānbúsì	improper	L5
不外乎	búwàihū	nothing else but	L10
不聞不問	bùwénbúwèn	be indifferent to sth; neither care to inquire nor to hear	L8
補習班	bǔxíbān	cram school	L3, (L7)
不幸	búxìng	unfortunate; unlucky; unfortunately ; misfortune; adversity;	L1, L2, L4, L15, …
不休	bùxiū	endlessly; ceaselessly (V 個不休)	L11

C

猜	cāi	to guess	L8, L21
財產	cáichǎn	property; assets	L2
材料	cáiliào	ingredient; material; data;	L10
采取	cǎiqǔ	to adopt; to take (a method, a way, etc.)	L4, L12, L22
擦肩而過	cājiānérguò	to pass by shoulder to shoulder/ to bump into each other without knowing	L7
藏	cáng	to hide	L10, L18
殘疾	cánjí	deformity, handicap	L6
餐巾	cānjīn	napkin (餐巾紙 = paper napkin)	L10
殘酷	cánkù	cruel; brutal	L7
慚愧	cánkuì	to be ashamed; to feel abashed	L7, L18
草地	cǎodì	lawn; meadow; field	L11
曾經	céngjīng	ever; once; formerly	L2, L4, L19
差	chà	poor; inferior; not up to standard	(review) L2
纏	chán	to tangle; to twine; to bind	L2
場	chǎng	一場比賽, 一場表演, 一場電影, 一場夢	L1
場合	chǎnghé	occasion	L9, L21
唱戲	chàngxì	to act in a Chinese opera or play	L10
暢銷	chàngxiāo	to sell in high volume; best-selling	L3
長征	chángzhēng	a long march; The Long March (Aug.1934 - Oct.1936)	L11
吵	chǎo	to make noise; to quarrel; noisy	L1
炒	chǎo	to stir-fry	(review) L10
炒冷飯	chǎolěngfàn	to heat leftover rice (to say or do the same old thing; to repeat without any new content)	L9
超過	chāoguò	to exceed; to surpass	L4, L12, L14
車禍	chēhuò	traffic accident	L1
成功	chénggōng	to succeed; successful; success;	L3, L6, L15
成績	chéngjì	grade; score; achievement	L7
成立	chénglì	to found; to establish	L4
成千上萬	chéngqiān shàngwàn	tens of thousands of	L8
城市	chéngshì	city, town	(review) L2
承受	chéngshòu	to bear; to endure	L9, L15
成語	chéngyǔ	(four-word) idioms	(review) L8

成員	chéngyuán	member	L4
稱贊	chēngzàn	to praise	L9
成長	chéngzhǎng	to grow up; growth	L3, L15
沉默	chénmò	to be silent; silent ; silence	L1, L5
遲	chí	late; delayed	L6
吃不消	chībùxiāo	can't take it; can't endure it	L10
吃得開	chīdekāi	to be popular; to get along well	L10
吃驚	chījīng	to be suprised; to be shocked; to be amazed	L10
吃苦	chīkǔ	to endure hardship	L3, L10
吃虧	chīkuī	to suffer loss; to be taken advantage of	L10
崇拜	chóngbài	to adore; to idolize; to worship	L7
充滿	chōngmǎn	to be full of, brimming with	L7, L9, L12
重慶	Chóngqìng	name of a city in China	L9
重新	chóngxīn	anew; afresh; re-	L7
丑聞	chǒuwén	scandal	L9
初	chū	the beginning of [used as a compond]	(review) L11
床頭	chuángtóu	headboard; the head of a bed	L5
創意	chuàngyì	originality	L10
創造性	chuàngzàoxìng	creativity	L3
創作	chuàngzuò	to create (artwork); creation	L11, L17, L19
傳統	chuántǒng	tradition, traditional	(review) L2
穿著	chuānzhuó	apparel; what one wears	L5
出版	chūbǎn	to come off the press; to publish (of books)	L3, L11, L19
出差	chūchāi	to go on a business trip	L7
處處	chùchù	everywhere; in all respects	L2
處罰	chǔfá	to punish; to penalize; punishment	L2, L4, L9, L20
除非	chúfēi	only if; only when; unless	L4, L6
出入	chūrù	come in and go out; go out and come in	L8
廚師	chúshī	cook, chief	L7, L10
出現	chūxiàn	to appear; to arise; to emerge	L2
此時此刻	cǐshícǐkè	at this very moment	L11
蔥	cōng	green onion; scallion (洋蔥 = onion)	L10
聰明	cōngming	intelligent; clever; smart	(review) L3
從此以後	cóngcǐyǐhòu	since then (此 = "this" in written expression)	L1
從前	cóngqián	in the past; before	L9
崔健	Cuī Jiàn	name of a Chinese singer	L11
存	cún	to save or accumulate (for future use); to store; to deposit	L1
村民	cūnmín	villager	L4
存在	cúnzài	to exist; being; existence	L6, L8, L20
錯誤	cuòwù	wrong; incorrect	L8

D

打退堂鼓	dǎ tuìtánggǔ	to beat the step-down-the-stage drum (to give up a pursuit without attaining one's goal; to give up)	L9
答案	dá'àn	answer (n.);	L3
打扮	dǎbàn	to dress up	L5
達到	dádào	to achieve; to reach (a number, a goal, or a standard)	L2, L14
打倒	dǎdǎo	to beat down	L4
大多數	dàduōshù	great majority; most	L3
大概	dàgài	general; approximate; probably; most likely	L1, L9
打鼓	dǎgǔ	to beat the drum (to feel uncertain; to feel nervous)	L9

待	dāi	to stay for a period of time	L5, L7
帶領	dàilǐng	to lead; to guide	L8, L12
代替	dàitì	to substitute for; to replace	L8, L9
大量	dàliàng	a large number; a great quantity	L8, L11, L13, L17
大陸	dàlù	mainland	(review) L11
淡淡	dàndàn	light; slight; lightly, slightly	L5
黨	dǎng	political party	L1, L4, L16, L17,
當初	dāngchū	at the beginning; in the first place;	L6, L7
當面	dāngmiàn	to sb.'s face; in sb's presence	L5
單身	dānshēn	unmarried; single	L6, L7
誕生	dànshēng	To be born, birth; to come into the world	L11
單位	dānwèi	unit (as an organization, department, division, section, etc)	L5, L20
擔心	dānxīn	to worry; to feel anxious	(review) L5
道	dào	一道菜	L10
到底	dàodǐ	after all; [used in a interogative sentence to get to the bottom of the matter]	(review) L3 口語, L8
刀叉	dāochā	fork and knife	L10
到處	dàochǔ	everywhere	(review) L5
道教	Dàojiào	Taoism/Daoism	L4
打破	dǎpò	to break; to smash	L2, L5, L17
大聲	dàshēng	loud；loudness; in a loud voice	(review) L3
大體上	dàtǐshàng	roughly; by and large;on the whole;	L8
答應	dāying	to agree to; to consent to	L5
打招呼	dǎzhāohu	to greet	(review) L9
大致	dàzhì	roughly; on the whole; approximately	L5
等於	děngyú	to be equal to; to be equivalent to; to amount to	L3
得意	déyì	to be proud of oneself; to be pleased with oneself	L11
典故	diǎngù	literary quotation	L8, L9, L17
電視臺	diànshìtái	TV station	L4
點頭	diǎntóu	to nod one's head; to signal one's agreement	L4
電子	diànzǐ	electronic	L7, L14
掉	diào	to drop; to fall; to shed	L7
頂	dǐng	to carry on the head; to stand up to; measure word for hat	L2
地區	dìqū	region; area; district	L10
敵人	dírén	enemy	L11
地位	dìwèi	status; position (in a society, a family, an organization, etc.)	L2, L16
地主	dìzhǔ	landlord; landowner	L2, L16
動不動就	dòng-búdòng jiù	easily; often (to have certain reaction)	L3
度	dù	degree	L11
鍛煉	duànliàn	to exercise; to workout;exercise (n.)	L5
隊	duì	a team; a row of people	L1
對待	duìdài	to treat	L9
對牛彈琴	duìniútánqín	to play lute for the cow (to speak to the wrong audience)	L8
對象	duìxiàng	object; boyfriend or girlfriend	L9
對於	duìyú	to; for; with regard to	L6, L15, L18, L19, …
獨立性	dúlìxìng	independence; (性, as a suffix, means "nature")	L3

頓	dùn	一頓飯	(review) L10
躲	duǒ	to hide; to dodge; to avoid	L5
多多少少	duōduō-shǎoshǎo	more or less	L3, L20
墮落	duòluò	to decline (morally); corruption; decay (of morals); indulgence	L11, L16
墮胎	duòtāi	to have an abortion; abortion	L2, L7
多余	duōyú	extra; surplus	L9
獨生子女	dúshēngzǐnǚ	the only child	L2, L3, L6,
讀者	dúzhě	reader (a person); readership	L3
E			
把...當耳邊風	ěrbiānfēng	to let something go in one ear and out the other; to turn a deaf ear to something	L9
二奶	èrnǎi	concubine; mistress	L2
兒童	értóng	children	L6, L13
F			
發表	fābiǎo	to publish; to release	L8, L17, L19, L21
發達	fādá	developed; advanced	L7
發呆	fādāi	to stare blankly; to daze off	L5, L7
法輪功	fǎlúngōng	Falun Gong	L4
煩	fán	to bother; annoying; vexed	L5
反對	fǎnduì	to oppose; to be against; to object to	L2, L4, L6, L12, …
反對黨	fǎnduìdǎng	opposition party	L4
放棄	fàngqì	to give up; to quit	L7, L9, L19
方式	fāngshì	way; method; style	L3, L9, L21
訪問	fǎngwèn	to visit and have an interview with; visit (n.)	L1, L19, L21
方向	fāngxiang	direction	(review) L11
防治	fángzhì	prevention and cure	L4, L22
凡是	fánshì	every; any; all	L11
范圍	fànwéi	scope; range	L9
反映	fǎnyìng	to reflect; to report	L9, L10, L15
反正	fǎnzhèng	anyway; in any case	L5
犯罪	fànzuì	to commit a crime	L2, L22
發送	fāsòng	to dispatch (letters, etc.); to hand out	L4
發現	fāxiàn	to find; to discover	(review) L3
發展	fāzhǎn	to develop, development	(review) L4
非法	fēifǎ	illegal; unlawful	L4
份	fèn	一份報紙, 一份早餐	(review) L6
紛飛	fēnfēi	to blow and to fly	L11
奉承	fèngcheng	to flatter	L9
諷刺	fěngcì	to mock; to lampoon; satire	L9
豐富	fēngfù	to enrich; abundant; plentiful	L6, L10, L14, L19
豐富多樣	fēngfù duōyàng	(to allow to choose from) many kinds and many categories	L10
風格	fēnggé	style	L11, L20
豐收	fēngshōu	bumper crop; a good harvest	L10
分手	fēnshǒu	to split up; to say good-bye	L6
佛教	Fójiào	Buddhism	L4

公事	gōngshì	business errand; official business	L2
貢獻	gòngxiàn	to contribute; contribution	L9, L12, L17
構成	gòuchéng	to constitute; to form	L8, L10
雇	gù	to hire	L7, L10, L18
孤兒院	gū'éryuàn	orphanage	L6
觀察	guānchá	to observe; to watch; observation	L5
廣	guǎng	broad, wide	(review) L11
冠軍	guànjūn	champion; championship; first place prize winner	L3
管理	guǎnlǐ	to manage, to supervise; management	L7, L19
官僚	guānliáo	bureaucratic; bureaucracy;	L4
觀念	guānniàn	concept；perception	(review) L2
關心	guānxīn	care for ; be concerned with; show solicitude for	(review) L1
慣用	guànyòng	idiomatic	L9
官員	guānyuán	official (n.)	L2, L4, L21
觀眾	guānzhòng	audience; viewer	L11, L16, L19
關注	guānzhù	to follow with interest; to pay close attention to	L1, L8, L19, L20
古代	gǔdài	ancient time	(review) L8
孤單	gūdān	alone; all by oneself; lonely	L6
固定	gùdìng	to fasten; to fix (and not change); fixed	L8
孤兒	gūér	orphan	L1, L4
古話	gǔhuà	old saying	(review) L10
規模	guīmó	scale; scope; extent	L4, L12, L13
規則	guīzé	rules; regulation	L8
估計	gūjì	to estimate; to evaluate; estimation	L5, L6
鼓勵	gǔlì	to encourage; encouragement	L2, L19
姑娘	gūniang	unmarried girl, young lady	L7
國民黨	Guómíndǎng	KMT: Chiang Kai-shek's political party；nationalist party	L4, L16
果然	guǒrán	as expected	L5
孤僻	gūpì	unsociable; eccentric (a negative usage); introverted	L3, L7
股票	gǔpiào	stock; shares	L8, L22
故事	gùshi	story; tale	(review) L1
股市	gǔshì	stock market	L8, L22
固執	gùzhí	stubborn	L8

H

哈佛	Hāfó	Harvard University	L3
海內外	hǎinèiwài	inland and overseas	L1
害怕	hàipà	to be afraid	(review) L4
海鮮	hǎixiān	seafood	L10
喊	hǎn	to shout; to yell; to cry out; to call a person	L3
行情	hángqíng	market quotations; market trend	L8
行業	hángyè	industry; profession; vocation	L2
韓裔	hányì	Korean-descendant	L6
毫不在乎	háobúzàihū	to not care about	L9
好奇	hàoqí	be curious, 好奇心=curiosity	(review) L6
好強	hàoqiáng	eager to put one's best foot forward; eager to proof one's capability	L7
合法性	héfǎxìng	legitimacy (合法 = legal; lawful)	L4
何況	hékuàng	much less; not to mention	L3, L7
河南	Hénán	name of a Chinese province	L4

恨不得	hènbùdé	to itch to; to be very anxious to (do something);	L3, L7
狠心	hěnxīn	to make up one's mind cruelly; cruel; cruel-hearted; heartless;	L7
何時	héshí	when (written expression)	L11
合資	hézī	joint-venture	L7, L12, L13
紅遍各地	hóng	to be hot; to be popular	L11
紅燒	hóngshāo	to braise or stew in soy sauce	L10
後悔	hòuhuǐ	to regret	L6
後來	hòulái	afterwards; later	(review) L1
懷裏	huáilǐ	bosom	L7
懷念	huáiniàn	to cherish the memory of; to think of	L1
懷疑	huáiyí	to suspect ; to have doubts; suspicions	L11, L17, L20
懷孕	huáiyùn	to be or to become pregnant	L2, L6.L9, L16
皇帝	huángdì	emperor	L3, L12
黄瓜	huánggua	cucumber	L10
環境	huánjìng	environment; surroundings	L4, L6, L14, L19
幻想	huànxiǎng	to fancy; illusion	L7
華人	huárén	Chinese people (including those who aren't Chinese citizens)	L1, L15, L19
話題	huàtí	subject (of talk); topic	L4
回	huí	to respond	L5
恢復	huīfù	to recover; to resume	L1, L19
回頭	huítóu	to turn one's head; to look back; later	L5, L19
回憶	huíyì	to recall; to look back upon; to reminisce; memoirs	L7
婚外關係	hūnwàiguānxi	extra-marital affair	L9
婚姻	hūnyīn	marriage	L6
活動	huódòng	activity	(review) L2
火箭	huǒjiàn	a rocket	L1
活潑	huópō	lively；full of life	(review) L3
胡思亂想	húsī luànxiǎng	to let one's mind wander; to let one's imagination run wild; to have fantasies	L5

J

繼	jì	following	L3
嫁	jià	(said of a woman) to marry; to marry off	L2
家教	jiājiào	private tutor	L3, L7
煎	jiān	to pan fry; to fry in a shallow oil	L10
肩膀	jiānbǎng	shoulder(s)	L7
堅持	jiānchí	to insist on; to persist in; to hold on	L8, L13
將	jiāng	a written usage that means 1) = 會：will (auxiliary verb) 2)= 把: as in 把書給我	L7, L16, L17, L18, …
薑	jiāng	ginger	L10
江澤民	Jiāng Zémín	name of former Chinese chairman	L4
講究	jiǎngjiu	to be particular about; to pay great attention to	L2, L10, L17
獎學金	jiǎngxuéjīn	scholarship; fellowship	L3, L7
漸漸	jiànjiàn	gradually; little by little	(review) L1
劍橋	Jiànqiáo	Cambridge; Cambridge University	L3
建議	jiànyì	to propose; to suggest; suggestion	L8
簡直	jiǎnzhí	simply; at all	L4
建筑	jiànzhù	to build; to erect; building; architecture	L8, L19, L22
驕傲	jiāo'ào	be proud of; arrogant; pride; to	L1
嬌慣	jiāoguàn	to spoil; to pamper; pampering	L3

叫好	jiàohǎo	to cheer on; to commend; acclaim	L3
交流	jiāoliú	to exchange; to communicate; communication; exchange; interchange;	L1, L14, L15, L17, …
教授	jiàoshòu	professor	L4, L16, L19
教訓	jiàoxun	to teach sb. a lesson; a lesson	L5, L12
教育	jiàoyù	to educate; education	L2, L3, L12, L15
加入	jiārù	to join	L1, L2, L13, L14
加速	jiāsù	to accelerate; to speed up (加速 = 加快速度 – sùdù-speed)	L1, L20
家庭	jiātíng	family	(review) L6
家長	jiāzhǎng	the parent or guardian of a child	L3
基本	jīběn	basic; fundamental 基本上=basically; by and large	L8
急匆匆	jí-cōngcōng	in a hurry	L5
激動萬分	jīdòng wànfēn	very agitated; excited	L11
基督教	Jīdūjiào	Christianity	L4
接	jiē	to pick up (a person)	(review) L6
結構	jiégòu	structure; construction	L8, L12, L17
解雇	jiěgù	to fire someone; to lay off	L7, L21
結果	jiéguǒ	result; finally; as a result; as it turns out	L3, L19
解決	jiějué	to resolve (a problem); to solve	L4, L10, L21
節省	jiéshěng	to economize; to use sparingly; to save; frugal	L7, L13
解釋	jiěshì	to explain; to interpret	L7
接受	jiēshòu	to accept; to take	L2, L14, L22
機構	jīgòu	institution; organization	L6, L21
幾乎	jīhū	almost	L11, L13, L16, 18
忌諱	jìhuì	to avoid as a taboo; to abstain from； taboo (n.)	L8
季節	jìjié	season	L10
激烈	jīliè	intense; fierce; violent(ly)	L3
記錄	jìlù	to record; to write down; record (n.)	L9
擠滿	jǐmǎn	to be at full capacity	L11
寂寞	jìmò	lonely, lonesome; loneliness	L6
禁不住/不禁	jīnbuzhù	can't help doing sth; can't refrain from	L10
警察	jǐngchá	police	(review) L11
警告	jǐnggào	to warn; to caution; warning;	L5
經濟	jīngjì	economic； economy	(review) L3
精力	jīnglì	energy; vigor	L3
經歷	jīnglì	to experience; to live through； experience	L11, L16
竟然	jìngrán	unexpectedly; to one's surprise	L2, L3, L4, L7…
精神	jīngshén	spirit; mind; vitality	L1, L14
精通	jīngtōng	to get a thorough knowledge of; to have a good command of	L10
儘管	jǐnguǎn	even though; in spite of	L5, L7, L8, L12,
經驗	jīngyàn	skill or knowledge from experience 有經驗 = experienced	(review) L4
競爭	jìngzhēng	to compete; to vie for; competition	L3, L12, L13
盡快	jǐnkuài	as soon as possible	L7
進入	jìnrù	to enter	L11
進行	jìnxíng	to process, to carry out; to be in progress	L1, L4, L6, L13…
既然	jìrán	since	L7, L8
即使…也	jíshǐ…yě	even if	L9
技術	jìshù	technique; skill; technology	L7, L13, L14, L19,
集體	jítǐ	collective; team	L6

舊	jiù	old; outdated	(review) L2
就算…也	jiùsuàn	even if	L4
繼續	jìxù	to continue; to keep on	(review) L7
急於	jíyú	to be impatient to; to be eager to	L2, L15
記者	jìzhě	journalist; reporter	L6, L22
集中	jízhōng	to concentrate; to focus on	L3
舉	jǔ	to raise; to lift; to hold up	L1
捐	juān	to donate	L1
捐款	juānkuǎn	to donate money; to contribute money; monetary contribution	L6, L20
決定	juédìng	to decide; decision	(review) L6
絕對	juéduì	absolute; absolutely	L4
決心	juéxīn	determination; resolution; (下決心= make up one's mind)	L6
聚會	jùhuì	to gather; gathering; get-together	L6
拒絕	jùjué	to refuse, to turn down; rejection	L7, L9
舉例	jǔlì	to give an example; to cite an instance	L8
巨人	jùrén	a giant (巨 = huge); gigantic	L1

K

開口	kāikǒu	to open one's mouth; to start to talk	L1, L5
開朗	kāilǎng	(of a person) open; cheerful; extroverted	L3, L7
開玩笑	kāiwánxiào	to joke, to make a joke of	(review) L10
開夜車	kāiyèchē	"to burn the midnight oil"	L9
抗議	kàngyì	to protest; to object; remonstrate; protest (n.)	L11, L17
靠	kào	to rely on, to depend on	(review) L4
靠	kào	to lean against	L5
烤	kǎo	to bake; to roast; to toast; to BBQ	L10
考慮	kǎolǜ	to consider; to think over	L7
棵	kē	一棵樹	(review) L5
可愛	kě'ài	cute; lovable; lovely	(review) L6
可憐	kělián	to have a pity on; pitiful; pitiable	L7
肯定	kěndìng	definitely; certainly; definite; surely; (to affirm: see also Lesson 3 for 否定)	L7
肯尼	kěnní	Kenny	L6
可惜	kěxī	unfortunately; it's a pity; it is too bad	L7
可笑	kěxiào	funny; silly; ridiculous	L6
空氣	kōngqì	air; atmosphere	L5, L17
控制	kòngzhì	to control; to dominate; control (n.)	L2, L12, L20
會計師	kuàijìshī	senior accountant; chartered accountant	L2
困難	kùnnan	difficult; difficulty	(review) L8

L

來不及	láibùjí	there's not enough time (to do sth) 來得及 = there's still time to do sth	L6
來源	láiyuán	source; origin	L9
來自	láizì	to come from	L1
辣椒	làjiāo	hot pepper; chili	L10
浪	làng	wave	L11
浪漫	làngmàn	romantic	L9, L11
籃球	lánqiú	basketball	(review) L1
壓迫	lǎobǎixìng	ordinary people	(review) L4
老婆	lǎopo	wife	L9, L10

瞞	mán	to hide the truth from a person	L7
茫然	mángrán	to feel lost; at a loss	L11
埋怨	mányuàn	to complain; to blame	L5
滿足	mǎnzú	to be fully satisfied, (讓人滿足/令人滿足= satisfying)	L6
毛澤東	Máo Zédōng	Mao Zedong	L2, L16
毛病	máobìng	illness; breakdown; defect	L6
冒險	màoxiǎn	to take a risk; at the risk of; risky	L6
每逢	měiféng	when; on every occasion	L6, L7
美好	měihǎo	happy and beautiful	L10
悶	mèn	boring; stuffy; suffocative (mēn)	L5
燜	mèn	to allow to simmer in a covered pot	L10
蒙古	ménggǔ	Mongolia	L9
夢想	mèngxiǎng	to dream; to vainly hope; an earnest wish	L7
免不了	miǎn-bùliǎo	to be unavoidable; bound to be	L3
面對	miànduì	to face; to confront	L3, L4, L6, L13
免費	miǎnfèi	free (of money)	L4
描寫	miáoxiě	to describe; to portray	L9, L15, L19
秘密	mìmi	secret; confidential	L5
迷迷糊糊	mímihúhu	in a daze; muddled	L5
明白	míngbai	to understand; clear; coherent; clearly; coherently	L11
名校	míngxiào	well-known schools	L3, L7
名義	míngyì	the name of; 以…的名義= in the name of; (名義上 = nominal; in name)	L6
名著	míngzhù	famous book; masterpiece; a classic	L3
民間	mínjiān	folk (adj.); nongovernmental	L4
民以食為天	mínyǐshíwéitiān	Food is the most important thing in the eyes of the people.	L10
民主	mínzhǔ	democratic democracy;	L4, L17, L19
迷信	míxìn	superstition; blind worship	L4
末	mò	the end of [used as a compond]	(review) L11
默不做聲	mòbú zuòshēng	to be silent	L8
默默地	mòmòdi	quietly; silently	L5
默契	mòqì	tacit understanding; privity; unvoiced pact]	L6, L14
陌生	mòshēng	strange; unfamiliar	L1, L6, L19
模式	móshì	model; mode	L3
某	mǒu	certain; some	L1, L20, L21
目前	mùqián	at present; at the moment	L2, L13

N

吶喊	nàhǎn	to shout loudly; loud shouts in support (of something)	L11
耐心	nàixīn	patience; patiently	L5
難道	nándào	[a word to strength one's rhetorical intonation]	L3, L7, L11
難得	nándé	hard to come by; rare; rarely	L7
難以想象	nányǐ-xiǎngxiàng	hard to conceive of ; unimaginable	L3
鬧笑話	nàoxiàohua	to make a fool of oneself	L8
內	nèi	within; inside	L2, L12
內心	nèixīn	innermost; of the heart	L11
能夠	nénggòu	be able to; be capable of	L6, L13, L14
能力	nénglì	ability; capacity for	L3
年紀	niánjì	age	(review) L7

強	qiáng	strong；powerful; better	(review) L3
強調	qiángdiào	to emphasize; to stress	L8, L17.L19, L20
強尼	Qiángní	Johnny	L6
千萬	qiānwàn	to be sure (usually used in an imperatival sentence)	(review) L2 口語, L8
謙虛	qiānxū	modest; modesty	L8
潛意識	qiǎnyìshi	sub-consciousness (意識 = consciousness, 潛= potential; to go under water)	L11
簽證	qiānzhèng	visa	L7
悄悄	qiāoqiāo	quietly	L11
氣氛	qìfen	atmosphere; air	L10, L17
氣候	qìhòu	climate	L10
騎驢找馬	qílǘ zhǎomǎ	to ride the donkey while looking for a horse (to retain while looking for something better (usually said of a job or a boyfriend or girlfriend)	L9
親戚	qīnqi	relatives; kinsfolk	(review) L6
青春	qīngchūn	youth (n.)	L9
青島	Qīngdǎo	Qingdao (a city in China)	L1
清華	Qīnghuá	name of a Chinese university	L7
請教	qǐngjiào	to consult; to ask for advice	L8
青椒	qīngjiāo	green pepper	L10
情景	qíngjǐng	scene; circumstances	L7, L10
情人	qíngrén	lover; sweetheart	L2
輕松	qīngsōng	to relax; relaxed; light; calm	L3
清新	qīngxīn	pure and fresh; fresh	L5
親近	qīnjìn	to approach; close (adj.); intimate	L9
其實	qíshí	actually; in fact; as a matter of fact	(review) L1
其他	qítā	other; else	L1
求婚	qiúhūn	to propose (a marriage)	L6
球賽	qiúsài	ball game (比賽 = game; to take part in the game)	L1
球員	qiúyuán	ballplayer	L1
秋雲	qiūyún	name of a girl	L6
氣溫	qìwēn	temperature	L11
企業	qǐyè	enterprise; corporation	L2, L12
其中	qízhōng	among (which, them, etc)	L8, L12, L17
妻子	qīzi	wife	L5, L16
娶	qǔ	to marry a woman; to take to wife	L2, L6, L10
全部	quánbù	total; all	L3
勸告	quàngào	to advise; to warn; to exhort; exhortation	L6, L10, L16
勸酒勸菜	quànjiǔ quàncài	to urge sb. to drink and eat more	L10
權利	quánlì	right (n.); interest	L2, L17, L20
取代	qǔdài	to replace; to take over	L4
卻	què	but; yet (used as an adverb. Also written as 䣐)	L1, L2, L5, L15, …
缺乏	quēfá	to lack; to be short of	L3, L12, L14, L16
群	qún	group; measure word "a group of" "a herd of"	L6, L7
群體	qúntǐ	collective unit; group	L9
群眾	qúnzhòng	the masses; the general public	L9
去世	qùshì	to pass away	L1, L12
取消	qǔxiāo	to cancel	L11, L20, P1132L21

R

然而	rán'ér	however	L2
認	rèn	to recognize	L5
人家	rénjiā	other people	(review) L1 口語, L5
忍不住	rěnbúzhù	can't help but do sth.	L7
扔	rēng	to throw; to toss; to throw away	L4, L6
仍舊	réngjiù	still; yet	L5
人工	réngōng	artificial；man-made; artificially	L6
仍然	réngrán	as usual; still (adv.)	L4, L7, L14, L18, …
人口	rénkǒu	population	(review) L2
人群	rénqún	a crowd of people	L5
人事處	rénshìchù	office of human resources	L7
忍受	rěnshòu	to endure; to suffer; to bear	L2, L3
認為	rènwéi	to think; to deem	(review) L1
人物	rénwù	figure; personage; character	L4, L22
任務	rènwù	mission; task	L9
忍心	rěnxīn	to have the heart to	L7
任性	rènxìng	capricious; willful; stubborn	L3
認真	Rènzhēn	serious, seriously; to take seriously; to take to heart	(review) L6
熱情	rèqíng	enthusiastic; warm; enthusiasm; warmth	L1
日常	rìcháng	day-to-day; daily (matters) (adj.)	(review) L9
日子	rìzǐ	days; date; life; livelihood	(review) L7
肉	ròu	meat	(review) L10
如	rú	as; as if; such as	L2, L9
軟綿綿	ruǎnmiánmián	as soft as cotton	L11
如此(as in 如此高興\如此興奮)	rúcǐ	as so; like that	L6
若	ruò	if	L6, L17, L22
入睡	rùshuì	to fall asleep	L5

S

散開	sànkāi	to disperse; to scatter	L5
三心二意	sānxīnèryì	cannot make up one's mind; to be of two minds	L8
色香味	sè xiāng wèi	color, smell, and flavor	L10
色鬼	sèguǐ	pervert;lady-killer	L5
色情	sèqíng	erotic; eroticism	L2
傻	shǎ	stupid; muddleheaded; silly	L5
殺菌	shājūn	to sterilize; to kill germs	L10
沙拉	shāla	salad	L10
傷	shāng	to hurt; to injure, wound; injury	L6, L18
傷腦筋	shāng nǎojīn	to cause sb. a headache; knotty; bothersome	L2, L3
傷害	shānghài	to hurt; to harm; harm; hurt	L7, L19
上火	shànghuǒ	to suffer from excessive internal heat (according to traditional Chinese medicine)	L10
商量	shāngliáng	to talk over; to consult with sb	(review) L7
商業	shāngyè	commerce ; trade; commercial	L7, L14
燒	shāo	to stew after frying or to fry after stewing; to cook	L10
勺子	sháozǐ	spoon	(review) L10
捨得	shěde	to willingly expend; not begrudge	L3, L7, L13
社會	shèhuì	society	(review) L2
社會主義	shèhuì zhǔyì	socialism	L11
深	shēn	deep	(review) L11

深藏不露	shēncáng bú lòu	to hide one's great ability; to be modest about one's skill	L8
省	shěng	province	L4, L19.L22
升	shēng	to rise; to promote	L11
生菜	shēngcài	an uncooked vegetable; lettuce	L10
生產	shēngchǎn	to produce; to manufacture; production	L2, L13, L21
生動	shēngdòng	lively; vivid	L8, L9
生意	shēngyì	busines, trade	(review) L2
生龍活虎	shēnglóng huóhǔ	to be energetic; doughty as a dragon and lively as a tiger -- full of vim and vigor	L8
生氣	shēngqì	to get angry; be angry at	(review) L3
總	shēngyì	always；consistently	(review) L2
聲音	shēngyīn	voice; sound	L11
生長	shēngzhǎng	to grow; growth	(review) L8
審判	shěnpàn	trial; to try; trial (n.)	L9
申請	shēnqǐng	to apply for; to apply to	L3, L7, L20
深入	shēnrù	to go deep into; to penetrate; intensively	L11
甚至	shènzhì	even; so much so that	L1
使	shǐ	to make; to cause; to enable (written expression. Similar to “讓”)	L1, L3, L15, L!6, ….
詩	shī	poem	L9
時代	shídài	times; era; age	L2, L20
十分	shífēn	very; fully	L6
是否	shìfǒu	是不是；whether	L11, L20
師傅	shīfu	master worker; a polite form to address blue-collar workers	L8
適合	shìhé	to suit; to fit; to be appropriate for	L9
實際	shíjì	practical; realistic; actual (實際上 = actually)	L1, L12
世紀	shìjì	century	L2, L13, L16
世界	shìjiè	world	(review) L4
時髦	shímáo	stylish; fashionable	L5, L13
失去	shīqù	to lose (something important and/or significant)	L11, L12, L15
事實	shìshí	fact; truth (事實上= in fact; as a matter of fact)	L7, L15
視為	shìwéi	把/被...視為	L2
實行	shíxíng	to carry out; to implement	L2
適應	shìyìng	to adapt to; to get with it; to fit in	L3, L14, L17
適用	shìyòng	to be applicable; suitable for use	L3
使用	shǐyòng	to use; usage	L4, L8, L17, L21
食慾	shíyù	appetite	L10
實在	shízai	indeed; really; honestly	L8, L15
首	shǒu	一首歌, 一首詩, 一首順口溜	(review) L9, L11
手冊	shǒucè	handbook; manual; pamphlet	L4
手段	shǒuduàn	means; measure; artifice	L6
收獲	shōuhuò	to harvest; to gather in the crops; to gain; the harvest; gain (n.)	L10
收集	shōují	to collect; to gather	L8
首輪	shǒulún	the preliminary round (of election) (首 = first; highest; supreme)	L1
手續	shǒuxù	procedure; formalities	L6, L7
手藝	shǒuyì	workmanship; skill	L8
受孕	shòuyùn	to become pregnant	L6
蔬菜	shūcài	vegetables; greens	L10

束縛	shùfú	to constrain; bondage; rigid control	L2, L12, L16
順口溜	shùnkǒuliū	rhymed, slang verse	L9
順利	shùnlì	smooth going; smoothly;	L4
說服	shuōfú/shuìfú	to persuade; to convince	L6, L19
碩士	shuòshì	Master's degree(M.A.)	L7
屬於	shǔyú	to belong to; to be part of; to be included in	L4, L6, L8, …
熟悉	shúxi	familar	(review) L9
四川泡菜	Sìchuān pàocài	Sichuan picked vegetables (泡菜＝ pickles)	L10
似乎	sìhū	it seems; as if; it looks like	L1, L2, L6, …
思考	sīkǎo	to reflect upon; to ponder over; to think deeply about	L11
私生活	sīshēnghuó	private life	(review) L9
思想	sīxiǎng	frame of mind, outlook, principles; thoughts	L11, L17
私營	sīyíng	privately-operated	L2
蒜	suàn	garlic (usually appears as 大蒜)	L10
隨	suí	to follow	L5
隨便	suíbiàn	casual, random, informal; as one wishes; careless	(review) L8
隨著	suízhe	along with	L9, L11, L13, L20
孫女	sūnnǚ	granddaughter	(review) L5
所	suǒ	一所學校, 一所房子, 一所醫院	L1
所謂	suǒwèi	what is called; so-called	L1, L2, L9, L18
俗語	súyǔ	common saying	L9, L17

T

踏	tà	to step on	L7
態度	tàidu	attitude; manner	L4
太極拳	tàijíquán	Tai-chi	(review) L5
太陽	tàiyáng	sun	L11
躺	tǎng	to lie (down); to recline	L5
嘆氣	tànqì	to sigh	L5, L7
逃犯	táofàn	escaped criminal; fugitive	L5
討論	tǎolùn	to discuss; to talk over	(review) L1
討厭	tǎoyàn	to dislike; to be disgusted with; to be fed up with;	L3
特別	tèbié	special; unusual; especially	(review) L1
特點	tèdiǎn	characteristic	(review) L11
特色	tèsè	characteristic, distinguishing feature	L8
踢	tī	to kick	L1
提	tí	to carry (in one's hand below the shoulders)	L1, L17, L19, …
提	tí	to mention; to bring up	L7, L9, L15
替	tì	to replace; for ; on behalf of	L1
天安門廣場	Tiānānménguǎngchǎng	Tiananmen Square	L11
天才	tiāncái	talented; talent; genius	L11
天津	Tiānjīn	name of a city in China	L6
天空	tiānkōng	the sky; the heavens	L6
天生	tiānshēng	innate; inborn; inherent	L6
甜酸雞	tiánsuānjī	sweet and sour chicken	L10
天真	tiānzhēn	naïve; childlike innocence	L7
挑	tiāo	1) to shoulder 2) to choose; to pick	L7
條件	tiáojiàn	condition	(review) L3
挑戰	tiǎozhàn	to challenge; challenge	L4, L11, L12, L17
提供	tígōng	to provide; to supply; to offer	L2, L4, L6, L12, …

題目	tímù	title; subject	(review) L9
聽從	tīngcóng	to obey; to listen to	L6
體育館	tǐyùguǎn	gymnasium; stadium	L11
通過	tōngguò	to pass; by means of	L4, L6, L14, L15…
統計	tǒngjì	to count up; statistics; census	L2, L13, L14, L22
同事	tóngshì	colleague	(review) L7
通俗	tōngsú	popular; common	L9
通訊	tōngxùn	communication (of using electronic technology)	L7, L20, L22
同意	tóngyì	to agree; to consent	(review) L4
同義詞	tóngyìcí	synonym(s); 反義詞：antonym(s)	L11
通知	tōngzhī	to inform; to notify; notice (n.)	L7
頭等	tóuděng	first-class	L10
頭發	tóufa	hair	(review) L1
偷偷	tōutōu	secretly; sneakily	L11
頭一個	tóuyígè	the first	L1
團體	tuántǐ	organization; group	L4, L19
土地	tǔdi	land	L7, L17
禿頂	tūdǐng	bald; bald-headed	L5
土豆絲	tǔdòusī	shredded potato (土豆 is also called 馬鈴薯 [mǎlíngshǔ]) (絲 = thread or thread like thing)	L10
推	tuī	to push	L5
退堂	tuìtáng	to leave the court	L9
推銷	tuīxiāo	to try to sell; to market	L6
退休	tuìxiū	to retire	L5, L9
脫褲子放屁	tuōkùzi fàngpì	to take off one's pants to fart (to do something that is unnecessary and superfluous)	L9
突然	tūrán	sudden; unexpected; suddenly	L1, L5, L18

W

外交	wàijiāo	diplomatic; diplomacy; foreign affairs	L1, L20, L22
外套	wàitào	overcoat; outer wear	(review) L5
網	wǎng	net; internet	L2
網絡	wǎngluò	internet	L7, L14, L20
望子成龍, 望女成鳳	wàngzǐchénglóng, wàngnǚchéngfèng	to hope that sons and daughters will grow up to be successful	L3
玩弄	wánnòng	to play with; to dally with men/women	L8
頑皮	wánpí	naughty; mischievous	L1, L3, L7
完全	wánquán	completely, entirely	(review) L2
偉大	wěidà	great (for achievement or personality); mighty	L1, L7
味道	wèidào	scent; flavor; taste	L9, L10
衛生	wèishēng	hygienic; sanitary hygiene; sanitation;	L4
危險	wēixiǎn	dangerous, danger	(review) L6
微笑	wēixiào	to smile; smile	L5
溫和	wēnhé	gentle; mild; moderate	L5
文化	wénhuà	culture	(review) L1
文化大革命	wénhuà dàgémìng	Chinese Cultural Revolution	L11, L15, L16
文雅	wényǎ	refined; educated; elegant	L9
文章	wen2zhang1	article; essay	(review) L8
臥室	wòshì	bedroom	L5
無比	wúbǐ	incomparable; unparalleled	L11
無處不在	wúchù búzài	to exist everywhere	L10, L20

無法	wúfǎ	unable; incapable (usually followed by two-syllable verb)	L3
五花八門	wǔhuā bāmén	a wide variety of; a motley variety of	L10
無話不說	wúhuà bùshuō	to talk about everything; to hide nothing	L10
誤會	wùhuì	to misunderstand; misunderstanding	L5
無奈	wúnài	can't help but; to have no choice (usually used as an adjective)	L9
無人能比	wúrén-néngbǐ	incomparable; beyond comparison	L3
無數	wúshù	countless; innumerable	L1
無私	wúsī	selfless; disinterested	L1, L4, L7
無所謂	wúsuǒwèi	to be indifferent; not matter	L6
舞臺	wǔtái	stage for performances	L11
無限	wúxiàn	unlimited; infinite	L6
五顏六色	wǔyán liùsè	colorful	L10
物質	wùzhì	material; substance	L2, L4

X

系	xì	school department	L7
吸毒	xīdú	to use drug	L7
蝦	xiā	shrimp (龍蝦 = Lobster)	L10
下崗	xiàgǎng	to be laid-off from a unit	L5, L9
嫌	xián	to dislike; to mind; to complain of	L5
現代	xiàndài	modern times; modern; contemporary	(review) L6
顯得	xiǎnde	to appear (to be); to seem	L9
項	xiàng	item; sub-category (measure word)	L1, L2, L16, L20
想不通	xiǎng bùtōng	cannot think through, cannot know why	L7
相對	xiāngduì	to be opposite, relative (opposite of "absolute")	L9
相聚	xiāngjù	to get together	L10
向來	xiànglái	always; all along	L10, L19
享受	xiǎngshòu	to enjoy; enjoyment	L1, L2, L6, L9
向往	xiàngwǎng	to yearn for; to look forward to	L10, L16
鄉下	xiāngxià	countryside	L10, L18
相信	xiāngxìn	to believe	(review) L4
閑話	xiánhuà	gossip;chitchat	L5
先進	xiānjìn	advanced	L10, L13
羡慕	xiànmù	to envy; to admire	L6
顯然	xiǎnrán	obvious; evident; obviously	L3
現象	xiànxiàng	phenomenon	L6, L19, L20
限制	xiànzhì	to restrict; restriction	L4, L6, L20
小心	xiǎoxīn	to be careful; to be cautious;careful	(review) L6
消化	xiāohuà	to digest; digestion	L10
小秘	xiǎomì	" little secretary;" i.e. a secretary who also acts as a mistress (秘書 = secretary)	L2
消滅	xiāomiè	to exterminate; to wipe out	L11
消失	xiāoshī	to disappear; to vanish	L9
笑盈盈	xiào-yíngyíng	smilingly	L5
下手	xiàshǒu	to put one's hand to; to start; to set about	L8
血	xiě	blood	L4
邪惡	xié'è	evil; malicious	L11
瀉肚子	xièdǔzi	to have a diarrhea; sometimes appear as 拉肚子	(review) L11
協議	xiéyì	an agreement	L7, L21
西紅柿	xīhóngshì	tomato (also called 番茄[fānqié])	L10

信封	xìn fēng	envelope	L7
性別	xìngbié	gender (性 = sex)	L2
興奮	xīngfèn	to be excited；hectic; 讓/令人興奮=exciting	(review) L6
幸福	xìngfú	happy, happiness	L6, L10
性感	xìnggǎn	sexy	L2
性格	xìnggé	personality; disposition; character (synonym: 個性)	L3
行李	xínglǐ	luggage; baggage	L1
形容	xíngróng	to describe (形容詞: adjective)	L8, L22
行為	xíngwéi	action; behavior	L4, L22
心靈	xīnlíng	soul; heart	L7
心事	xīnshì	sth. weighing on one's mind; a load on one's mind	L5
信息	xìnxī	information	L8, L14
胸	xiōng	chest	L5
犧牲	xīshēng	to sacrifice; to do something at the expense of another	L9
系統	xìtǒng	system; systematically	L10
希望	xīwàng	to hope; hope	(review) L3
選	xuǎn	to select; to choose	L1, L4
宣布	xuānbù	to announce; to declare	L11, L20, L21
選舉	xuǎnjǔ	to elect; to select by vote; election	L4
炫耀	xuànyào	to show off; to flaunt	L8
選擇	xuǎnzé	to select; to choose; election; choice	L3
許多	xǔduō	many, much, a great deal of	(review) L1
學問	xuéwen	learning; knowledge (有學問 = knowledgeable)	L10
學院	xuéyuàn	college (for a higher degree)	L4
學者	xuézhě	scholar	L10, L19
尋找	xúnzhǎo	to seek; to search for	L9, L18
壓力	yālì	pressure	L3
演唱會	yǎnchànghuì	music concert with vocals	L11

Y

様	yàng	type, kind	(review) L10
養家	yǎngjiā	to support the family (養 = to raise; to provide food)	L4
洋女人	yángnǚren	foreign woman(洋= foreign; ocean)	L7, (L13)
嚴格	yángé	to be strict; rigid	(review) L3
眼淚	yǎnlèi	tears	L7, L16
言行	yánxíng	words and deeds	L5
嚴重	yánzhòng	critical; serious (said of problems or illnesses)	L2
嚴重性	yánzhòngxìng	ponderance	(review) L4
搖滾	yáogǔn	rock and roll	L11
姚明	Yáomíng	name of a famous Chinese basketball player	L1
邀請	yāoqǐng	to invite; invitation	L6
搖頭	yáotóu	to shake one's head	L5, L7
謠言	yáoyán	rumor	L11
壓迫	yāpò	to oppress; to repress; oppression	L2, L4, L17
押韻	yāyùn	to rhyme; to have a correspondence of terminal sounds of words or of lines of verse	L9
夜郎自大	Yèlángzìdà	to be too proud of oneself out of ignorance; ignorant boastfulness;	L8
耶魯	Yēlǔ	Yale University	L3

一敗涂地	yíbàitúdì	to suffer a crushing defeat; to suffer a complete loss	L8
一般	yībān	general; ordinary；generally	(review) L3
一輩子	yíbèizi	lifetime; a lifetime of;as long as one lives;	L6
一成不變	yìchéng búbiàn	invariable; immutable and never-changing	L8
一旦	yídàn	once; in case; now that	L2, L13
一帆風順	yìfān fēngshùn	as smooth and pleasant as a perfect sailing	L8
以及	yǐjí	and; as well as; along with	L2, L16, L19, L20, …
意見	yìjiàn	opinions; view; objection and complain	L8
一見鍾情	yījiàn zhōngqíng	fall in love at first sight	L8
因此	yīncǐ	hence; therefore	L4, L8, L9, L10
贏	yíng	to win; to beat in competition	L3, L4, L15
影響力	yǐngxiǎng-lì	power of influence (力 can be a suffix meaning "power or ability", such as in 創造力, 想象力, 適應力)	L4
英雄	yīngxióng	hero	L1, L12
營養	yíngyǎng	nutrition (有營養 = nourishing; nutritious)	L10
引起	yǐnqǐ	to cause; to arouse; to attract (notice)	L4, L5, L9, L17, …
印象	yìnxiàng	impression	L3, L19
一片	yípiàn	a slice; a stretch (of land, water); a scene of (rejoicing, sound)	L3
一切	yíqiè	everything; all	L7
一生	yìshēng	a lifetime; all of one's life	L1, L3, L15
一無所有	yìwúsuǒyǒu	to have nothing at all in the world	L11
一向	yíxiàng	all along, as always (until the present)	L3, L6
醫學	yīxué	medical science	L6
一陣子	yízhènzi	a period of time	L6, L7
一直	yīzhí	all along; always; continuously	(review) L6
用餐	yòngcān	to dine	L10
勇敢	yǒnggǎn	brave; courageous	L3
用功	yònggōng	to study hard；diligent; studious	(review) L3
擁有	yōngyǒu	to own; to possess	L6, L7, L20
永遠	yǒngyuǎn	forever; always	L1
由	yóu	by; through	L6
游	yóu	to swim; usually appear as "游泳"(yóuyǒng)	(review) L10
友好	yǒuhǎo	friendly; amicable	L1, L21
幽默	yōumò	humorous (幽默感 = sense of humor)	L9, L10
有趣	yǒuqù	interesting; amusing	L9
幼小	yòuxiǎo	immature; infantile	L7, L18
優秀	yōuyòu	outstanding; excellent	L10, L16, L17
由於	yóuyú	due to; because of; in that	L2, L4, L15, L19
猶豫	yóuyù bùjué	to remain undecided to poise; (猶豫=to hesitate)	L8
於	yú	in; on (written expression)	L1
與	yǔ	and (in written Chinese)	(review) L11
原本	yuánběn	original; originally; formerly	L3, L4, L15, L17
原來	yuánlái	original, former	(review) L4
原諒	yuánliàng	to excuse; to forgive; forgiveness	L7
圓夢	yuánmèng	to fulfill a dream or a goal	L3, L7
願意	yuànyì	to be willing to	L2
原因	yuányīn	cause; reason	(review) L6

愚笨	yúbèn	foolish; stupid	L8
與此同時	yúcǐ-tóngshí	at the same time; meanwhile	L3, L20
樂隊	yuèduì	orchestra; band	L11
岳母	yuèmǔ	mother-in-law (wife's mother)	L5
樂壇	yuètán	musical circles (of people); music world	L11
愚公移山	Yúgōng yíshān	to be as determined as the old man's attempt to move the mountain	L8
運動鞋	yùndòngxié	sneakers	(review) L7
運動員	yùndòngyuán	sportsman; athlete	L1
允許	yǔnxǔ	to allow; to permit; permission	L4
於是	yúshì	thereupon; consequently	L5, L6, L17

Z

在乎	zàihu	to care about; to mind	L5, L7
在世	zàishì	to be alive	L5
在於	zàiyú	to lie in; to reside in; to be found in	L11
咱們	zánmen	we;us (include the listner)	(review) L7
暫時	zànshí	temporary; for the time being	L7, L14
造成	zàochéng	to cause; to create (sth. unpleasant)	L7, L17, L19, L20…
遭遇	zāoyù	to encounter (unhappy thing); misfortune	L6, L9, L16
增加	zēngjiā	to increase; to add	L10
增進	zēngjìn	to enhance	L10
增長	zēngzhǎng	to increase; to grow; growth	L2, L13, L18
責任	zérèn	duty; responsibility	L3
炸	zhà	to deep-fry	(review) L10
著急	zháojí	to be worried; to feel anxious	(review) L7
蒸	zhēng	to steam (清蒸 = to steam in clear soup)	L10
政策	zhèngcè	policy	L2, L6, L19, L20
正常	zhèngcháng	normal; regular；normally	L6
政府	zhèngfǔ	government	(review) L2
正好	zhènghǎo	exactly right; coincidently right (adj.)	L5
爭取	zhēngqǔ	to fight for; to strive for	L2
正確	zhèngquè	correct (adj.); right	L8, L16
正式	zhèngshì	formal; official	L4, L15
爭議	zhēngyì	controversy	L4, L19
掙扎	zhēngzhá	to struggle; a struggle	L11, L15
震撼	zhènhàn	to shake, to shock; shock (n.) , shaking,	L11, L15, L16
針頭	zhēntóu	pinhead; needle tip; 打針= to give an injection	L4
真正	zhēnzhèng	genuine; really	L6, L11
指	zhǐ	to point to, to refer to	L8, L9
織	zhī	to knit; to weave	L5
之	zhī	的 in written Chinese [as in 在此之前]	(review) L8
治病	zhìbìng	to treat disease; to cure illness	L4
支持	zhīchí	to support; to back	L4, L13, L17, L20
值得	zhídé	to be worth; to deserve	L1, L3, L20
制度	zhìdù	system	L9, L17
指教	zhǐjiào	to give advice or comments to; advice or comments	L8
直接	zhíjiē	direct; directly; (間接: inderct; indirectly)	L8
智商	zhìshāng	IQ(intelligence quotient)	L6
職業	zhíyè	occupation; profession; vocation	L1
至於	zhìyú	as for; as to	L8, L14, L15, L18…

指責	zhǐzé	to blame; to accuse	L9, L21
執政	zhízhèng	to be in power; to be in office; to be at the helm of the state	L4, L17, L19
重擔	zhòngdàn	heavy burden; heavy responsibility	L7
中華	zhōnghuá	China; the Chinese nation	L2
中介	zhōngjiè	agency	L6
重男輕女	zhòngnánqīngnǚ	to value the male child only; to prefer sons to daughters	L2, L6
重視	zhòngshì	to value highly; to attach importance to	L3, L4, L9
中心	zhōngxīn	center	(review) L10
中央	zhōngyāng	center; middle; central	L4
中醫	zhōngyī	Chinese medicine (西醫=western medicine)	L4
終於	zhōngyú	finally; eventually	L1, L3, L5, L18
皺眉頭	zhòu-méitóu	to frown	L5
週末	zhoūmò	weekend	(review) L3
煮	zhǔ	to boil, to cook	(review) L10
抓	zhuā	to seize; to grab	L5, L16, L18
裝聾作啞	zhuānglóng zuòyǎ	to pretend to be ignorant of sth.; pretend ignorance	L8
專輯	zhuānjí	music album	L11
專家	zhuānjiā	expert	L8, L22
專門	zhuānmén	special; specialized; specially	L10, L20
賺錢	zhuànqián	to make money; to make a profit	L1, L4, L7
專業人員	zhuānyè rényuán	professionals	L2
主管	zhǔguǎn	to be in charge of; the person in charge	L2
主觀	zhǔguān	subjective; subjectivity; (客觀 = objective; objectivity)	L8
追求	zhuīqiú	to pursue; to seek；to woo	L1, L11
準	zhǔn	accurate; precise	L8
準確	zhǔnquè	precise; accurate	L8
桌布	zhuōbù	table cloth	L10
主席	zhǔxí	chairman	L4
自大	zìdà	arrogant	L8
資本主義	zīběnzhǔyì	Capitalism	L11
自不量力	zìbúliànglì	to do sth. beyond one's ability; be unaware of one's own limitation	L8
資料	zīliào	data, document	L6, L14
字面	zìmiàn	literal; literal meaning	L8
自然	zìrán	natural; nature	L4
自殺	zìshā	to commit suicide; suicide (n.)	L7, L16
自私	zìsī	selfish	L1, L7
仔細	zǐxì	careful; attentive; closely; carefully	L2, L5, L6
享受	zǒng		(review) L2
宗教	zōngjiào	religion	L4, L21
總統	zǒngtǒng	president (of a country)	L4, L21
走火入魔	zǒuhuǒ-rùmó	to have blind faith in; to be possessed by the Devil	L4
組合	zǔhé	to compose; to assemble; composition;, combination	L8
罪犯	zuìfàn	criminal (n.)	L9
最終	zuìzhōng	finally; at last;at the end	L8
尊敬	zūnjìng	to respect; to honor	L1, L12, L15
座	zuò	一座山，一座建筑	(review) L8

坐冷板凳	zuò lěng-bǎndèng	to sit on the cold bench (to be idled from important tasks)	L9, L15
左宗棠雞	Zuǒ Zōngtáng jī	General Tso's Chicken	L10
作風	zuòfēng	style; style of work; method of doing something	L4, L14
坐井觀天	zuòjǐng guāntiān	to look into the sky from sitting in a well -limited outlook; to take a narrow view of things	L8
佐料	zuǒliào	sauce	L10
作用	zuòyòng	effect; function	L10
組織	zǔzhī	to organize; organization	L2, L4

第一冊詞彙 英文索引(Volume 1 English Vocabulary Index)

A

ball game (比賽 = game; to take part in the game)	球賽	qiúsài	L1
ballplayer	球員	qiúyuán	L1
basic; fundamental 基本上=basically; by and large	基本	jīběn	L8
basketball	籃球	lánqiú	(review) L1
to be afraid	害怕	hàipà	(review) L4
to be applicable; suitable for use	適用	shìyòng	L3
be curious, 好奇心=curiosity	好奇	hàoqí	(review) L6
to be excited; hectic; 讓/令人興奮=exciting	興奮	xīngfèn	(review) L6
to be forced to; to be compelled to	被迫	bèipò	L7, L13
to be hot; to be popular	紅遍各地	hóng	L11
to be in power; to be in office; to be at the helm of the state	執政	zhízhèng	L4, L17, L19
be proud of; arrogant; pride; to	驕傲	jiāo'ào	L1
to be strict; rigid	嚴格	yángé	(review) L3
to be sure (usually used in an imperatival sentence)	千萬	qiānwàn	(review) L2 口語, L8
to be worried; to feel anxious	著急	zháojí	(review) L7
to bear; to endure	承受	chéngshòu	L9, L15
to beat down	打倒	dǎdǎo	L4
to beat the drum (to feel uncertain; to feel nervous)	打鼓	dǎgǔ	L9
to beat the step-down-the-stage drum (to give up a pursuit without attaining one's goal; to give up)	打退堂鼓	dǎ tuìtánggǔ	L9
bedroom	臥室	wòshì	L5
beef steak	牛排	niúpái	L10
at the beginning; in the first place;	當初	dāngchū	L6, L7
the beginning of [used as a compond]	初	chū	(review) L11
to believe	相信	xiāngxìn	(review) L4
to belong to; to be part of; to be included in	屬於	shǔyú	L4, L6, L8, …
benefits; welfare (see also Lesson 6 福利院)	福利	fúlì	L9
to blame; to accuse	指責	zhǐzé	L9, L21
blood	血	xiě	L4
to blow and to fly	紛飛	fēnfēi	L11
to boil, to cook	煮	zhǔ	(review) L10
boring; stuffy; suffocative (mēn)	悶	mèn	L5
To be born, birth; to come into the world	誕生	dànshēng	L11
bosom	懷裏	huáilǐ	L7
bossy ; overbearing; high-handed	霸道	bàdào	L3
to bother; annoying; vexed	煩	fán	L5
to braise or stew in soy sauce	紅燒	hóngshāo	L10
brave; courageous	勇敢	yǒnggǎn	L3
to break; to smash	打破	dǎpò	L2, L5, L17
trial; to try; trial (n.)	審判	shěnpàn	L9
broad, wide	廣	guǎng	(review) L11
Buddhism	佛教	Fójiào	L4
to build; to erect; building; architecture	建筑	jiànzhù	L8, L19, L22
to bump into the nail (to be rebuffed)	碰釘子	pèngdīngzi	L9
bumper crop; a good harvest	豐收	fēngshōu	L10
bureaucratic; bureaucracy;	官僚	guānliáo	L4
"to burn the midnight oil"	開夜車	kāiyèchē	L9
businees, trade	生意	shēngyì	(review) L2
business errand; official business	公事	gōngshì	L2
to go on a business trip	出差	chūchāi	L7

to consider; to think over	考慮	kǎolǜ	L7
constant; constantly	不斷	búduàn	L9, L14
to constitute; to form	構成	gòuchéng	L8, L10
to constrain; bondage; rigid control	束縛	shùfú	L2, L12, L16
to consult; to ask for advice	請教	qǐngjiào	L8
to continue; to keep on	繼續	jìxù	(review) L7
to contribute; contribution	貢獻	gòngxiàn	L9, L12, L17
to control; to dominate; control (n.)	控制	kòngzhì	L2, L12, L20
controversy	爭議	zhēngyì	L4, L19
to cook (dishes); cooking	烹調	pēngtiáo	L10
cook, chief	廚師	chúshī	L7, L10
to coordinate; in step with	配合	pèihé	L10
correct (adj.); right	正確	zhèngquè	L8, L16
corrupt (adj.); rotten (morally, ethically)	腐敗	fǔbài	L11, L21
to count up; statistics; census	統計	tǒngjì	L2, L13, L14, L22
countless; innumerable	無數	wúshù	L1
countryside	鄉下	xiāngxià	L10, L18
countryside; village	農村	nóngcūn	L1, L2, L4
craftsman	工匠	gōngjiàng	L8
cram school	補習班	bǔxíbān	L3, (L7)
to create (artwork); creation	創作	chuàngzuò	L11, L17, L19
creativity	創造性	chuàngzàoxìng	L3
criminal (n.)	罪犯	zuìfàn	L9
critical; serious (said of problems or illnesses)	嚴重	yánzhòng	L2
a crowd of people	人群	rénqún	L5
cruel; brutal	殘酷	cánkù	L7
to make up one's mind cruelly; cruel; cruel-hearted; heartless;	狠心	hěnxīn	L7
cucumber	黃瓜	huánggua	L10
to cultivate; to foster; to educate	培養	peíyǎng	L3, L14
culture	文化	wénhuà	(review) L1
to curse; to scold; to criticize; to reprimand	罵	mà	L9
cute; lovable; lovely	可愛	kěài	(review) L6

D

dangerous, danger	危險	wēixiǎn	(review) L6
to dare to	敢	gǎn	(review) L5
data, document	資料	zīliào	L6, L14
days; date; life; livelihood	日子	rìzǐ	(review) L7
day-to-day; daily (matters) (adj.)	日常	rìcháng	(review) L9
in a daze; muddled	迷迷糊糊	mímihúhu	L5
的(de) in written Chinese [as in 在此之前]	之	zhī	(review) L8
to decide; decision	決定	juédìng	(review) L6
to decline (morally); corruption; decay (of morals); indulgence	墮落	duòluò	L11, L16
deep	深	shēn	(review) L11
to deep-fry	炸	zhà	(review) L10
definitely; certainly; definite; surely; (to affirm: see also Lesson 3 for 否定)	肯定	kěndìng	L7
deformity, handicap	殘疾	cánjí	L6
degree	度	dù	L11
democratic democracy;	民主	mínzhǔ	L4, L17, L19

E

the end of [used as a compond]	末	mò	(review) L11
endlessly; ceaselessly (V 個不休)	不休	bùxiū	L11
to endure hardship	吃苦	chīkǔ	L3, L10
to endure; to suffer; to bear	忍受	rěnshòu	L2, L3
enemy	敵人	dírén	L11
to be energetic; doughty as a dragon and lively as a tiger -- full of vim and vigor	生龍活虎	shēnglóng huóhǔ	L8
energy; vigor	精力	jīnglì	L3
engineering; project	工程	gōngchéng	L7, L14
to enhance	增進	zēngjìn	L10
to enjoy; enjoyment	享受	xiǎngshòu	L1, L2, L6, L9
to enrich; abundant; plentiful	豐富	fēngfù	L6, L10, L14, L19
to enter	進入	jìnrù	L11
enterprise; corporation	企業	qǐyè	L2, L12
enthusiastic; warm; enthusiasm; warmth	熱情	rèqíng	L1
envelope	信封	xìn fēng	L7
environment; surroundings	環境	huánjìng	L4, L6, L14, L19
to envy; to admire	羡慕	xiànmù	L6
to be equal to; to be equivalent to; to amount to	等於	děngyú	L3
equal; equality	平等	píngděng	L2, L16
erotic; eroticism	色情	sèqíng	L2
escaped criminal; fugitive	逃犯	táofàn	L5
to estimate; to evaluate; estimation	估計	gūjì	L5, L6
even if	就算…也	jiùsuàn	L4
even if	即使...也	jíshǐ...yě	L9
even though; in spite of	儘管	jǐnguǎn	L5, L7, L8, L12, ….
even; so much so that	甚至	shènzhì	L1
ever; once; formerly	曾經	céngjīng	L2, L4, L19
every; any; all	凡是	fánshì	L11
everything; all	一切	yíqiè	L7
everywhere	到處	dàochǔ	(review) L5
everywhere; in all respects	處處	chùchù	L2
evil; malicious	邪惡	xié'è	L11
exactly right; coincidently right (adj.)	正好	zhènghǎo	L5
to exceed; to surpass	超過	chāoguò	L4, L12, L14
to exchange; to communicate; communication; exchange; interchange;	交流	jiāoliú	L1, L14, L15, L17, …
an exclamation; a particle	噢	ō	L11
to excuse; to forgive; forgiveness	原諒	yuánliàng	L7
to exercise; to workout;exercise (n.)	鍛煉	duànliàn	L5
to exist everywhere	無處不在	wúchù búzài	L10, L20
to exist; being; existence	存在	cúnzài	L6, L8, L20
to experience; to live through； experience	經歷	jīnglì	L11, L16
expert	專家	zhuānjiā	L8, L22
experience	經驗	jīngyàn	(review) L4
to explain; to interpret	解釋	jiěshì	L7
to express; to deliver	表達	biǎodá	L8, L11, L17, L21
to exterminate; to wipe out	消滅	xiāomiè	L11
extra; surplus	多余	duōyú	L9

H

to have no choice	別無選擇	biéwúxuǎnzé	L4
to have nothing at all in the world	一無所有	yìwúsuǒyǒu	L11
to have the heart to	忍心	rěnxīn	L7
headboard; the head of a bed	床頭	chuángtóu	L5
to heat leftover rice (to say or do the same old thing; to repeat without any new content)	炒冷飯	chǎolěngfàn	L9
heavy burden; heavy responsibility	重擔	zhòngdàn	L7
hence; therefore	因此	yīncǐ	L4, L8, L9, L10
hero	英雄	yīngxióng	L1, L12
to hide	藏	cáng	L10, L18
to hide one's great ability; to be modest about one's skill	深藏不露	shēncáng bú lòu	L8
to hide the truth from a person	瞞	mán	L7
to hide; to dodge; to avoid	躲	duǒ	L5
high-ranking; senior; superior	高級	gāojí	(review) L2
to hint; to imply; hint(n.)	暗示	ànshì	L9, L16
to hire	雇	gù	L7, L10, L18
history	歷史	lìshǐ	(review) L1
to hold the post of; be engaged in; to do	幹	gàn	L7
honest, frank	老實	lǎoshi	L5, L18
Hong Kong and Taiwan	港臺	Gǎng Tái	L11
to hope that sons and daughters will grow up to be successful	望子成龍, 望女成鳳	wàngzǐchénglóng, wàngnǚchéngfèng	L3
to hope; hope	希望	xīwàng	(review) L3
hot pepper; chili	辣椒	làjiāo	L10
however	然而	rán'ér	L2
humorous (幽默感 = sense of humor)	幽默	yōumò	L9, L10
in a hurry	急匆匆	jí-cōngcōng	L5
to hurt; to harm; harm; hurt	傷害	shānghài	L7, L19
to hurt; to injure, wound; injury	傷	shāng	L6, L18
hygienic; sanitary hygiene; sanitation;	衛生	wèishēng	L4
I			
idiomatic	慣用	guànyòng	L9
(four-word) idioms	成語	chéngyǔ	(review) L8
if	若	ruò	L6, L17, L22
illegal; unlawful	非法	fēifǎ	L4
illness; breakdown; defect	毛病	máobìng	L6
immature; infantile	幼小	yòuxiǎo	L7, L18
immediately	馬上	mǎshàng	(review) L2
immediately; in a fast pace; ; to hurry up	趕快	gǎnkuài	L8
to be impatient to; to be eager to	急於	jíyú	L2, L15
to be too impatient to wait	迫不及待	pòbùjídài	L5
impression	印象	yìnxiàng	L3, L19
improper	不三不四	bùsānbúsì	L5
to improve; improvement	改善	gǎishàn	L4, L14, L21
in accordance with; to follow (an instruction, a regulation)	按照	ànzhào	L3, L8, L16
to be in charge of; the person in charge	主管	zhǔguǎn	L2
in; on (written expression)	於	yú	L1
incomparable; beyond comparison	無人能比	wúrén-néngbǐ	L3

many, much, a great deal of	許多	xǔduō	(review) L1
Mao Zedong	毛澤東	Máo Zédōng	L2, L16
market quotations; market trend	行情	hángqíng	L8
marriage	婚姻	hūnyīn	L6
to marry a woman; to take to wife	娶	qǔ	L2, L6, L10
(said of a woman) to marry; to marry off	嫁	jià	L2
master worker; a polite form to address blue-collar workers	師傅	shīfu	L8
Master's degree(M.A.)	碩士	shuòshì	L7
material; substance	物質	wùzhì	L2, L4
means; measure; artifice	手段	shǒuduàn	L6

Measure words

一場比賽, 一場表演, 一場電影, 一場夢	場	chǎng	L1
一道菜	道	dào	L10
一頓飯	頓	dùn	(review) L10
一份報紙, 一份早餐	份	fèn	(review) L6
一副...的樣子, 一副眼鏡	副	fù	L5
一棵樹	棵	kē	(review) L5
一首歌, 一首詩, 一首順口溜	首	shǒu	(review) L11
一所學校, 一所房子, 一所醫院	所	suǒ	L1
一座山, 一座大樓	座	zuò	(review) L8

M

meat	肉	ròu	(review) L10
medical science	醫學	yīxué	L6
member	成員	chéngyuán	L4
to mention; to bring up	提(to mention)	tí	L7, L9, L15
mission; task	任務	rènwù	L9
to misunderstand; misunderstanding	誤會	wùhuì	L5
to mock; to lampoon; satire	諷刺	fěngcì	L9
model; mode	模式	móshì	L3
modern times; modern; contemporary	現代	xiàndài	(review) L6
modest; modesty	謙虛	qiānxū	L8
Mongolia	蒙古	ménggǔ	L9
more or less	多多少少	duōduō-shǎoshǎo	L3, L20
mother-in-law (wife's mother)	岳母	yuèmǔ	L5
to move someone's emotions; to feel touched (讓人感動的= touching)	感動	gǎndòng	L4
much less; not to mention	何況	hékuàng	L3, L7
music album	專輯	zhuānjí	L11
music fans (迷 = fans)	歌迷	gēmí	L11
musical circles (of people); music world	樂壇	yuètán	L11

N

naïve; childlike innocence	天真	tiānzhēn	L7
the name of; 以…的名義= in the name of; (名義上 = nominal; in name)	名義	míngyì	L6

Names

Linda	琳達	Líndá	L6
Kenny	肯尼	Kěnní	L6
name of a Chinese singer	崔健	Cuī Jiàn	L11
name of a famous Chinese basketball player	姚明	Yáomíng	L1

opinions; view; objection and complain	意見	yìjiàn	L8
to oppose; to be against; to object to	反對	fǎnduì	L2, L4, L6, L12, …
to be opposite, relative (opposite of "absolute")	相對	xiāngduì	L9
opposition party	反對黨	fǎnduìdǎng	L4
to oppress; to repress; oppression	壓迫	yāpò	L2, L4, L17
orchestra; band	樂隊	yuèduì	L11
ordinary people	壓迫	lǎobǎixìng	(review) L4
organization; group	團體	tuántǐ	L4, L19
to organize; organization	組織	zǔzhī	7
original, former	原來	yuánlái	(review) L4
original; originally; formerly	原本	yuánběn	L3, L4, L15, L17
originality	創意	chuàngyì	L10
orphan	孤兒	gūér	L1, L4
orphanage	孤兒院	gū'éryuàn	L6
other people	人家	rénjiā	(review) L1 口語, L5
other; else	其他	qítā	L1
otherwise; or else	否則	fǒuzé	L4, L6, L9, L18
outstanding; excellent	優秀	yōuyòu	L10, L16, L17
overcoat; outer wear	外套	wàitào	(review) L5
to own; to possess	擁有	yōngyǒu	L6, L7, L20
Oxford; Oxford University	牛津	Niújīn	L3

P

to pan fry; to fry in a shallow oil	煎	jiān	L10
the parent or guardian of a child	家長	jiāzhǎng	L3
to be particular about; to pay great attention to	講究	jiǎngjiu	L2, L10, L17
to pass away	去世	qùshì	L1, L12
to pass by shoulder to shoulder/ to bump into each other without knowing	擦肩而過	cājiānérguò	L7
to pass on; to hand down	流傳	liúchuán	L9
to pass; by means of	通過	tōngguò	L4, L6, L14, L15…
in the past; before	從前	cóngqián	L9
to pat the horse's butt (to flatter excessively; to be a sycophant; to lick sb.'s shoes)	拍馬屁	pāimǎpì	L9
to pat; to slap	拍	pāi	L9
patience; patiently	耐心	nàixīn	L5
Peking duck	北京烤鴨	Běijīng kǎoyā	L10
personality; disposition; character (synonym: 個性)	性格	xìnggé	L3
to persuade; to convince	說服	shuōfú/shuìfú	L6, L19
pervert;lady-killer	色鬼	sèguǐ	L5
phenomenon	現象	xiànxiàng	L6, L19, L20
piano	鋼琴	gāngqín	L3
to pick up (a person)	接	jiē	(review) L6
Ping-Pong; table tennis	乒乓球	pīngpāngqiú	L1
pinhead; needle tip; 打針= to give an injection	針頭	zhēntóu	L4
to play lute for the cow (to speak to the wrong audience)	對牛彈琴	duìniútánqín	L8
to play with; to dally with men/women	玩弄	wánnòng	L8
to play; to be engaged	搞	gǎo	L7
poem	詩	shī	L9

to come off the press; to publish (of books)	出版	chūbǎn	L3, L11, L19
to publish; to release	發表	fābiǎo	L8, L17, L19, L21
to punish; to penalize; punishment	處罰	chǔfá	L2, L4, L9, L20
pure and fresh; fresh	清新	qīngxīn	L5
to pursue; to seek；to woo	追求	zhuīqiú	L1, L11
to push	推	tuī	L5
to put one's hand to; to start; to set about	下手	xiàshǒu	L8
Q			
quiet	安靜	ānjìng	(review) L1
quietly	悄悄	qiāoqiāo	L11
quietly; silently	默默地	mòmòdi	L5
R			
radish	蘿卜	luóbo	L10
to raise; to lift; to hold up	舉	jǔ	L1
reader (a person); readership	讀者	dúzhě	L3
reason	理由	lǐyóu	L4, L21
to recall; to look back upon; to reminisce; memoirs	回憶	huíyì	L7
recession of (economy; market); financial depression;	不景氣	bùjǐngqì	L7, L22
to recognize	認	rèn	L5
to record; to write down; record (n.)	記錄	jìlù	L9
to recover; to resume	恢復	huīfù	L1, L19
refined; educated; elegant	文雅	wényǎ	L9
to reflect upon; to ponder over; to think deeply about	思考	sīkǎo	L11
to reflect; to report	反映	fǎnyìng	L9, L10, L15
reform and open to the outside world	改革開放	gǎigékāifàng	(review) L2
to refuse, to turn down; rejection	拒絕	jùjué	L7, L9
region; area; district	地區	dìqū	L10
to register for/in	報	bào	L3
to regret	後悔	hòuhuǐ	L6
relatives; kinsfolk	親戚	qīnqi	(review) L6
to relax; relaxed; light; calm	輕松	qīngsōng	L3
religion	宗教	zōngjiào	L4, L21
to rely on, to depend on	靠	kào	(review) L4
to remain undecided to poise; (猶豫=to hesitate)	猶豫	yóuyù bùjué	L8
to replace; for ; on behalf of	替	tì	L1
to replace; to take over	取代	qǔdài	L4
resentful; unsatisfied; discontented	不滿	bùmǎn	L9
to resolve (a problem); to solve	解決	jiějué	L4, L10, L21
to respect; to honor	尊敬	zūnjìng	L1, L12, L15
to respond	回	huí	L5
to be responsible for; to be in charge of; responsible	負責	fùzé	L6, L14
to restrict; restriction	限制	xiànzhì	L4, L6, L20
result; finally; as a result; as it turns out	結果	jiéguǒ	L3, L19
to retire	退休	tuìxiū	L5, L9
revolution	革命	gémìng	L11
[a word to strength one's rhetorical intonation]	難道	nándào	L3, L7, L11
to rhyme; to have a correspondence of terminal sounds of words or of lines of verse	押韻	yāyùn	L9
rhymed, slang verse	順口溜	shùnkǒuliū	L9
富裕(fùyù = rich)的商人; rich businessman	富商	fùshāng	L2, (L12, L16)

1) to shoulder 2) to choose; to pick	挑	tiāo	L7
to shout loudly; loud shouts in support (of something)	吶喊	nàhǎn	L11
to shout; to yell; to cry out; to call a person	喊	hǎn	L3
to show off	賣弄	màinong	L8, L9
to show off; to flaunt	炫耀	xuànyào	L8
to show up; to make public appearances	露面	lòumiàn	L11
to show,to express	表示	biǎoshì	L8, L20, L21
to show; to manifest; performance	表現	biǎoxiàn	L9, L15, L19
shredded potato (土豆 is also called 馬鈴薯 [mǎlíngshǔ]) (絲 = thread or thread like thing)	土豆絲	tǔdòusī	L10
shrimp (龍蝦 = Lobster)	蝦	xiā	L10
Sichuan picked vegetables (泡菜 = pickles)	四川泡菜	Sìchuān pàocài	L10
side; near by	旁邊	pángbiān	(review) L5
to sigh	嘆氣	tànqì	L5, L7
to sigh over sth.;to exclaim out of surprise	感嘆	gǎntàn	L8, L10
to sign	簽	qiān	L7, L14, L15
to be silent	默不做聲	mòbú zuòshēng	L8
to be silent; silent ; silence	沉默	chénmò	L1, L5
to allow to simmer in a covered pot	燜	mèn	L10
simply; at all	簡直	jiǎnzhí	L4
since	既然	jìrán	L7, L8
since then (此 = "this" in written expression)	從此以後	cóngcǐyǐhòu	L1
to sing and praise	歌頌	gēsòng	L11
singer	歌手	gēshǒu	L11
to sit on the cold bench (to be idled from important tasks)	坐冷板凳	zuò lěng-bǎndèng	L9, L15
the sky; the heavens	天空	tiānkōng	L6
a slice; a stretch (of land,water); a scene of (rejoicing,sound)	一片	yípiàn	L3
to smile; smile	微笑	wēixiào	L5
smilingly	笑盈盈	xiào-yíngyíng	L5
smooth going; smoothly;	順利	shùnlì	L4
sneakers	運動鞋	yùndòngxié	(review) L7
socialism	社會主義	shèhuì zhǔyì	L11
society	社會	shèhuì	(review) L2
as soft as cotton	軟綿綿	ruǎnmiánmián	L11
songs	歌曲	gēqǔ	L11
soul; heart	心靈	xīnlíng	L7
source; origin	來源	láiyuán	L9
"spare the rod,spoil the child"	不打不成器	bùdǎ-bùchéngqì	L3
special; specialized; specially	專門	zhuānmén	L10, L20
special; unusual; especially	特別	tèbié	(review) L1
spirit; mind; vitality	精神	jīngshén	L1, L14
to split up; to say good-bye	分手	fēnshǒu	L6
to spoil; to pamper; pampering	嬌慣	jiāoguàn	L3
spoon	勺子	sháozǐ	(review) L10
sportsman; athlete	運動員	yùndòngyuán	L1
stage for performances	舞臺	wǔtái	L11
to stare blankly; to daze off	發呆	fādāi	L5, L7
status; position (in a society,a family,an organization,etc.)	地位	dìwèi	L2, L16

to stay for a period of time	待	dāi	L5, L7
to steam (清蒸 = to steam in clear soup)	蒸	zhēng	L10
to step on	踏	tà	L7
to sterilize; to kill germs	殺菌	shājūn	L10
to stew after frying or to fry after stewing; to cook	燒	shāo	L10
sth. weighing on one's mind; a load on one's mind	心事	xīnshì	L5
still; yet	仍舊	réngjiù	L5
to stir-fry	炒	chǎo	(review) L10
stock market	股市	gǔshì	L8, L22
stock; shares	股票	gǔpiào	L8, L22
story; tale	故事	gùshi	(review) L1
strange; unfamiliar	陌生	mòshēng	L1, L6, L19
strong；powerful; better	強	qiáng	(review) L3
structure; construction	結構	jiégòu	L8, L12, L17
to struggle; a struggle	掙扎	zhēngzhá	L11, L15
stubborn	固執	gùzhí	L8
to study abroad	留學	liúxué	(review) L7
to study hard；diligent; studious	用功	yònggōng	(review) L3
stupid; foolish; clumsy	笨	bèn	L3
stupid; stupefied; muddleheaded; silly	傻	shǎ	L5
style	風格	fēnggé	L11, L20
style; style of work; method of doing something	作風	zuòfēng	L4, L14
stylish; fashionable	時髦	shímáo	L5, L13
sub-consciousness (意識 = consciousness,潛= potential; to go under water)	潛意識	qiǎnyìshi	L11
subject (of talk); topic	話題	huàtí	L4
subjective; subjectivity; (客觀 = objective; objectivity)	主觀	zhǔguān	L8
to substitute for; to replace	代替	dàitì	L8, L9
to succeed; successful; success;	成功	chénggōng	L3, L6, L15
sudden; unexpected; suddenly	突然	tūrán	L1, L5, L18
to suffer a crushing defeat; to suffer a complete loss	一敗涂地	yíbàitúdì	L8
to suffer from excessive internal heat (according to traditional Chinese medicine)	上火	shànghuǒ	L10
to suffer loss; to be taken advantage of	吃虧	chīkuī	L10
to suit; to fit; to be appropriate for	適合	shìhé	L9
sun	太陽	tàiyáng	L11
superstition; blind worship	迷信	míxìn	L4
to support the family (養 = to raise; to provide food)	養家	yǎngjiā	L4
to support; to back	支持	zhīchí	L4, L13, L17, L20
surface (see grammar for "表面上")	表面	biǎomiàn	L2
to be suprised; to be shocked; to be amazed	吃驚	chījīng	L10
to suspect ; to have doubts; suspicions	懷疑	huáiyí	L11, L17, L20
sweet and sour chicken	甜酸雞	tiánsuānjī	L10
to swim; usually appear as "游泳"(yóuyǒng)	游	yóu	(review) L10
synonym(s); 反義詞：antonym(s)	同義詞	tóngyìcí	L11
system	制度	zhìdù	L9, L17
system; systematically	系統	xìtǒng	L10
T			
table cloth	桌布	zhuōbù	L10

tacit understanding; privity; unvoiced pact]	默契	mòqì	L6, L14
Tai-chi	太極拳	tàijíquán	(review) L5
to take off one's pants to fart (to do something that is unnecessary and superfluous)	脫褲子放屁	tuōkùzi fàngpì	L9
to take turns	輪流	lúnliú	L6
talented; talent; genius	天才	tiāncái	L11
to talk about everything; to hide nothing	無話不說	wúhuà bùshuō	L10
to talk over; to consult with sb	商量	shāngliáng	(review) L7
a tall person；個兒/個子 = height of a person	高個兒	gāogèr	L5
to tangle; to twine; to bind	纏	chán	L2
Taoism/Daoism	道教	Dàojiào	L4
to teach sb. a lesson; a lesson	教訓	jiàoxun	L5, L12
a team; a row of people	隊	duì	L1
tears	眼淚	yǎnlèi	L7, L16
technique; skill; technology	技術	jìshù	L7, L13, L14, L19,…
temperature	氣溫	qìwēn	L11
temporary; for the time being	暫時	zànshí	L7, L14
tens of thousands of	成千上萬	chéngqiān shàngwàn	L8
to thank; to acknowledge; thanks (n.)	感謝	gǎnxiè	L2, L4
the first	頭一個	tóuyígè	L1
the masses; the general public	群眾	qúnzhòng	L9
the only child	獨生子女	dúshēngzǐnǚ	L2, L3, L6,
thereupon; consequently	於是	yúshì	L5, L6, L17
to think; to deem	認為	rènwéi	(review) L1
this year；the current year	本年度	běnniándù	L3
this; that; the aforementioned (used in written Chinese or formal speech)	該	gāi	L10, L14, L15, L22
to throw oneself onto; to pounce on	撲	pū	L7
to throw; to toss; to throw away	扔	rēng	L4, L6
Tiananmen Square	天安門廣場	Tiānānménguǎn gchǎng	L11
times; era; age	時代	shídài	L2, L20
title; subject	題目	tímù	(review) L9
to sb.'s face; in sb's presence	當面	dāngmiàn	L5
to; for; with regard to	對於	duìyú	L6, L15, L18, L19,…
tomato (also called 番茄[fānqié])	西紅柿	xīhóngshì	L10
tool	工具	gōngjù	L8, L10, L17
total; all	全部	quánbù	L3
tradition，traditional	傳統	chuántǒng	(review) L2
traffic accident	車禍	chēhuò	L1
to train; training	培訓	péixùn	L7, L14, L21
to treat	對待	duìdài	L9
to treat disease; to cure illness	治病	zhìbìng	L4
trouble; troublesome	麻煩	máfan	(review) L9
to try to sell; to market	推銷	tuīxiāo	L6
to turn one's head; to look back; later	回頭	huítóu	L5, L19
to tutor; to coach; tutoring	輔導	fǔdǎo	L7
TV station	電視臺	diànshìtái	L4
type,kind	樣	yàng	(review) L10

U			
unable; incapable (usually followed by two-syllable verb)	無法	wúfǎ	L3
to be unavoidable; bound to be	免不了	miǎn-bùliǎo	L3
an uncooked vegetable; lettuce	生菜	shēngcài	L10
under no circumstance [used for exhortation or a friendly warning]	千萬	qiānwàn	(review)L2 口語, L8
to understand; clear; coherent; clearly; coherently	明白	míngbai	L11
to understand；to acquaint oneself	了解	liǎojiě	(review) L4
unexpectedly; to one's surprise	竟然	jìngrán	L2, L3, L4, L7…
unfortunate; unlucky; unfortunately ; misfortune; adversity;	不幸	búxìng	L1, L2, L4, L15,…
unfortunately; it's a pity; it is too bad	可惜	kěxī	L7
unit (as an organization,department,division,section,etc)	單位	dānwèi	L5, L20
to unite; to ally; united	聯合	liánhé	L11
unlimited; infinite	無限	wúxiàn	L6
unmarried girl,young lady	姑娘	gūniang	L7
unmarried; single	單身	dānshēn	L6, L7
unsociable; eccentric (a negative usage); introverted	孤僻	gūpì	L3, L7
to urge sb. to drink and eat more	勸酒勸菜	quànjiǔ quàncài	L10
to use drug	吸毒	xīdú	L7
to use or take advantage of; to exploit	利用	lìyòng	L9
to use; usage	使用	shǐyòng	L4, L8, L17, L21
V			
to value highly; to attach importance to	重視	zhòngshì	L3, L4, L9
to value the male child only; to prefer sons to daughters	重男輕女	zhòngnánqīngnǚ	L2, L6
to vary in thousands of ways; kaleidoscopic change	千變萬化	qiānbiàn wànhuà	L10
vegetables; greens	蔬菜	shūcài	L10
very; fully	十分	shífēn	L6
villager	村民	cūnmín	L4
visa	簽證	qiānzhèng	L7
to visit and have an interview with; visit (n.)	訪問	fǎngwèn	L1, L19, L21
voice; sound	聲音	shēngyīn	L11
W			
to warn; to caution; warning;	警告	jǐnggào	L5
wave	浪	làng	L11
way; method; style	方式	fāngshì	L3, L9, L21
we,us (include the listener)	咱們	zánmen	(review) L8
weekend	週末	zhōumò	(review) L3
well-known schools	名校	míngxiào	L3, L7
what is called; so-called	所謂	suǒwèi	L1, L2, L9, L18
when; on every occasion	每逢	měiféng	L6, L7
when (written expression)	何時	héshí	L11
是不是；whether	是否	shìfǒu	L11, L20
wife	妻子	qīzi	L5, L16
wife	老婆	lǎopo	L9, L10
a written usage that means 1) = 會：will (auxiliary verb) 2)= 把: as in 把書給我	將	jiāng	L7, L16, L17, L18,…

to be willing to	願意	yuànyì	L2
to willingly expend; not begrudge	捨得	shěde	L3, L7, L13
to win; to beat in competition	贏	yíng	L3, L4, L15
within; inside	內	nèi	L2, L12
women	婦女	fùnǚ	L2
words and deeds	言行	yánxíng	L5
to work hard	努力	nǔlì	(review) L7
worker,farmer,and solder	工農兵	gōng nóng bīng	L11
workmanship; skill	手藝	shǒuyì	L8
world	世界	shìjiè	(review) L4
to worry; to feel anxious	擔心	dānxīn	(review) L5
to be worth; to deserve	值得	zhídé	L1, L3, L20
would rather	寧可	nìngkě	L5
wrong; incorrect	錯誤	cuòwù	L8
Y			
Yale University	耶魯	Yēlǔ	L3
to yearn for; to look forward to	向往	xiàngwǎng	L10, L16
young	年輕	niánqīng	(review) L1
youth (n.)	青春	qīngchūn	L9
Z			
zero	零	líng	(review) L1

4716717R0

Made in the USA
Charleston, SC
06 March 2010